Hetero

THE SUNY SERIES

HORIZONS OF CINEMA

MURRAY POMERANCE | EDITOR

Also in the series

William Rothman, editor, *Cavell on Film*

J. David Slocum, editor, *Rebel Without a Cause*

Joe McElhaney, *The Death of Classical Cinema*

Kirsten Thompson, *Apocalyptic Dread*

Francis Gateward, editor, *Seoul Searching*

Michael Atkinson, editor, *Exile Cinema*

Bert Cardullo, *Soundings on Cinema*

Paul S. Moore, *Now Playing*

Robin L. Murray and Joseph K. Heumann, editors,
Ecology and Popular Film

William Rothman, editor, *Three Documentary Filmmakers*

Hetero

Queering Representations of Straightness

Edited by

Sean Griffin

SUNY PRESS

Published by
State University of New York Press, Albany

Printed in the United States of America

For information, contact State University of New York Press, Albany, NY
www.sunypress.edu

Production by Marilyn P. Semerad
Marketing by Anne M. Valentine

Library of Congress Cataloging-in-Publication Data

Hetero : queering representations of straightness / edited by Sean Griffin.
p. cm. — (SUNY series, horizons of cinema)
Includes bibliographical references and index.
ISBN 978-1-4384-2617-4 (hbk. : alk. paper)
ISBN 978-1-4384-2618-1 (pbk. : alk. paper)
1. Heterosexuality in motion pictures. 2. Motion pictures—United States—History. I. Griffin, Sean.

PN1995.9.H45H48 2009
791.43'653—dc22 2008028298

10 9 8 7 6 5 4 3 2 1

Contents

Illustrations

Introduction

SEAN GRIFFIN

A FEW YEARS AGO, HARRY BENSHOFF and I signed a contract to write a textbook for courses on cinema and diversity (Benshoff and Griffin 2003). Both of us had taught such courses at a variety of universities and colleges, and so we felt reasonably well equipped to tackle such a project. The book would be divided into four sections: race, class, gender, and sexuality. To keep abreast with recent film scholarship, we felt including a chapter on "whiteness" in the race section, as well as a chapter analyzing filmic representations of masculinity in the gender section, was important. Yet neither of us had really consciously considered an in-depth analysis of cinematic representations of heterosexuality in the sexuality section. Without discussing it, we both seemed to feel that we needed to use the space to educate students on the cinematic history of homosexuality and other "nonstraight" sexual identities, rather than talking about heterosexuality. Yet in doing so, we came to realize (partly through others who also noticed this omission) that in neglecting to analyze heterosexuality, we were still possibly granting heteronormativity a sense of power.

I open this anthology with this anecdote because our realization not only seemed to apply to the first draft of the textbook, but also to the general application of queer theory in cinema and media studies since the advent of the "queer moment" in academia in the early 1990s. In sexuality studies, little investigation has been done with regard to how heterosexuality functions as a social construct—how it must continually reify its primacy through repeated rehearsals, performances, and announcements. This collection attempts to redress this imbalance, shifting the application of queer theory in media studies away from the social construction of minoritized sexualities and toward the heterosexual dominant to deconstruct its conceptual stability. In other words, these chapters posit that if queer theory is to break down effectively the barriers of sexual identity, it needs not only to examine marginalized sexualities, but it also needs to deconstruct the love that *does* dare to speak its name—over and over again until one is almost unaware of hearing it.

The Foundations of Hetero Studies

Many of the formative texts of queer theory laid the groundwork for undertaking the deconstruction of heterosexual identity—specifically announcing that all sexualities are social constructs. In fact, long before the "queer moment" blossomed, writers such as Lisa Duggan (1983) and Jonathan Ned Katz examined the social invention of heterosexuality and its subsequent enforcement. Michel Foucault's work was a history of the entire concept of sexuality, proposing sex as a discourse, a power relation between and among a multiplicity of various medical, legal, and social discourses (and between sexualities themselves; Foucault 1978, 1985, 1986). In this history, he examined a variety of sexual practices and identity formations. Judith Butler's examination of the performativity of all sexual identity, and Eve Kosofsky Sedgwick's (1985, 1990) call for a universalizing view of sexuality similarly implicate heterosexuality in their theoretical work.

In the ensuing years, two general trends emerged linking queer theory and heterosexuality in academic discourse. The first was devoted to "queering" certain heterosexual cultures and practices, such as S/M culture and same-sex affection and sexual acts among self-identified heterosexuals (Califia; Duberman, Vicinus, and Chauncey). In doing so, such investigations point out the blurred lines between supposedly rigid sexual categories—queering aspects of heterosexuality. The second trend examined the concept of the "straight queer"—an individual who identifies as heterosexual, yet still considers him or herself "queer," outside normative heterosexuality.[1] The idea of "straight queers" has often been a problematic concept among nonheterosexuals and, as Calvin Thomas puts it in his introduction to *Straight with a Twist: Queer Theory and the Subject of Heterosexuality*, straight queer academics spend much of their time trying "not to arrogate, confiscate, or seize queer theory's varied conceptual tools and put them to straight use" (3).

Thomas's anthology focuses mainly on "the general problematic of straight negotiation of queer theory" (4). How can a straight person write about a marginalized sexual identity? How can a straight person read or watch through a "queer subjectivity"? Such questions are important—but they obfuscate how heterosexuality itself, even at its most normative and approved of, can be "queer." The anthology's subtitle, "the subject of heterosexuality," ends up referring to "the heterosexual subject" engaging with queer theory rather than queer theory engaging with heterosexuality. Similarly, dissections of things such as heterosexual S/M culture and nongay same-gender sex tends to pull such desires, concepts, or activities into the realm of the nonnormative, constructing a minoritized view of sexuality in which normative heterosexuality is still shielded from the realm of queerness.[2]

Several reasons are possible for this reticence to zero in on normative heterosexuality with a queer magnifying lens. First, the reworking of the term "queer" began not in academic ivory towers but on the streets with radical activists, who very much invested the term "queer" as the binary opposite of "straightness" (Duggan 1996). Queer activism rose out of a literally life-and-death struggle for marginalized sexualities to be acknowledged and addressed in the wake of the AIDS crisis. Hence, in the early stages of queer theory, it should not have been surprising that there was felt a need to explore and discuss sexualities that had been historically castigated, erased, or both. Drawing back the veil on histories and reception practices that had been ignored and censored for generations took precedence over giving attention to heterosexuality. Heterosexual academics felt the need to respect that imperative or were criticized if some felt that they were not respecting it in their articles or conference papers. For example, Jacqueline Foertsch, in her article "In Theory if Not in Practice: Straight Feminism's Lesbian Experience," details the "lengthy, emphatic, multivoiced attack" to a self-identified heterosexual "'using' a lesbian subject position" at a conference presentation (55). The use of "queer" by activists specifically to define themselves as "everything *not* straight" seems to battle actively against applying the concept to heterosexuality. Whereas the subsequent use of "queer" by academics deconstructs the ideology of sexuality in general, this activist-based definition seems to have affected the work done by queer theorists and kept the focus away from conceptions of straightness or heteronormativity.

Another possible reason for the relative lack of attention to the social construction of heterosexuality may be that because heterosexuality is so intricately tied into the ideology of patriarchy, some academics may have felt that any analysis of it crosses out of queer theory into gender studies. The work of feminist scholars such as Laura Mulvey, Mary Ann Doane (1992), Molly Haskell, and numerous others might seem to cover representations of heterosexuality in great depth. Long before queer theory's rise, Monique Wittig's landmark essay, "The Straight Mind," focused on the "obligatory relationship between 'man' and 'woman,'" attempting to lay bare the power of heterosexuality's invisibility in culture (107; see also Rich). Yet, queer theory has brought out new ideas and areas of study that lie beyond the foci of gender studies. Judith Butler, for example, took from feminist theories to help lay the foundation for queer theory in *Gender Trouble: Feminism and the Subversion of Identity*, critiquing earlier feminist conceptions of sexuality, including Wittig's (120–128). Continuing in this vein, heterosexual identity is more than just or only patriarchy and concepts of gender.

Studies in sexuality could learn from further developments in gender studies (and race studies as well). In the late 1980s, a growing body of feminist criticism began to focus on the social construction of masculinity, moving beyond an earlier felt need to devote time to the marginalized histories and issues of women (Penley and Willis; Boone and Cadden; Lehman). Similar to this shift in the application of feminist theory, the more recent boom in "white studies" has opened up entire new areas for discussing and conceptualizing race and ethnicity (Bernardi; Dyer 1997; Hill; Rogin). Both of these developments have turned attention to the dominant ideological positions, attempting to unseat their power as an almost unspoken "default" core from which everything else is defined.

Similarly, queer theory needs to draw out the bland, white bread, vanilla, missionary position, monogamous, married, patriarchal form of heterosexuality and point out it is just as much a social construct as any minoritized sexuality. Just as Richard Dyer (1997) has pointed out that part of whiteness's power is its practical invisibility, the omnipresence of heterosexuality in society is often not fully recognized. Precisely the sense that heterosexuality is "bland" or "vanilla" gives it such power. Conceiving of heterosexuality as some sort of "default" sexual identity creates the same sense of cultural invisibility that race scholars are attempting to tear down in social conceptions of "white." "Straight queers" (and those who would argue about the concept) need to stop worrying about the legitimacy of their "outsider" badges—stop interrogating those areas of their sexual identity that make them feel "nonnormative"—and start deconstructing those aspects of their heterosexual identity that *are* considered normative. Shifting the focus in this way can become another way in which the academic concept of queer can link up with queer activism. When everything—including normative heterosexuality—is considered queer, then the terms of sexual identity (as well as concepts of normal or abnormal sexuality) will cease to have meaning and real social change may be accomplished.

Heteronormativity and Heterosexualities

A small but growing interest in deconstructing the heterosexual paradigm has begun to emerge (Dixon; Richardson; Sullivan). This scholarship has often focused on heterosexual ritual: ceremonies that mark an individual's coming of sexual age (such as bar or bat mitzvahs, or quinceañeras), traditions of dating (high school proms), weddings, and celebrations of childbirth. Weddings in particular underscore the theatricality of heterosexuality, and wedding culture has become a budding area of academic inquiry in cinema and beyond (Freeman; Geller; Ingraham; Manekar; Otnes and Pleck; Wallace; Wexman). Through such rituals, heterosexuality is conspicuously displayed with the community supporting or enforcing its standards of sexual identity. The emphasis on following detail (something old, something new, something borrowed, something blue) and order (the regular guests are seated followed by the immediate family, then the bridal party enters, then the groom, and lastly the bride) stresses the highly structured nature of heterosexuality. Motion pictures and other cultural texts can also be seen as ritualized performances of heterosexuality. The prevalence of (and audience expectation for) "boy-meets-girl, boy-loses-girl, boy-gets-girl" narratives exemplify the reinscription of heteronormative traditions.

Ironically, such ritualized performativity attempts to present heterosexuality as natural, ahistorical, and self-evident. It does so by presenting heterosexuality functioning smoothly and simply, bereft of complications (we are never in any doubt that boy *will* get girl). Such ritual performance of heterosexuality (whether in ceremony or in media) also supports other ideological concepts. This is most obvious with regard to gender (boy gets girl, not girl gets boy; father gives the bride away). The history of matrimonial and childbirth celebrations are also intricately tied to notions of community identity, helping support national, ethnic, and racial cohesion. Furthermore, the growth of capitalism has used heterosexuality and its rituals to further its own aims (from inciting heterosexual desire in advertising to the multimillion dollar wedding industry). The interweaving of heteronormativity with ideologies of gender, race, and economics works even further to essentialize it even as it is so lavishly and repeatedly enacted.

Yet, as Butler theorizes, such multiple discourses create overlaps and contradictions. Anyone who has ever been involved in organizing a wedding, for example, generally finds that such celebrations of heterosexuality are not straightforward and simple—rather they are fraught with tension as various individuals struggle over what they consider "ideal" or even "proper." Posing as celebrations of a univocal heterosexuality, ritualized performances more specifically enforce *heteronormativity*. The term "heteronormative"—standardizing heterosexuality as the only healthy and normal desire—is usually invoked to discuss how nonheterosexual desires are marginalized in the process. Yet, heteronormativity also hegemonically negotiates heterosexual desire itself, attempting to assert one "proper" heterosexuality and deny or pathologize the multiple other forms of heterosexuality that exist.

For example, intergenerational conflict over wedding plans has become common fodder for comedians, advice columnists, and screenwriters, exposing that what is considered acceptable heterosexual behavior now (a couple living together before marriage, for example) was not condoned in the past. Structures of sexuality and gender also create conflict, juxtaposing heterosexual desire with patriarchal norms that assert men prefer to socialize with each other than with women (and vice versa). Traditional assertions of patriarchy also usually involve men denying emotion or interdependence (often through displays of violence or power), making commitment to a woman difficult. Similarly, patriarchal traditions have often denied or demonized a woman's own heterosexual desires. Capitalism's need to maintain and increase consumption has resulted in offering ideal images of heterosexuality (the perfect sexual partner, wedding, family) that consistently lie just out of reach to keep the individual unfulfilled and needing to buy more. Thus, capitalism instills in heterosexual individuals a constant sense of self-judgment and insecurity. Such attitudes are most obvious when issues of class are wedded (pardon the pun) to sexual desire—worries about having enough money to attract a partner or actual prohibitions of having relationships across class or caste lines. Similarly, while heterosexual rituals often also function as ethnic or racial celebrations, race and sexuality can come into pitched (and often violent) conflict when heterosexual desire crosses perceived racial lines.

Differences in race, ethnicity, or nationality also often result in differences in notions of acceptable heterosexuality. What may be considered shocking in one culture may be accepted as part of the social system in another. For example, polygamy had been officially outlawed in the West for centuries, while it was still common practice in other areas of the world. Such a comparison may connote Orientalist notions of "oversexed" non-Western cultures, yet other aspects depict the West as being more sexually open. For example, certain public displays of heterosexual affection (holding hands, quick pecks on the hand or cheek) became accepted in the West by the start of the twentieth century, whereas such behavior is *still* regarded as improper in certain other regions (areas of the Middle East, for example). During the 1930s, at the height of the Production Code in Hollywood, studio films showed many heterosexual embraces but erased the existence of prostitution; during the same period, Japanese films never showed an on-screen kiss, but did often acknowledge the geisha system as an accepted part of the larger community. Such conflicts are exacerbated when cultures come into contact with each other (such as when Allied forces after World War II made certain that Japanese films started including on-screen kissing). Most particularly, while same-sex activity went on around the globe, the conceptual categories of "heterosexuality" and "homosexuality" themselves were devised in Europe and the United States, definitions that conflicted with how other cultures defined sexual behavior. As such, many post-colonial societies consider homosexuality and certain types of heterosexual behavior (particularly involving women's sexuality) to be Western inventions that are corrupting their communities. (The global reach of Hollywood film has often been implicated in these charges.) The United States and Europe, on the other hand, have historically displaced certain sexual desires they consider inappropriate onto foreign cultures, regarding Africans, Native Americans, Asians, and Arabs (not to mention, at times, European nationalities such as Irish, Italians, and Spaniards) as overly sexualized or improperly sexualized.

Once recognized, the multiple levels of conflict over heterosexuality amply reveal it not as a simple essentialism but a heavily contested terrain. Current events have highlighted this struggle. In 2003, the U.S. Supreme Court struck down all laws against "sodomy" that had been used to criminalize homosexuality (although, when many of these laws were initially passed, they criminalized heterosexual sodomy as well). In this action, the long-standing distinction that heterosexuality was the only completely legal and sanctioned form of sexual behavior in the land was eliminated. Yet, even before the high court's decision, another conceptual battle was being waged over the ultimate institution of heteronormativity: marriage. In 1996 various groups and politicians banded together to ensure that marriage could only be used to define heterosexuality by passing the federal Defense of Marriage Act. While the legislation's title claims to be defending the institution of marriage, it more specifically tries to protect traditional concepts of heterosexuality. Expanding marriage beyond straight couples would take away yet another part of heterosexuality's ability to define itself as different from homosexuality (Warner 1999). As state and local governments began granting marriage licenses to lesbian and gay couples in 2005 (in California and in Massachusetts, as well as in areas of Oregon, New Mexico, and New York), even more drastic attempts to keep marriage within the domain of heterosexuality were attempted. By 2007, twenty-six states had created heterosexual-only definitions of marriage to their constitutions, and attempts to amend the U.S. Constitution are ongoing. By 2007, however, nine states and the District of Columbia had granted same-sex couples some form of civil union acknowledgments or partnership rights.

The struggle over definitions of marriage and other negotiations of heteronormativity are often embodied in "civilized" debates, op-ed pieces, and peaceful demonstrations. Heterosexuality may appear so endemic an institution that it only needs Althusserian Ideological State Apparati (extravagant weddings, baby showers) to maintain its dominance, but Repressive State Apparati are sometimes frighteningly called forward to keep everything in check. Societies regularly resort to overt pressure and violence to establish one vision of heteronormativity over the other. Lynchings, stonings, riots, and imprisonment all work to terrorize the heterosexual man or woman into performing heterosexuality properly. Men regularly elect to undertake various rituals of violence, such as fraternity hazing, sports, and the military, as part of their induction into patriarchal heterosexuality. Women also commonly go through rituals of physical duress as part of their training—such as foot binding, starvation diets, and plastic surgery.

The Changing Screen Image of Heterosexuality

One of the strongest ways to expose the construction of various identities lies in showing how their concepts have changed over time. Work done in race studies and in lesbian/gay studies provide two apt examples. Scholars of race and ethnic identity have pointed out how Irish and Eastern European immigrants to the United States were originally not accepted into the category of "white," and had to fight to be included (Ignatiev; Negra). Similarly, historians of sexuality have detailed how definitions of homosexuality have shifted from "gender inversion" to "object choice" (Chauncey; D'Emilio and Freedman; Faderman). In addition, numerous scholars have specifically recounted the evolution of social attitudes toward sex in the United States (D'Emilio and Freedman; Lystra; Rothman; Seidman).

Motion pictures provide ample evidence of the shifting conceptions of heterosexuality. Although manifest expressions of same-sex desires were strictly forbidden for a large part of the history of filmmaking across the globe (and, in some areas, still are), images of heterosexuality have tended to be the stock-in-trade of cinema almost since its inception (going back at least as far as the infamous Edison kinetoscope close-up of May Irwin and Edgar Rice kissing). Most fictional narratives include some heterosexual romance, even if it has to be wedged into the plot uncomfortably. Men and women since the start of the twentieth century have taken lessons from movies in how to talk to the opposite sex, how to date, and even how to kiss. In other words, film has been a primary resource for training individuals in how to behave heterosexually (with audience members in theater balconies or at drive-ins often practicing what they have learned right there in front of the screen). The power struggles over what constitutes appropriate heterosexuality have continuously affected filmmaking (and again have often descended to threats of punishment and violence). In various eras and locations, police have arrested filmmakers, theater owners, and even audiences over films that were thought to have stepped over the line. Yet, even with such outcry and oversight, depictions of heterosexuality altered as the twentieth century progressed.

Early cinema often exposed a range of heterosexual behaviors. For example, numerous U.S. silent pictures, including *Ramona* (1910), *Birth of a Nation* (1915), and *Broken Blossoms* (1919)—all directed by D. W. Griffith—dealt with interracial heterosexual desires. Similarly, early Indian cinema often dramatized people loving across caste lines. Motion pictures also emerged as roles for women in the United States and Western Europe were shifting. The figure of the vamp—a highly eroticized female who lured men to their doom with her charms—became a popular recognition of women's newly empowered heterosexual desires. Such acknowledgement was not endorsement, however. In these narratives, only one type of heterosexuality was sanctioned—chaste same-race (and often same-class) courtship leading to monogamous marriage. All other forms were officially regarded as "unhealthy," much like the pathologization of homosexuality. Racial or intercaste mixing was often regarded as unnatural, and films about such desires inevitably led to tragic (and violent) consequences. Films often associated heterosexual vamps such as Theda Bara and their prey with alcoholism and, at times, hints of drug abuse—if not syphilis and other venereal diseases.

Demonizing such heterosexual desires or practices did not always placate critics, however, because the films acknowledge nonetheless that such desires did (and do) exist. (Also, by the 1920s, Hollywood became increasingly synonymous in the public imagination with heterosexual licentiousness, calling up images of wild parties and scandalous affairs.) Consequently, filmmakers felt pressure to treat not only same-sex desires but also certain opposite-sex desires as unmentionable. The establishment of the Production Code stands as the most elaborate example of regulating definitions of heteronormative behavior. The Code specifically forbade mention of miscegenation (interracial sex), prostitution, premarital sex, or extramarital sex. Incest was considered so taboo, it was not even mentionable within the Code itself. Attempts to regulate films existed prior to the Code however, and not just in the United States. City and state censor boards, as well as a Supreme Court ruling that denied motion pictures freedom of speech, led several films during the silent era to depict forms of heterosexuality quite literally as "loves that dared not speak their names."

One of the last silent films made at MGM was the Greta Garbo melodrama *A Woman of Affairs* (1928). An adaptation of *The Green Hat*, a novel dealing with premarital and extramarital heterosexual sex, as well as unwed pregnancy and—most notoriously—venereal disease, the studio took full advantage of the absence of sound to get around censors.[3] When Garbo's character is accused by her brother of being sexually promiscu-

Figure 1. A worried David (Johnny Mack Brown) and an intrigued Diana (Greta Garbo) in their honeymoon bed in *A Woman of Affairs* (1928). *Photo courtesy of MGM/The Kobal Collection.*

ous, we see him angrily start to hurl a profanity at her, followed by the intertitle "You——!" The film cuts to a reverse shot of her reacting to the following word . . . without the viewer being able to see his mouth finish the epithet. Later on, when Garbo is hospitalized, her former lover asks a companion what could have brought her to this state. An intertitle has the fellow saying, "You didn't know?" followed by a two-shot of them as he explains the situation. Again, we have no intertitle that overtly reveals the cause, but this time alert lip-readers can see actor Lewis Stone say, "She was pregnant." The strongest example of this strategy occurs during the key moment when the female protagonist's new husband commits suicide on their honeymoon night. The scene has no intertitles to help us understand why the husband is nervous, what the men at the door want—much less why they have handcuffs and why subsequently he jumps out the window to his death. And the eventual denouement, which changes the husband's secret from syphilis (as it was in the novel) to being guilty of embezzlement, seems vastly out of proportion to the passion of the moment presented. In fact, the overwrought signals are very akin to the not-so-subtle hints usually used in Hollywood films of the era to suggest a secret homosexual past. While D. A. Miller famously theorized how homosexuality in cinema is often veiled in connotative ways, *A Woman of Affairs* reveals that heterosexuality was also sometimes subject to such mystification.

While a strict heteronormativity was asserted in classical Hollywood cinema, the existence of other forms of heterosexuality could be found hiding in the margins. Studio films indicated heterosexual activity through metaphor during the Production Code era: dissolving from a couple embracing to waves cashing or fireworks exploding (or, in the notorious final shot of *North by Northwest* [1959], a train going into a tunnel). While prostitutes were officially absent from Production Code–era films, once could still find plenty of "dance-hall hostesses" and "saloon girls." Furthermore, exploitation films sold themselves by promising to show or discuss the types of sexuality the Code did not allow, such as premarital or interracial sex, but framed within warnings of catastrophe, such as venereal disease or unwed pregnancy (Schaefer).

After World War II the desire by many postwar Europeans to throw off censorship restrictions associated with dictatorial regimes helped lead to more explicit representations of sexuality in cinema. Italian neorealists, the French New Wave, and international auteurs such as Ingmar Bergman and Federico Fellini attempted new ways of portraying heterosexual desire. These films mirrored increasingly relaxed attitudes about premarital sex and (hetero)sexual experimentation. Simultaneously, American filmmakers (such as Otto Preminger) chipped away at the force of the Production Code. Mention of unwed pregnancies, prostitution, abortions, and teenage sex, along with pictures revealing more and more of the human body, began to proliferate. With the onset of greater sexual liberation in the 1960s and early 1970s (and as the United States and other countries shifted from censorship to classificatory ratings systems), several important films interrogated the politics of heterosexuality in uncompromising ways (*WR; Mysteries of the Organism* [1971, Yugoslavia], *Last Tango in Paris* [1972, Italy/France], *In the Realm of the Senses* [1976, Japan], and *Salo, or 120 Days of Sodom* [1976, Italy]). Many of these films showed how heterosexual patriarchal notions often still held sway even within the so-called sexual revolution. Many exposed the power dynamics that often infuse sexual desire. Others pointed out the limits of sexual liberation without an accompanying change in the socioeconomic order.

The sexual revolution was followed by a general cultural backlash (partly fueled by growing fears of sexually transmitted diseases such as herpes and AIDS) that saw a variety of attempts to reassert "traditional values"—which generally meant reestablishing the patriarchal heterosexual family unit. British Prime Minister Margaret Thatcher promoted a "heritage" culture that translated into numerous British films taking place in a nostalgic era of Victorian propriety. In the United States, under the Reagan Administration, "slasher" horror film became popular, visiting violent retribution on young people who had premarital sex (with particularly grisly focus on punishing sexually active women). By the 1990s, however, the complexity of heterosexual relations once again was being explored in greater depth by filmmakers such as Pedro Almodovar and Katherine Breillat, as well as in individual pictures, including *The Cook, The Thief, His Wife and Her Lover* (1989, U.K.), *Henry and June* (1990, U.S.), *Kids* (1995, U.S.), *Baise Moi* (2000, France), *Intimacy* (2001, U.K./France), and *Lust, Caution* (2007, Taiwan).

Whither Hetero Studies?

This anthology focuses squarely on cinema to study the differing social constructions of heterosexuality, supporting that focus with the work of a legacy of queer theorists. The collection exposes how concepts (and representations) have shifted across time and cultures, but also examines the silent assumption of heterosexuality that gives the concept its ideological power (that is, its simultaneous omnipresence and its invisibility). The articles enter in various ways into the timeline and ideological matrices presented earlier, expanding the discussion and analysis of certain moments, industries, texts, or figures in the hegemonic negotiation of heterosexuality. The chapters have been arranged in a generally chronological order: the first chapters deal with classical Hollywood and other industries during the same era; Michael DeAngelis's chapter, roughly at midpoint, transitions the anthology into the modern era. Organizing in this manner highlights the hegemonic negotiations over heterosexualities and heteronormativity. Yet, the chapters can also be ordered around certain issues: the affect of class or economic issues on sexuality, for example, or definitions of heteronormativity beyond WASP U.S. culture. Most strongly, an emphasis is found across several articles on the performativity of sexual identity, attempting to take heterosexuality from its unspoken invisible centrality and expose the methods and manners of its public practice.

In invoking Butler's theories of performativity, many of the contributors point out the tension and anxiety placed on individuals to enact successfully their heterosexual identity. Whereas many in lesbian and gay studies have emphasized the emotional and psychological oppression of the "closet" that lesbians, gay men, and other queer individuals have faced for generations, pressures are also brought to bear on straight people to "live up to" expectations (much as men are granted certain privileges but also face numerous pressures within a patriarchal society). Straight-identified people charged with hate crimes against queer individuals have often invoked what is called the "homosexual panic" defense. Such a defense posits this panic as a brief moment of intense mental anguish and trauma over being thought queer that results in violence. In contrast, many of the chapters herein argue that rather than a sudden outburst, the demands of heteronormative performativity create an ongoing and deeper sense of "heterosexual panic." Such a panic arises from the ever-present sense that one not only watches others to "see how it's done" (how to ask someone for a date, how to kiss, how to be a parent), but also that everyone is watching back and judging. Thus, discussion of the performance of heterosexuality in many of these articles also includes how observation is structured into the texts.

Victoria Sturtevant's opening chapter on the films of William Haines provides a perfect entry into heteronormative performativity by examining how a self-identified gay man portrayed straight romantic roles. Sturtevant argues that Haines used his outsider's viewpoint comically to overstate his characters' heterosexuality, thereby emphasizing the construction of sexual identity. At the end of her chapter, she suggests that such overt performativity may have had a hand in Haines's decline from popularity during the depth of the Great Depression, a time when images that supported rather than undermined essentialist concepts of heterosexual masculinity were desperately desired.

Mary Beth Haralovich takes up this topic as well in her examination of the advertising and publicity around the MGM melodrama *A Free Soul* (1931), which catapulted Clark Gable to stardom through his naturalized performance of brute male heterosexual desire. Yet Haralovich's main focus lies in how Hollywood films often display a range of heterosexual possibility, even if eventually favoring one type over others. In particular, extending the thoughts she expressed earlier in her well-known essay, "Advertising Heterosexuality," she describes how film advertising "flirts" with diverse heterosexualities to attract an audience's gaze. In the case of *A Free Soul*, such flirting is exemplified in the image of star Norma Shearer and her character facing various options of heterosexuality: Marriage or an affair? Clark Gable's character or Leslie Howard's? A working wife or stay-at-home wife?

David Lugowski's study of images of male heterosexuality in Yiddish American films also stresses the impact of the Great Depression (and the growing conflict in Europe) on struggles over definitions of heteronormativity, showing how a desire for an image of a naturalized physically strong heterosexual masculinity within Jewish communities contradicted other earlier cultural ideals of manhood. Three Yiddish-language films of the 1930s display a softer male image, one that today may connote queerness, but was held at the time within Jewish culture as acceptable (and even prized) heterosexual masculinity. Furthermore, Lugowski includes the impact of mainstream Hollywood films (such as *A Free Soul*) on these changing attitudes, pointing out that not just outside the United States did certain cultures have to negotiate their own concepts of heterosexuality against those of dominant Hollywood cinema.

Louise Wallenberg, in studying Swedish male stars of the 1930s, similarly discusses alternate visions of the heterosexual male ideal that arose when cultural notions of heteronormativity were under contestation. Similar to how the first articles implicate the U.S. economic crisis in attitudes about heterosexuality, Wallenberg asserts that the rise of Social Democracy and the decline of aristocratic rule overtly impacted debates over sexual behavior. She links notions of the heterosexual family unit with social discourse about national pride (thereby creating additional pressure to embody successfully the heterosexual construct to be a proper citizen). Both Lugowski and Wallenberg expose that definitions of heteronormativity were not universally agreed on, displaying the diversity of various national or ethnic conceptualizations of acceptable straightness.

Much of the pressure to enact successful heteronormativity is tied to enforcing gendered norms of behavior as countless feminist scholars have shown. Adrienne McLean's study of Eleanor Powell describes how the complex interstices of gender and sexuality impacted the career of one particular female star. While conventionally feminine in appearance and typically involved in formulaic courtship narratives, Powell's sheer competence as a dancer was itself regarded as problematic to the expectations of heteronormativity in the United States at the time. The pressures to embody one particular vision of heterosexuality are also the focus of David Gerstner's discussion of Vincente Minnelli's epic melodrama *Home from the Hill* (1960). Somewhat similarly to Sturtevant's arguments about Haines's performances, Gerstner reveals how the film exposes the difficulties of reconciling the demands of patriarchal masculinity to the demands of heteronormativity (not to mention small-town American class division).

Michael DeAngelis contributes an insightful and in-depth examination of the myriad issues that faced heterosexual women and men in the United States during the so-called sexual revolution of the late 1960s and early 1970s. Looking at several films—some of them generally forgotten today—DeAngelis explores how mainstream films often expressed the bewilderment and befuddlement major upheavals in sexual politics caused during this time.

Similar to Lugowski and Wallenberg, Bhaskar Sarkar showcases the sexual structure of another culture (this time popular Mumbai cinema), and the connections between notions of sexuality and notions of national identity. All three also invoke the importance of the family structure in linking cultural identity and sexuality. Writing about contemporary India, however, Sarkar's discussion strongly accentuates the impact of an increasingly global economy on negotiating what constitutes "proper" heterosexual behavior in India. He also describes how postmodernist commodification helps regulate current attitudes about heterosexual desire. Sarkar also analyzes how heterosexuality at the turn of the millennium increasingly must confront and deal with the growing awareness (and growing acceptance) of homosexuality.

While Haralovich examines the range of sexual possibility available to women (or at least to female film characters) in the United States in the early 1930s, Diane Negra discusses the range currently available to them. In a cultural overview of what many call an era of "postfeminism," Negra uncovers the new pressures (or hetero panic) facing women today. Like Sarkar, Negra reveals how the advanced stages of capitalism in the postmodernist era have impacted representations of female heterosexuality by simultaneously imposing rigid structures of time as "natural" (the moment of sexual maturity, of marriage, of motherhood) and pressuring women to somehow "overcome" time (such as extending the years of sexual activity, both the onset and the end).

Kevin Heffernan complements Negra's chapter by laying out the state of contemporary "heterosexual panic" for American men. While Negra surveys film, television, newspaper and magazine stories, and best-selling books in her discussion, Heffernan zeroes in specifically on the career and films of Ben Stiller. Just as McLean uses Powell, Heffernan's star study uses Stiller's image to present the dilemmas and contradictions of heterosexuality. In particular, Heffernan points out the constant fear that social determinations of "unsuccessful" heterosexual masculinity will be deemed homosexual (paralleling arguments Lugowski makes).

An auteur study rather than an examination of a star, Allan Campbell's survey of Quentin Tarantino's oeuvre shows that the difficulties of reconciling the demands of patriarchal masculinity to the demands of heteronormativity did not disappear with the sexual revolution. Campbell points out how Tarantino's films often show heterosexual desire complicated by mixed expectations. While associated strongly with a straight male viewpoint, Tarantino often verges on queer desire through the representation of intense homosocial bonds between men or by creating sexually desirable women who often display conventionally masculine attributes.

Harry Benshoff brings the anthology to its completion by analyzing *Brokeback Mountain* (2005), generally regarded as a landmark film in the history of representations of homosexuality, as a film about heterosexuality. In so doing, he brings together several strains that filter through the collection (performativity, the ties to economics, the paradoxical expectations of male heteronormativity, and the impact of greater awareness of homosexuality on definitions of heterosexuality). As with all the chapters, Benshoff's piece reveals the potential of looking at heterosexuality with the tools of queer theory.

While this volume provides numerous examinations of the construction of heterosexuality in film, a wealth of potential exploration still remains. How heterosexuality has been depicted in preclassical Hollywood cinema (not to mention the wide range of other national cinemas), in experimental films or documentaries, on television, or on the Internet or other new media are not addressed (see Becker). And this is the main point of the anthology—to call for new examinations and new mindsets. In no way does this call claim that queer theory and sexuality studies should abandon the highly valuable and needed study of lesbian, gay, bi, transgendered, and other minoritized identities. Rather, what is needed is to broaden the scope of how queer theory is applied or put into practical use. It is time that queers—straight or otherwise—turn toward normative heterosexuality and start chanting, "We're here, *you're* queer . . . get used to it."

Notes

1. Sedgwick (1993) has been instrumental in arguing this concept, forthrightly considering herself as a "straight queer."

2. Duberman, Vicinus, and Chauncey provides a perfect example of this conceptualization. Rather than looking at twentieth-century South African mining society or British boarding-school friendships of the 1800s as constructions of a variety of sexualities including heterosexuality, the collection subtitles itself *Reclaiming the Gay and Lesbian Past*—thus claiming all of this research as outside the boundary of heterosexuality.

3. The novel's fame for sexual situations led the studio to retitle the film and to scour its mention from the credits, which only read "from *the story* by Michael Arlen."

1

Victoria Sturtevant

Stop the Wedding!

William Haines and the Comedy of the Closet

The hero encounters a pretty young woman of his acquaintance and offers to walk her home. Reluctantly she accepts and allows him to carry her groceries for her. Hoping to extend the walk, the young man intentionally drops the eggs so they will have to go back. When she insists that she really did not need the eggs, he drops the jam as well. Very soon, all the young woman's purchases are a mess on the sidewalk, and she storms into her house, outraged. The hero, nonplussed, carves another notch in what he calls his "sheik belt," a device he uses to keep count of the women he claims are in love with him. It is just another day in the life of a William Haines hero.

William Haines was a gay comic actor who ranked first in the U.S. exhibitor's poll for the year 1930 and scored in the top five every year from 1926 to 1931. The scene just described comes from his best-known film, *Brown of Harvard* (1926), a college football movie that became an archetype for most of his later roles: a brash, cocky young man sets out to conquer the world, he meets a nice young woman, but offends her with his arrogant courtship. Time passes, and the young hero makes some mistakes, suffers a loss, undergoes a personal transformation, finds success, and wins the love of the heroine. It is a fairly conventional formula, but in Haines's hands, it usually veered toward the outrageous. Haines's performances tended to invest his characters with so much arrogance and mischievous energy that the first half of the film easily overwhelms the second—there is not enough humble pie in the world to counteract the orgy of egotism that usually envelops a William Haines hero. His narcissism, his destructiveness, and his contempt for women are all symptoms of childishness, of an arrested development that the film must finally reverse. Every William Haines picture is, in the end, about growing up. And in this task, they always fail.

William J. Mann's 1999 biography of the star is titled *Wisecracker: The Life and Times of William Haines, Hollywood's First Openly Gay Star*. Although Haines lived an unabashed life in Hollywood with his lover Jimmy Shields, the label "openly gay" remains problematic. Haines did refuse to participate in the Hollywood culture of fictive heterosexual courtship, and according to Anthony Slide, Haines was the only gay star of the 1920s who insisted on bringing his lover to social functions, dinner parties, and studio events (29). The end of his career followed Haines's refusal to comply with Louis B. Mayer's order that he stop living with Shields and accept a fake marriage with a studio-approved woman. A victim of the Production Code Administration crackdown of 1934, Haines made two films on Poverty Row, then left the film industry for good. His refusal of the culture of fictive heterosexuality was genuinely courageous, and by reinventing himself as a successful interior designer, Haines excelled in a new profession without ever giving up or lying about his relationship with his partner. Joan Crawford famously called Haines and Shields, who enjoyed fifty years together, "the happiest married couple in Hollywood" (Mann, xv). We have many reasons to celebrate his legacy as an actor who refused to trade his partner or his identity for his career.

However, Mann's label "openly gay" is meant to be provocative, rather than definitive. He describes Haines's career in ways that pit the star's refusal to lie or disguise his identity against the studio's interest in casting him in heterosexual roles, on-screen and off-screen. Mann uses the term "wisecracker" as emblematic of the coded ways Haines's films and the media would refer to his homosexuality—the star had adapted a style of physical exuberance and sly wit drawn from the gay subculture of Greenwich Village, where he spent his early twenties. Through the outrageousness of his performances and the sly evasive joking of his media interviews (he always insisted in print that he was engaged to the much

Figure 2. An autographed publicity photo of William Haines, circa 1930. *Author's personal collection.*

older character actress Polly Moran), information about his sexuality was available for those who could read between the lines, but not imposed on those who could not or would not. In Mann's account, conservative Louis B. Mayer was predictably uncomfortable with Haines personally and professionally, but Haines was such a profitable commodity that the studio was content with this bargain.

Ronald Gregg, in contrast, argues that MGM was just as invested in Haines's game of ambiguity as the star himself and indeed encouraged its star to reach out through his publicity and film roles to a sophisticated gay or gay-friendly audience in urban centers (82). These audiences would have been expected to recognize and enjoy the gender and sexual ambiguities being celebrated because the late 1920s and early 1930s saw the development of a brief "pansy craze," particularly in New

York. During the late years of prohibition, an elaborate underground socioeconomic network developed to accommodate the public demand for alcohol. Middle-class heterosexual consumers encountered the gay underworld through the mechanism of the speakeasy. By the end of the 1920s, they also began to consume the mystique of homosexual subcultures in increasingly public and daring ways—Broadway productions, nightclub acts, Greenwich Village balls, Vaudeville, and gay bars were all developing campy gay-themed shows and events popular with a Prohibition-era urban populace, already flouting the law with their consumption of bootleg alcohol, and seeking new illicit thrills to explore (Chauncey, 310–311). The lesbian novel *The Well of Loneliness* found an enthusiastic national audience in 1929 (Hall 1929). Gregg argues that the studio consciously embraced the pansy craze in its promotion of Haines and his films. Not until the Great Depression produced a backlash against the social upheaval of the 1920s did gay culture make a hasty retreat. The Production Code intervention gave MGM an excuse to dump the rapidly cooling Haines along with other gay stars.

Intriguingly, Haines's films do certainly contain references to his homosexuality—an occasional ad-libbed comment, a swish of the hips, or a code word here and there. In *Show People* (1928), he wears an apron and cooks dinner for a male friend. In *Hollywood Revue of 1929* (1929), he rips some of the clothes off emcee Jack Benny. In *Way Out West* (1930), his "queerest" film, a cowboy calls out the name of the maid, "Pansy!" and Haines replies, "I'm the wildest Pansy you ever picked!" But these moments contrast with the many other scenes that show Haines aggressively pursuing women, performing athletic feats, or engaging in heteronormative social activities with other men. David Lugowski has shown how Hollywood's representations of homosexual male characters in the 1930s were primarily understood to be effeminate or fey, the "sissy" stereotype (Lugowski 1999, 5). The robust and pranksterish Haines is not a sissy. Physically muscular and energetic, Haines's roles after *Brown of Harvard* were nearly always athletes, military cadets, and criminals.

For the very sophisticated, a gay subtext could certainly have been read into Haines's characters' homosocial relationships with other men in sport- and military-themed films such as (all from MGM) *Tell It to the Marines*, *Brown of Harvard* (both 1926), the baseball movie *Slide, Kelly, Slide* (1927), the race car movie *Speedway*, the boxing movie *The Duke Steps Out*, and the sailor-on-leave comedy *Navy Blues* (all 1929). But for most viewers, Haines's athleticism, his comfortable association with the outdoors, and his social confidence were themselves proof of his normal, healthy heterosexuality. Perhaps the duality of his image is best summed up in the title of his 1929 comedy *A Man's Man*. Instead of concentrating on how this title can be read as a reference to the star's homosexuality, I want to emphasize here how it must have also been read "straight," as a genuine affirmation of Haines's masculinity.

Indeed, Haines's outrageous star persona was something of a "camp" version of "straight." Constantly ad-libbing, clowning, cavorting, and overplaying his courtship, Haines invests his performances of heterosexuality with an outsider's appreciation of the extent to which heterosexual masculinity can be seen as absurd. The writing of a typical William Haines formula picture represents courtship as a series of destructive and manipulative acts leading up to a quick redemption and the final clinch. Added to this, Haines's performances in these films push the outrageous potential of these plots to their outer limits, emphasizing the privilege and arrogance of heterosexual masculinity, while viewing that masculinity as innately comic. Working together, the narrative and Haines's performance create a vision of heterosexuality that is so strained, so excessive, that they rupture the mythology that heterosexuality is normative and omnipresent.

The dominance of heterosexuality relies on the mythology that it is the natural, the healthy, indeed the only mode of human existence. It must render invisible the ways in which it is performed, incomplete, or chosen by man or woman. Precisely because Haines's performances of heterosexuality were performed and incomplete, his career offers a unique "queering" of straight masculinity and particularly of the institution of marriage as a centerpiece of male heterosexual privilege. In looking not at Haines's buddy movies, but two of his many romantic comedies, I discuss what "playing straight" meant for this star. We conventionally look at the closet, the process of passing for straight, as a process of obscuring any behavior that might give notice of one's gay identity. Instead, I want to look at Haines's passing as a process of *layering on* the trappings of heterosexuality. It is useful to compare the act of closeting oneself to gender cross-dressing. That is, when film characters cross from an unmarked category (masculinity) to a marked one (femininity), it is usual to see those characters put on coded items—jewelry, wigs, stuffed bras. When crossing from a marked to unmarked category, it is usual to see characters taking off or obscuring—cutting hair, removing jewelry, binding breasts. The cultural tendency to see only the marked category (in this case femininity) as constructed and performed is reflected in this process.

In crossing from a marked category to an unmarked category, then, the gay star performing heterosexuality is in a similar position to women performing masculinity. Judith Halberstam, in her book, *Female Masculinity*, points out that drag kings (female entertainers who dress like men) make visible the ways masculinity is an "outrageous performance," of predictable and definable acts, gestures, costumes, and linguistic habits. By showing the ways these features of masculinity can be put on, the drag king specifically undermines the apparent naturalness or invisibility of male identity (Halberstam 1998, 235). So in light of heterosexuality's centuries-old claims to be natural, rather than achieved, understanding the extent to which straight identity functions as a performance must also begin at the margins, at the place where that performance is self-conscious and indeed outrageous. William Haines's enactments of heterosexual characters are bold excesses; they render hetero-masculinity not as a natural category but rather an outrageous performance, marked by privilege, aggression, and a set of codified and artificial situations and actions, centering on the most central ritual of heterosexual privilege, the marriage ceremony.

I concentrate here on two romantic comedies that end with an arrested wedding scene. The silent *Show People* with Marion Davies, and the early sound film *The Girl Said No* (1930) with Leila Hyams, are connected by their wedding-stopping climaxes, where the Haines character prevents his leading lady from marrying the wrong man. The wedding, of course, is among the most potent symbols in American cinema culture and has enjoyed a long precinematic history as the happy ending that ties everything together. Its inverse, the dramatic wedding-stopping scene, offers all the pageantry of the big wedding finale, combined with an emotional climax that is not stale and ritualized (I do), but rather transgressive and exhilarating (stop the wedding!). In the hands of a star such as William Haines, whose performances of heterosexuality are simultaneously incomplete and overtly constructed, the wedding-stopping scene takes on two important connotations, both in critique of heteronormative institutions. First, by stopping the leading lady from marrying an overbearing and financially privileged man, he makes visible the ways that economic and social pressures can make marriage an imprisoning institution for women. They toy with the idea of playful feminist rebellion in a way that helped lay the groundwork for the screwball comedy of the mid-1930s. But second and more complexly, by stealing the bride away from a rival, these wedding-stopping scenes become the clearest expressions of Haines's outrageous performances of heteronormativity, where masculine pride and patriarchal privilege are acquired through competition with other men and possessive domination of women. In this sense, while the Haines characters often become least likable in these aggressive wedding scenes, his provocative interpretation of straight masculinity powerfully explodes the illusory naturalness and harmlessness of male heterosexual privilege.

A Man's Man

In the late silent and very early sound era, Haines's characters were commonly read as "real men," middle-class heroes of wit and drive. Irving Thalberg, in a speech at the University of Southern California in 1929, used Haines as an example of the new leading man of the talking era, "The idealistic love of a decade ago is not true today. William Haines, with his modern salesman attitude to go and get it, is more typical" (Mann, xii). The irony of Thalberg's characterization of Haines as a "typical" heterosexual suitor should be apparent, but it is also a testament to the way the closet performances of Haines could be and often were read as genuine representatives of heterosexual courtship. One newsletter of the William Haines Club referred to the star as "the greatest actor on the screen, typical of the finest in American manhood" (Mann, 165).

Like Rock Hudson, whose romantic comedy heroes were nearly always contrasted with the smaller, nervous "sissies" played by Tony Randall, the impression that Haines was a paragon of heteronormativity was usually helped along a bit by the casting of a scrawny, privileged milquetoast as Haines's rival for the affections of the heroine. This rival was overtly coded as a sissy, and audiences would have interpreted him as being far more sexually suspicious than the robust and witty Haines. Haines's fun-loving low-culture vibrant masculinity contrasted with the joyless high-culture effeminacy of his rival. Vito Russo argues, "From the bespectacled, bookish Harold Lloyd to the 'sensitive' student Tom Lee in *Tea and Sympathy*, a certain amount of anti-intellectualism is basic to the ingredients of the sissy stereotype" (31). Haines's characters sneer at these rivals, make fun of their glasses, their books, their devotion to their studies, and their courtly manners with women. In *Brown of Harvard*, Haines finds a hymnal in another student's room and proceeds to call the rival "deacon" for the rest of the film.

The schoolboy hierarchy that denigrates obedience, book-learning, politeness, and religion is the founding moral order of a Haines movie. His characters' outrageous behaviors were often read not as homosexual camp, but as juvenile pranksterism. The reviews for Haines's films occasionally used the kinds of code words that hinted at his homosexuality, such as "wisecracker." But more often, they referred to his verbal and physical exuberance in language that connoted boyish excess. In a review of *The Duke Steps Out*, *Variety* calls him "the screen's top disciple of juvenile egotism" (Mann, 160). *Life*'s Harry Evans calls him "the most popular smart aleck of the screen," describing the star in the youthful slang that Haines helped popularize (25). Robert Sherwood describes the dramatic arc in *Slide, Kelly, Slide*, "Having had his comeuppance,

Kelly changes from a loud-mouthed, self-assertive pest into a saddened, chastened, even tearful boy" (24). *New York Times* critic Mordaunt Hall tended to be quite hard on Haines's outrageous performances of youthful masculinity and peppered his reviews with exasperated references to Haines's immaturity. In panning *The Girl Said No*, Hall labels Haines "impertinent" and "hair-brained [*sic*]" (Hall 1930, 3). Hall describes the star's performance in *Telling the World*, in terms that recall an overactive child: "Mr. Haines is always boisterous, dancing around, and never still." In his more positive review of *A Tailor Made Man*, Hall's highest terms of praise are to place the thirty-something Haines at last among the adults, claiming that the film is "proof that maturity comes in time to those who wait."

The cinematic logic that treats Haines as a naughty boy—and therefore both harmless and justified in his rebellions against the feminizing institutions of church, school, family, and society—places him within the tradition of American boyhood that had emerged in the early 1900s and was still gaining momentum as the Great Depression began. The bad boy Haines shows a contempt for his weakling good boy rival that taps into a dark underside of the debate over how to raise American boys, a debate that tended to valorize the bad boy as the healthy and heterosexual one, while casting the good boy as timid and sexually suspicious.

Victorian models of middle-class boyhood encouraged young men to cultivate obedience, respect, and delicate manners. Frances Hodgsen Burnett's sentimental novel *Little Lord Fauntleroy* was published in 1886, and immediately gained an international following. It inspired one of the first merchandising booms in the history of popular novels when copies of Fauntleroy's infamous velvet suit became available, followed by dolls and even perfumes (Wilson, 235). But for all the acclaim and attention given to Burnett's pretty little boy, he quickly became the symbol of the "sissy" and helped focus the energies of a tremendous backlash against the "feminizing" of American boys. Several articles were written, organizations founded, and alternate children's books published to defend "natural" or "normal" masculinity against the suspicious effeminacy typified by the velvet menace. Indeed, although he was popular in his day, Fauntleroy was nearly the last text to defend obedient, gentle boyhood as an ideal.

Around the turn of the twentieth century, influential psychologist G. Stanley Hall popularized a new notion of boyhood, that young boys were "savages" and needed to replicate the stages of human civilization as they grew up. Hall argued that boys' development was stunted when mothers and educators tried to force obedience and refinement on them. Instead, he advocated a system of education that acknowledged and channeled their "savage" instincts into a productive basis for civilized adult masculinity (J. Grant, 833). This was one of many emerging theories that advocated some degree of roughness, naughtiness, and pranksterism as normal and healthy activities for young boys, necessary antidotes to the feminizing influences of modern life. By about 1920 most experts agreed that boys should be physically robust, attracted to adventure and competition, and willing to get into school-yard fights to defend themselves (J. Grant, 845). The "real boy" enjoyed mischief and chafed at cultural norms coded feminine, such as dress, manners, and sometimes church. The obedient Fauntleroy, alas, was a mama's boy.

The scientific literature of the early twentieth century reinforced the notion that a mother's attempts to turn this savage into a model citizen could result in his homosexuality, the signs of which would be his "display of femininity, his neurotic disposition, and/or his inability to form 'normal' sexual relationships with women besides his mother" (Gregg, 84). Based on Freud's diagnosis of homosexuality as a boy's failure to properly dissociate his own identity from his mother's, a newly public discussion of male homosexuality occurred in these years, a discussion that was intensively focused on how mothers treat their male children (J. Grant, 836).

Increasingly, popular prescriptions for normal boyhood began to center around freeing the boy from the mother's excessive influence. Between 1900 and 1920 the development of institutions such as the YMCA and the Boy Scouts were responses to urbanization and industrialization, two social changes that undermined the ideal of white masculinity, which in the United States had often been based in the conquest of the open land (Mechling, 219). As urban fathers went off to factory, clerical, or managerial jobs, they left boys in the home with their mothers or in schools characterized by an increasingly female teaching staff (Macleod, 47). Public figures such as Teddy Roosevelt advocated the idea that boys needed exercise, rugged outdoor activities, discipline, and wholesome male role models. Experts on boy culture advocated these activities to counteract the two negative extremes to which modern boys were subject—urban gangland delinquency and "soft" feminine dependency. Of the two extremes of "bad" boyhood—the mischievous delinquent and the neurasthenic "sissy"—the mischievous boy was by far preferable.

So in reading the antipathy between Haines and his more civilized rival in terms of a school-yard economy of masculine health versus feminized neurosis, how his campy, outrageous performances could be read as expressions of normal, if juvenile, heterosexuality is easy to see. Gaylyn Studlar has shown how Douglas Fairbanks exemplified an idealized boyish exuberance in his films of the late 1910s and early 1920s (21). Neither as robust nor as wholesome as Fairbanks, Haines's star persona edged more toward the naughty boy, the charismatic trickster whose bad behavior stems from a contempt for the rules of adult society that is altogether missing from the healthy optimistic athleticism of Fairbanks's films. Wickedly boyish disdain for all things feminine informs the Haines character's aggression against the wedding ceremony, a confluence of all the things the mischief-loving "real" boy hates—feminine décor, religion, formality, fancy dress, sentimentality, and the imposition of rules. By placing these wedding-stopping scenes near the end of the films, these two narratives allow the Haines character to remain in a state of arrested development. Instead of growing up, abandoning their playful narcissism, and joining an orderly adult society, these heroes bring their spirit of irreverent disorder to the symbolic site of heterosexual closure, the wedding ceremony.

Show People

Show People, directed by King Vidor, is a film about Peggy Pepper (Marion Davies) a young rube from Georgia trying to break into the movies. She puts on airs about her future stardom, but has no luck gaining access to studio work until she meets Billy Boone (William Haines) who gets her a bit part in a slapstick comedy. Peggy shows up at the studio thinking she will star in a drama, but is instead hit in the face with a spray of seltzer water when she makes her first grand entrance. Her reaction is so natural that the director is impressed with her gift for comedy, and she soon becomes Billy's regular costar in low-budget comic features, including one where she rides a pig in a Keystone Cops style chase seen. Soon, however, Peggy hits the big time, moving up to "High Art" studios and starring in costume epics. Changing her name to Patricia Pepoire, and forgetting Billy, Peggy agrees to marry her pretentious new costar, the fey European Andre Telefair. Billy stops the wedding by spraying Peggy with seltzer water, ruining her hair and makeup, and reminding her of the fun she used to have with Billy.

Show People is an altogether remarkable film for its constant "in" jokes about Hollywood—including numerous sequences where other MGM stars wander the lots of High Art studios, including Marion Davies (whom Peggy disdains) and Charlie Chaplin (whom she fails to recognize without his hat and mustache). One of these in jokes could well be the several references to William Haines's homosexuality, including two scenes where he fixes Peggy's makeup. These moments are very tender challenges to conventional masculinity, where Billy nurtures others in a playful and devoted way. Billy Boone is a genuine alternative to compulsory heterosexuality for Peggy because he defies narrow definitions of masculine identity. His association with lowbrow comedy justifies his gender flexibility, making his camping and his attire a play on the world of drag. Peggy seems to be "herself" in the comedy scenes, only putting on "drag" when she has become a big dramatic star and finds herself elaborately costumed, lying about her background to a bevy of attentive reporters. The fact that this dress-up game is only play does not occur to Peggy until the juvenile Billy attacks her with the seltzer. By behaving childishly, Haines helps her liberate herself from the stultifying adult world and reenter the joyful child's world of comedy.

But the wedding is not the final scene of the film. In a short epilogue, Peggy arranges for High Art Studios to hire Billy, turning the tables on the original dynamic of the relationship, where Billy secured a job for Peggy. She arranges their reunion as a surprise to Billy, so he comes on the lot in costume, dressed as a soldier for a *Big Parade* style World War I picture, not knowing who his costar will be. With the cameras rolling, Peggy, dressed as a French peasant girl, exits a building and the two come together for the final clinch, in front of the cameras. This new scenario, the romantic drama, forces Billy to meet Peggy on her own terms, which represents a compromise between the lowbrow humor of pigs and seltzer water and the highbrow nonsense of the regal wedding ceremony. In Peggy's happy ending, they will play dress-up together, but in the service of a grown-up narrative. She cannot force Billy to act like an adult, but she can at least force him to dress like one. He puts on the costume of the soldier, and the audience knows it is a costume, a form of drag for this ambiguously sexed performer. But they play the game together.

The Girl Said No

The Girl Said No, directed by Sam Wood, is also a comedy, but it is a talkie and a much more aggressive film all around. No longer matched with a star of equal prominence, Haines plays opposite Leila Hyams, a second-tier contract player who would shortly leave her film career entirely to get married. So the power dynamic between the two favors Haines at every turn, leaving Hyams without punch lines, big scenes, or major close-ups. Added to this, Haines's rapid-fire delivery and flexible voice frequently overpower Hyams's soft and hesitant speech. This romantic comedy pushes the genre's tendency to valorize masculine pursuit of a female love object to such an extreme that it reveals the ways such courtship can be dangerous and predatory. To contemporary audiences, the title sounds very much like a reference to date rape, and the film is not far off that mark. It contains some deeply uncomfortable scenes where the Haines character essentially traps Hyams—in a car, in her apartment, in her office—and she is physically vulnerable to attack. Buttressed by the way his speech outpaces and outshines the other performers (except the indomitable Marie Dressler in a welcome supporting role), Haines runs rampant through the narrative, enacting a particularly outrageous and trying form of heterosexual masculine privilege. William Mann calls this film one of Haines's "most dislikable" performances, yet it was made in Haines's most successful year, was considered a "gigantic moneymaker" for MGM, and was quite profitable (166). *New York Times* reviewer Mordaunt Hall also detested the film, but noted that the audience greeted several scenes with "loud and prolonged laughter" (Hall 1930, 3).

Haines plays Tom Ward, a young football star just home from college. Tom is a typical Haines character in the sense that he is both physically strong and socially juvenile. When he arrives home from college, he embraces his mother until she protests, "You're hurting me!" and then shakes his father's hand so hard the older man responds "Ouch!" He then proceeds to torment the family maid, Pauline (played by Haines's "fiancée," Polly Moran), attempting to trip her as she walks by. His reentry into the family home is rough, physically exuberant, and marked by his privileged pranksterism.

In contrast to his physical strength, Haines uses his voice in ways that are explicitly childish through much of this early talkie. He speaks baby talk when he wants to overcome another character's logic. When Mary cries, he whines, "Then I'll cry, too," and begins to pantomime boo-hooing to mock hers. When he visits her workplace, Mary asks him to wait outside in the lobby, and he replies in baby talk, "Mommy, do I gotta sit on the bench to see Mr. Sutton?" He prances out of the office, in a gesture modern audiences would read as gay, but in this film also signifies youthful mischief, an extension of the baby-talk act. When Mary is unwilling to talk to him, Tom plays both sides of the conversation, adopting a high voice for her dialogue and a low voice for his own. Again, the spectacle of Haines impersonating a woman, simpering, "Hello Tom, me fine buckaroo," is indisputably camp. But the playfulness of it, even its contempt for the conventions of heterosexual courtship, is connected to the bad boy sensibility appropriate to masculinity of the era.

Having established his disdain for courtly conventions, the juvenile prankster Tom pursues Mary with a slangy, snarky single-mindedness that suggests the new youth culture of the 1920s. Kay Bailey argues that coeducational high schools, college campuses, urban amusements, and integrated workplaces of the early twentieth century brought about a situation in which "youth were segregated increasingly by age and decreasingly by gender" (78). As a result, new rules of courtship developed among peer groups in defiance of the conventional rules the older generation handed down. As the generations differentiated themselves, "sex quickly became the key issue in the struggle that ensued" (78). Haines's performances of reckless heterosexual courtship, then, are an expression of this new peer-group identity, which defined itself by sexual experimentation and a rejection of the courtly rituals of earlier generations. In wooing the object of his desire, the Haines hero transposes the naughty boy's resistance to maternal influence into an assault on an earlier generation's rules of proper behavior. But as with *Show People*, differentiating between an assault on the institution of courtship and an assault on the woman being courted is difficult.

Tom's aggressive heterosexuality is most clearly represented in three scenes revolving around cars. The cars in this film become signifiers of heterosexual masculine normalcy, the lure of freedom, machinery, and sexual conquest all rolled into one. Strikingly, Tom's character is defined most boldly through these three car scenes, although none of the three cars he drives is even his own. They are borrowed emblems of heterosexual privilege, one of the film's few unconscious nods to Haines's out-of-place role as an aggressive young heterosexual Romeo. In the first scene of the film, a convertible is seen in long shot, racing a train to an intersection, and narrowly beating it through the crossing. His young female passenger expresses panic, but Tom calms her down with a kiss. The kiss causes him to run the car into a tree, after which she exclaims, "My new car!" revealing that the car he has been driving so recklessly is not even his own. We see a bullet hole in the car's windshield, but for reasons unknown. As Tom pulls up the car in front of his family's house, he asks the young lady's name. The result of this breakneck introduction to young Tom Ward is an efficient portrait of young masculine privilege gone out of control.

The second car scene takes place when Tom is out carousing with his friends and encounters an old college rival, the stuffy Melvin McAndrews (Francis X. Bushman Jr.), whom Haines calls a "four-eyed, bird-brained, button-headed mama's boy." When McAndrews's date, the lovely Mary Howe (Hyams), tries to tell Tom about his rival's new job with Sutton and Co., Tom snidely replies, "What do they make, doilies?" transposing the threat of homosexuality onto McAndrews, whose thin frame, pince-nez glasses, and impeccable manners make him sexually suspect. Making a play for Mary, Tom bribes a waiter to dump soup in McAndrews's lap. The date thus hastily ended, McAndrews goes out to fetch his car while Mary waits at the curb. Tom filches McAndrews's car and pulls up in front of the café, where Mary climbs in, not realizing that her tormentor is driving. Tom quickly drives away, ignoring Mary's pleas to be let out, and teasing her by speeding and veering close to a tree when she refuses to kiss him. This scene is one of the film's most painful, as Tom endangers the pair and she refuses his advances with increasing desperation. Weeping into her handkerchief, she whimpers, "You're a brute." "I know it," he replies, "but what was it brought out the brute in me? Aw, you're a prairie fire, darling, with stars in your hair and banjos in your voice. Can I help it if I try to get lucky?" Eventually, Mary devises the strategy of dropping her hankie out the window and asking Tom to return for it. When he gets out of the car to fetch it for her, she slides over to the driver's seat and speeds away.

Although Mary comes out the victor, this scene is quite uncomfortable to watch. Again, it ties the recklessness of Tom's driving to the aggressiveness of his heterosexual courtship. Unlike the young lady in the first scene, Mary is an extremely unwilling participant in his game of kissing and crashing. And unlike the opening scene's convertible, the closed nature of McAndrews's car, especially a drawn shade in the tiny rear window, points to the car's increasing function in American sexual ritual as a place of relative privacy where young people could go to be alone (Bailey, 86). That very enclosure is the source of the threat to Mary, who cannot call for help or escape Tom's advances. Only when she gets control of the car (as vehicle, as machine, and as sexual meeting place) does she get control of the relationship. It is the first of two episodes in which she will be literally abducted by her outrageous suitor.

Following this car episode, Tom's father dies, and the cocky Tom is forced to sober up, take care of his family's finances, and look for work. Mary warms up to the somewhat less boorish new Tom, but explains to him that because she has no family, she has to marry to achieve financial security. McAndrews wants to marry her and buys her $5,000 in bonds as a wedding gift. With this confirmation that McAndrews has virtually purchased her hand, the film makes explicit the fact that heterosexual marriage for Mary is a choice between a man who wants to buy her and a man who wants to steal her.

Tom crashes the wedding. Unable to convince Mary to leave with him, he ties her up in torn bedsheets and hauls her out a bedroom window into a car he has borrowed from his employer. As the two are driving away, the whole McAndrews clan behind them, Mary pleads with Tom to take her back. The dialogue in this exchange is symptomatic of Tom's character, and the broad shifts in tone and logic that characterize this film. Stopping the car, he sneers at her, in the deepest and strongest voice he uses throughout the film:

TOM: All right, you goofy little fat-head, get out of here. I got a good notion to slap you, too, just to knock some sense into your silly head. Go on, get out. I never liked you anyhow.

MARY: Why Tom!

TOM: You think I'd go to jail for you? Get out.

MARY: Well, gee, I didn't want you to go to jail.

TOM: Well, do something about it.

MARY: But what?

TOM: Why you scared canary . . . you dumb blonde Annie . . . marry me!

MARY: All right, when you put it that way.

TOM: Why didn't you say that before?

MARY: Well, I didn't have a good excuse!

TOM (grinning, and embracing her): Baby!

As they embrace, McAndrews finally catches up to the car, but Tom stalls him by pulling Mary's bonnet-style wedding veil over his head to blind him as the pair drives away. By using the veil to blind and humiliate Melvin McAndrews, Tom again projects the suspicion of effeminacy onto another character. The real boy has been differentiated from the sissy, won the girl, and all the threatening feminine trappings of the wedding have been left behind.

The wedding-crashing scene in this film is obviously more aggressive than the one in *Show People*. Again, the car is both an emblem of Tom's masculine power and a tool to isolate Mary so she cannot get help. Mary's complicity is an appallingly convenient plot device that underlines the power of Tom's constant refusal to grant her any will, to acknowledge that the girl has said "no." He calls her names and threatens to strike her. She responds with a kind of relief, pleased to have a good excuse finally to say "yes." Significantly, however, Mary is not leaving marriage behind like Peggy did, but she is actually contracting herself to marry her abductor. In ruining her wedding, Tom was not inviting the bride to leave behind the world of adult responsibility and come out to play, but rather replacing the sissy suitor with the masculine one. However, the notion of play is still very much present in Tom's sudden change from suitor to antagonist. He turns on her in a way that is so unexpected and so narratively unjustified that reading it as anything but play is difficult. His words sound like something he just heard in a gangster movie, the hand raised as if to hit her is held at an awkward angle, and the timing of his lines suggests that the character is trying out a new tactic that he just thought up. His expression lacks consistency, coherence, and naturalness. It is an outrageous performance.

Conclusion: After Haines

The boyish William Haines could play out a violent and aggressive heterosexual narrative like the one in *The Girl Said No* with some degree of irony, some sense in his character that the whole process of romantic courtship is a child's game, and the cherished norms of heterosexual masculinity are the behaviors of a naughty boy. With the advent of sound, his playful masculine masquerades led down a path that distinctly influenced later performers. Lee Tracy's speedy salesman's talk, James Cagney's rat-a-tat-tat delivery, and Clark Gable's bemused sarcastic tone all owe a debt to William Haines's vocal technique. But while William Haines took advantage of the radical disjunction between his strong masculine body and his childish, ever-shifting voice for comic effect, his successors did not. Haines's style was quickly eclipsed by men whose performances enhanced the idea that aggressive masculinity is natural, physical, and unperformed.

By about 1931, robust and energetic stars such as Tracy, Cagney, and Gable, as well as Paul Muni, Edward G. Robinson, Charles Bickford, Victor McLaglen, Gary Cooper, and Robert Montgomery, had risen above most of the more romantic leading men of their generation, and above the juvenile Haines as well. This new cohort of actors frequently played characters with some combination of traits that included sexual aggression, street smarts, fast-talking persuasiveness, cynical contempt for tradition, and physical toughness. Mark LaSalle has argued that this generation of pre-Code men produced a unique vision of "new-fashioned heroes whose manhood was an authoritative force—not pretty boys, not cannon fodder, not pawns of the system, but dangerous men" (xiii). These "dangerous" men enacted an often-violent vision of masculinity that explicitly defined itself against and at the expense of femininity, just as the real boy had defined itself against the sissy. Famously, Cagney's breakthrough role in *The Public Enemy* (1931) required him to shove a grapefruit into Mae Clarke's face and to push his mother. The bit was successful enough to bear repetition. Cagney kicked Virginia Bruce in the caboose in *Winner Takes All* (1932), and he dragged Mae Clarke around by the hair in *Lady Killer* (1934).

By most accounts, this physical aggression toward women was met with considerable popular approval. The grapefruit scene became a touchstone for the cinema's new masculinity. Gilbert Seldes wrote in 1937:

> Men found the movies feminized and the great change came when Mr. Cagney in *Public Enemy* was being annoyed by Mae Clarke and rudely ground half a grapefruit into her face. From that time on it became common form for the tough guys of the picture to kick and slap their women around on the slightest provocation and roars of delight rose from the throats of men who had up to that time found nothing satisfactory in pictures except for the newsreel and Mickey Mouse. (Quoted in Crafton, 539)

Just as the feminizing effects of urban life and modernization had produced a backlash valorizing bad boys as a national ideal, the Great Depression's many "feminizing" stresses on masculinity, including joblessness, social instability, and the increased presence of women in the workplace, produced a demand to see dominant men on the screen. Physical violence helped reintegrate the body of the film hero and protect it against the twin stresses of both cinematic and social disintegration. Whereas William Haines's campy humor relied on an incoherence of body and voice, the celebrated new man of the talkies required precisely the opposite. The artful incoherence of Haines's naughty-boy persona was translated into a masculinity that relied on violent action to achieve the appearance of naturalness and coherence. In the years after Haines left the screen, masculinity was no longer an outrageous performance.

2

Mary Beth Haralovich

Flirting with Hetero Diversity

Film Promotion of *A Free Soul*

In a 1982 essay in *Screen* I explored the conventions of classical Hollywood film poster advertising: the art and design that present a film in one-sheet posters, lobby cards, and newspaper ads. The heterosexual couple has long been central to film advertising, to the invitation to cinema and the promise of cinematic pleasure. In film promotion (posters and publicity, inclusive), narrative strategies, star expectations, and studio production values conjoin with ideologies of courtship, attraction, and love. The poster places the couple within the process of formation—a man and a woman poised as simultaneously drawn together and kept apart—at a point of narrative tension that will be resolved by seeing the film in the movie theater. Using the advertising and publicity surrounding *A Free Soul* (1931), this chapter looks deeper into the heterosexual impulses of classical Hollywood film promotion to explore the quality of desire and the diversity of available heterosexuality.

Heterosexual masculine and feminine identities are important to the promotion of *A Free Soul* and to the desire for cinema. In *On Flirtation,* Adam Phillips observes that flirtation has an "implicit wish to sustain the life of desire" (xvii–xviii). Film promotion (whether in magazines, newspapers, or theater lobbies) has a flirtatious relationship with the filmgoer. Through its visual address and tease of information, film promotion entertains desire for a particular film and sustains desire for the pleasures of the cinematic institution. In the classical Hollywood period, these pleasures were often invitations to blur the boundaries of class and gender norms. Yet, as film promotion from different communities indicates, such flirtatious invitations could only go so far. Flirting with race and sexual orientation was beyond consideration.

"To Love as I Please!"

In their visual address, classical film posters tend to truncate human bodies to focus on the heads of stars. The eyes and the face are the windows to the character. The close-up of the star-in-character is arrayed not only to-be-looked-at, but also to look back or toward the viewer actively—to flirt, to invite interest in the story of the film. In her study of the theory of the close-up, Mary Ann Doane makes several observations that can help us understand the centrality of the star's face in film promotion.[1] The close-up in a film and in film promotion are both "a sign, a text, surface which demands to be read" (94). Unlike the close-up in a film, the film promotion face is under no compunction to avoid direct address with the spectator. The mute face of film promotion participates in a narrative, but one that is removed from the "relentless temporality of the narratives unfolding" (97). One narrative that the film promotion face participates in and conveys is heterosexuality.

In *Creating the Couple: Love, Marriage and Hollywood Performance*, Virginia Wright Wexman examines how Hollywood film narrative enjoins the formation of a companionable and monogamous heterosexual couple. In film posters, rather than being propelled toward one ideal companion, characters can be presented with choices, with options for companionship and partners. Thus, a poster presents a character flirting with the options at the cusp of choices and possibilities. Which one will he or she choose? How will he or she choose? In her study of gender and advertising, Anne Cronin finds that advertising "can articulate a range of narratives of self that traverse different zones or dimensions of self, context, historical location and text-based image" (110). Promotion for *A Free Soul* illustrates the importance of heterosexual identities to the "narratives of self" offered to the filmgoer.

Norma Shearer plays a post-1920s independent thinker who chooses a sexual affair with a gangster (manly Clark Gable, in a breakout role) instead of marriage to an admirer from her social class (softly masculine Leslie Howard). A 2001 Pacific Film Archive synopsis suggests *A Free Soul*'s vigorous pre-Code status:

> . . . Norma Shearer gives Jan an uncomplicated sexual aggressiveness, and a steely self-possession that doesn't temper in the face of both violent and passive attempts by men and family to control her. Ultimately a morality tale about freedom's perils, the film's first half lives up to the pre-Code era's sometimes exaggerated reputation for sexual freedom. A playfully incestuous interchange opening the film is probably more provocative to today's sensibilities; it prepares us for the frankness to follow. (Amazonas)

Jan Ashe (Norma Shearer) is the carefree daughter of alcoholic attorney Stephen Ashe (Lionel Barrymore) who defends gangster Ace Wilfong (Clark Gable) on a murder charge. Jan, engaged to polo-player Dwight Winthrop (Leslie Howard), begins an affair with Ace. When Ace wants to marry Jan, Stephen is appalled. Ace retreats to his apartment where sultry Jan awaits him. She is interested in an affair but not marriage. Stephen discovers Jan and Ace together. Stephen mourns Jan's "miserable backstairs affair." In an angry moment, Ace shoves Jan ("take it and like it") and announces they will be married the next morning, or he will ruin Jan's reputation. To save Jan, Dwight shoots and kills Ace. Jan visits Dwight in jail, weeping in his arms. She searches for her father Stephen and finds him drunk in a dive. At Dwight's trial, Stephen's honest questions and Jan's honest answers reveal her affair with Ace and her father's failures. Stephen collapses and dies on the courtroom floor. Jan decides to leave town. Dwight, free from jail, promises to follow her.

In *A Free Soul*, a woman acts on her desire for independence from the expedient behaviors expected from her upper-class and gender. The woman's independent thinking and actions are an impediment to the companionable couple. As she seeks her way, she rejects the opportunity to settle into romantic love and marriage with a "'suitable' partner" (Wexman, 13), a gentleman of her own class. Instead, she opts for what *New York Times* critic Mordaunt Hall (1931) described as an "unfortunate and unnatural affection" for a rough gangster. She ends the film as she began it, independent and unmarried. The invitation to experience Jan's free-spirited femininity in *A Free Soul* easily merges the star power of Shearer with the dramatic role of an independent woman, an object of desire who is interested in heterosexual desire, but is not bound by courtship or the goal of marriage. *A Free Soul*'s poster advertising celebrates her decisiveness and individual freedom, at the same time warning that Jan dangerously crosses the boundaries of gender propriety.

In some early 1930s films, the couple is at risk due to prostitution or trading sex for rewards (such as *Blonde Venus* [1932], *Red Headed Woman* [1932], and *Baby Face* [1933]). In *A Free Soul*, Jan enjoys an independence developed from the 1920s period of first-wave feminism and entertainment: shorter hair and shorter skirts, women's suffrage, free-spirited Jazz Age youth culture. The promotion of *A Free Soul* uses these historical advances for women to flirt with the possibility of Jan Ashe's heterosexuality as a femininity fortified by attributes associated with masculinity.

Figure 3. Advertisement for *A Free Soul*, *Photoplay* inside back cover (August 1931).

Among *A Free Soul's* national campaign was a full-page inside back cover of *Photoplay* (August 1931). This ad sought to connect with film fan readership by evoking the implications of the contemporary state of woman's conditions ("She was born in an age of FREEDOM! Who could blame her for seeking the sweet fruits of living?") and the assumed promiscuity of a divorced woman with its reference to Shearer's previous film, *The Divorcee* (1930)—"She wasn't a divorcee but she believed that strangers could kiss!" A sketch of Shearer in close-up dominates the ad. Three photos present Jan/Shearer in medium two-shot with each of the three men. With Leslie Howard, "She was bored—she wanted a new thrill!" With Clark Gable, "She gambled with love—but found the stakes too high." With Lionel Barrymore, "'Shearer superb—Barrymore magnificent' say the critics." Heterosexuality with Howard is boring, with Gable dangerous—and with Barrymore implicitly nonexistent in favor of shared professionalism.

Local promotions for the film also reflect this flirtation with female sexual emancipation, as can be seen in two city newspapers (the *Des Moines Register* and the *Cedar Rapids Gazette*). The first newspaper ad in the *Register* for the film's run at the Des Moines theatre declares in large type, "I can take care of myself in your man's world!" This copy anchors a photo of smiling and beautiful Norma Shearer in medium-shot, leaning toward the viewer, raising a glass of bubbling champagne in a toast. Her words are addressed to men, "your man's world." With vivacious confidence, she is ready to engage the world of men (June 19, 1931).

The day before the film's opening in Cedar Rapids, the ad in the *Gazette* similarly addressed the reader directly, promising, "the daring version of Adela Rogers St. John's novel" in which "you meet *A Free Soul*—free with love—free with kisses—daring shame—never once regretting!" (June 26, 1931). In a long-shot photo, Shearer in a gown and Gable in tuxedo face each other, his hands on her waist, her arms on his shoulders. The ad exploited women's changing social position ("She was born in an age of freedom! Who could blame her for seeking the sweet fruits of living?") and teased with its lurid pleasures ("A sordid affair with a gambler—flouting life's conventions—it's thrilling drama!"). Both ads invite the desire to see a glamorous woman push the boundaries of heterosexual norms.

These national and local campaigns for *A Free Soul* suggest audience recognition of diverse heterosexual identities for women, "narratives of self" that can be seen as oppositional to quiet domestic life. Two recent studies of women—as readers and as cinemagoers—find that 1930s-era movies provided women with alternative visions of female heterosexuality. In her study of the historical romance from 1918 to 1939,

Sallie McNamara situates "the development of a new market of erotic literature by women for a female audience" within a larger popular culture environment that includes other "leisure pursuits" such as cinema and dancing (83). McNamara finds that for female readers of historical romance, "fantasy and daydream . . . can offer scope or material as the basis for transgression and/or a challenge to gender roles and moral codes" (84).

In her study of the memories of 1930s British cinemagoers, Annette Kuhn finds that the women respondents had "dreams of a better, more beautiful self, dreams nourished and given expression through cinema culture. For cinema, above all, offered new models of femininity" (132). As Roger Dooley noted about Jan Ashe's model of femininity, "her money is no obstacle to happiness, but, rather, enables her to experiment and get away with unconventional conduct impossible for a girl without an impregnable bank account" (48). Money gives Jan the freedom to act and provides a realistic motivation for her glamorous gowns. Even if this financial model of femininity was not attainable or realistic for moviegoers, Kuhn found that "[i]n the 1930s, cinema culture provided a space in which young women could at least imagine themselves just as beautiful, interesting and adventurous as film stars" (133). Adventure and transgression, fantasy and daydream, glamour and beauty: the film promotion for pre-Code *A Free Soul* offered Norma Shearer as Jan Ashe, acting on her desires for independent heterosexuality.

"A Woman Can't Get Away with It!"

While these studies confirm the availability of diverse modes of femininity for female viewers, *A Free Soul* could also engage male pleasure in women's cinematic heterosexuality. Mr. Houlston, one informant in Kuhn's study, "contends, the cinema was for him—and indeed for others—a source of education in sexual matters as well as of pleasurable looking" (154). For Mr. Houlston, the cinema was flirtatious. "What he found most intriguing was not so much overt display as the tease of the partly revealed female body and the brief glimpse of the forbidden" (157). Dressed and poised for glamour and sexuality, female stars appeared in fan magazines and postcards, ready to be objects of male and female heterosexual gazes. Embraced within the visual pleasure of MGM production values, Norma Shearer as Jan is shown coiffed and wearing cute ensembles and glamorous gowns.

A tie-up in *Photoplay* presented Shearer in boudoir attire. "Norma Shearer can well afford to look regal. . . she wears this knockout negligee in 'A Free Soul' which you must see. It's tangerine velvet, girls, with one of the trains that are simply 'tripping'!" Shearer stands in a pose common to MGM women in their films: chest and chin forward, hands on hips, right knee bent. Her pose displays her body in the clinging and shiny gown that appeared as a visual motif in the posters for *A Free Soul*. The *Photoplay* tie-up and the film's ad campaign remind film culture to objectify Jan/Shearer and thus recuperate her heterosexuality: "Norma Shearer. . . Never so gorgeous, so lavishly gowned, so utterly bewitching."

Negotiated limits to heterosexual diversity extended beyond glamorous display of movie stars. Local promotion included warnings about the consequences of female liberation and, in one community, *A Free Soul* apparently raised issues of propriety. The aforementioned ad in the *Des Moines Register* starts with an assertion of independence, but the words positioned next to Shearer's head tease and warn:

> "I'll travel my own road!" she cried. "I want to be free to do as I please—to live as I please—to love as I please!" And then she found that her kind of freedom costs more than it was worth–that men might play at this game without being hurt but a woman *can't get away with it!* (emphasis in original)

Below the close-up of Shearer are four sketches that display Jan/Shearer in four poses. One is a long-shot of Jan/Shearer in décolletage and the body-hugging gown (which we now know is the tangerine velvet negligee). She looks off, displayed to-be-looked-at. In the other three sketches, Jan/Shearer is in an embrace with each of three men with text that offers information about each relationship. With one man, ambiguous yet evoking Gable, she pushes against him, "She knew it was madness when she started. But little did she realize that for him it would end with a bullet . . . for her—?" With a man recognizable as Howard, she appears comfortable, "Three men—three loves—three conflicting desires. And she tried to satisfy them all." The third sketch is Jan/Shearer in a hug with a disheveled Barrymore: "Superb performances by Shearer and Barrymore hailed by the critics as the season's best." This large and detailed ad promises parties, glamour, and sex as well as the perils of adventures in heterosexuality. Jan's assertion of independence at the top of the page becomes, at the bottom of the page, three relationships in which she subsumes her desires to give each man what he wants from her (June 19, 1931).

Other ads for *A Free Soul* in the *Register* were smaller and provided less detail of heterosexual diversity. The ad that announced the film's upcoming engagement (June 18, 1931) attempted to entice with a medium-shot glamour photo Shearer in décolletage and gown. The text was boilerplate promotion of the Hollywood cinematic institution, rather than this particular film: "A drama unfolds itself on the screen which excels the previous glories of Miss Shearer," and "a great star's greatest triumph!" The ad from later in the film's run (June 21, 1931) used a long-shot photo of Shearer in décolletage and clinging gown, looking out at the viewer. This ad promised a story that is "Gay! Daring! Truthful! Modern!" and used Jan's attributes of independence ("I've been taught to live my own life"), but with a warning and innuendo ("And she lived it!—Dangerously . . . Seeking the sweet fruits of living . . . traveling the high road of forbidden adventure!").

Reviews in the *Cedar Rapids Gazette* at first celebrate, but later indicate some concern with, the amount of flirting with heterosexual diversity used in promoting the film. Of course, the newspaper reviews might be taken, wholly or in part, from reviews the studio wrote. What matters to this study is that the exhibitor chose to put the review into circulation, to print the review in the newspaper as a means of engaging the local audience. In the *Cedar Rapids Gazette* in the 1930s, the reviews appear to be an amalgam of prepared materials and locally written copy.

To announce the engagement of *A Free Soul*, an enthusiastic review promises "something special . . . a gala event for the reason that Cedar Rapids is the first city of its size in the country to see this picture at a popular scale of prices." The review praises Barrymore ("the most effective characterization he has done before the cameras") and Howard ("one of the most accomplished of stage players and rapidly becoming a prime favorite in pictures"). For Gable, the review finds him "much better cast . . . as the ruthless, domineering gambler with whom Miss Shearer pleases to have a sordid affair than he was as a Salvation Army drummer in 'Laughing Sinners' with Joan Crawford in which he was recently seen here." For Shearer, the review finds that she goes "many steps farther . . . in flouting life's conventions, but she handles the part perfectly," suggesting that Shearer brings decorum to the representation of woman's desire.

A second review of *A Free Soul* appeared in the Sunday entertainment pages (June 28, 1931), praising all the performances and providing more information about the heterosexual options in the film, Gable as "the ruthless domineering gambler" and Howard as the "honorable gentleman and considerate devoted suitor." The attributes of Shearer's Jan are repeated verbatim in the film's ads: "free with her love, free with her kisses, daring shame to be 'A Free Soul.'" The page featured a long-shot photo of Shearer and Gable in Ace's apartment. She is in a gown, sitting forward on the edge of a couch while he, in tuxedo, leans into her intensely.

Near the end of *A Free Soul*'s run, a third *Gazette* review commented on the importance of high-quality performances for a film with a difficult topic (June 29, 1931). This review praised the "excellent work" of the players, "which should remove any shred of doubt concerning the manner in which the powerful story of unrestricted love is portrayed . . . because the story must be well done to keep from being distasteful." The film may have presented some controversy in Cedar Rapids because this review concludes with what appears to be a defense: "'A Free Soul' is one picture that cannot be accepted impassively. There will be some reaction, favorable or unfavorable, which is a compliment of the highest order to any picture." More editorial about film art than review, this piece suggests the thoughtful and communicative relationship that the Cedar Rapids exhibitor and newspaper had with the local audience.

In flirting with but still limiting heterosexual diversity, the film's promotion of the lead woman follows a structure similar to what Lea Jacobs has observed about the narrative of *Blonde Venus*, the productive "division between character and star" that confines Helen's womanly domesticity to the home and reveals her sexuality when she performs on stage. Jacobs writes, "the sexuality that Helen must hold back, that cannot achieve expression in the domestic space, is displaced to the space of the stage and the image of the star" (104). A similar duality plays out in the promotion of *A Free Soul:* Jan's sexuality (conveyed by Shearer) is celebrated in newspaper and magazine posters for the film, whereas fan magazine articles celebrate the performer's monogamy with MGM production head Irving Thalberg. Shearer is sexual in the character of Jan and wifely as Mrs. Thalberg. Thus, Shearer's star image places her securely within a heterosexual couple and tempers her displayed sexuality in her films.

Leading up to and during the run of *A Free Soul*, *Photoplay* continued its coverage of the Shearer-Thalberg marriage as the union of a companionable couple. In August 1930, one year before the release of *A Free Soul*, a story about Shearer's real life marriage to Thalberg pondered the paradox of the working woman and wife: "Will Norma Shearer retire? Read the answer in this fascinating story of a girl who found that love and a career can mix!" and "The star and her producer-husband, proud and happy in the discovery that their married life and their careers blend blissfully." But it is not easy. *Photoplay* (May 1931), two months before the release of *A Free Soul*, explained the attributes that allowed Shearer to manage the stresses of career and marriage: "How Norma Shearer Got What She Wanted: a steel will and driving ambition overcame her handicaps and brought her love and success." This story of a woman who reaches career heights raises the question, "But has she missed anything in her fight for fame?" The fan and reader can know that this is but one installment in the story of Norma Shearer's marriage.

In "'He Is Her Boss, You Know, as Well as Her Husband': Norma Shearer and the Place of Working-Wives in the Early 1930s," Tim Connelly observes that Shearer's publicity presented her as a modern woman and then relegated her to the role of Thalberg's wife through appeals to romantic love and cautionary tales about the perils of becoming a successful woman outside of marriage. Connelly finds that fan coverage of Shearer was dominated by "the high-profile nature of her marriage." In her relationship with Thalberg, Shearer "must defer to his authority as head of production . . . [and] to his authority as husband and head of the household." Yet, the promotion of *A Free Soul* uses the star power of Norma Shearer to fashion the dramatic role of an independent woman and her desire for choice. Shearer's star image seemed to manage easily the diverse heterosexuality of the independent woman and woman's desire in the 1930s.

"Honorable and Devoted" versus "Ruthless and Domineering"

In addition to presenting the film's pre-Code adventures in female heterosexuality, *A Free Soul*'s promotion explores the heterosexuality of its younger male stars. For Gable and Howard, *A Free Soul*'s promotion develops the conflicting masculine heterosexual attributes that they bring to their roles in the film: Ace/Gable's violent sexual attractiveness and Dwight/Howard's quiet passivity. Despite reviews that recognize Barrymore's return to the screen and the strength of his performance as Stephen Ashe (for which Barrymore would receive the 1930–1931 Academy Award for actor), Barrymore's marquee value recedes in favor of Gable, a younger man with matinee idol exploitation value.

With his 1931 breakout performances (*A Free Soul, Night Nurse, Possessed, Susan Lenox: Her Rise and Fall*), Gable became a masculine sensation on-screen and in film promotion. In "Clarke [*sic*] Gable's Balls: Real Men Never Lose Their Teeth," Joe Fisher notes that Gable entered the Quigley Publications Top Ten in 1932, where he remained secure for ten years (35). Fisher credits Gable with being "arguably the first leading man to bring [to the screen] 'real' masculine power—the power to tame and control women and land (and less masculine men)" (38). In the film and in promotion, theatrically trained British actor Leslie Howard was arrayed against Gable's "raw, brutal, uncivilized power" and "sex appeal" (36). *A Free Soul*'s promotion attempted to shore up Howard's masculine attributes to establish, or perhaps to confirm, his attractiveness to women.

Leslie Howard appeared in *Photoplay* (October 1931), two months after the second run of *A Free Soul* ("in which he made a minor part important by the sincerity of his playing"). A promotion still from *A Free Soul* of Howard and Shearer in medium-close two-shot looking dreamily into each other's eyes, occupies the top half of the page, above the title, "A Nervous Wreck! Don't be fooled by Leslie Howard's famous suavity—he's really as jittery as a stampeded herd of jumping beans." The story attempted to move Howard from the inaccessible high art pedestal of theater and make him more ordinary, that is, more American ("Offhand, you'd hardly know he was English."). The apologetic tone of this single story about Howard contrasted sharply with the tactility and number of stories about Gable.

Photoplay used Clark Gable's performance in *A Free Soul* in a series of three stories that found the new star to be an exemplar of masculinity. *Photoplay* swooned before his manliness. "'What a Man!'—Clark Gable" (October 1931) featured a production still of Gable and Shearer in *A Free Soul* and one of Gable and Greta Garbo in *Susan Lenox*. "Dastardly villain though he was, thousands of girls rubbed their eyes, felt their own pulses race into high and murmured dazedly, 'How long has this Gable person been going on?'" Fisher comments, "Gable's allure was somewhere between savagery and sadism" (36). In many of Gable's early 1930s films, his characters were violent toward women. Fisher finds "Gable's actual and threatened violence" to be "an 'acceptable' objective correlative for sex" (37) and a strong basis of his appeal.

In November 1931, "Why Women Go Crazy about Clark Gable" pondered why audiences preferred Gable's "uncompromising domination" and "indifference" to women to Howard's "noble self-sacrificing." *Photoplay* asked, "Is it that the ladies and gentlemen of the audience have been fed up with too much superhuman nobility, hearts of gold, and all that sort of thing in our motion picture actors?" The article contends that Gable's attraction stems partially from an attribute that he takes from women: mystery. "Mystery has been monopolized by women. Clark Gable has stolen one of their most potent weapons and turned it on them."

In August 1932, "Will Clark Gable Last?" argued against giving Gable film roles that would develop his versatility as an actor. The story used stills from two films with Shearer and Gable with captions that compared the power of their screen performances. In the still from *A Free Soul*, Shearer and Gable are in medium two-shot, she pushing against and away from him: ". . . Norma's fine performance paled beside the brisk virility of Gable. In this, the picture that brought him fame, he created a type—the brutal, knock-'em-around hero—and became a sensation overnight." In the still from *Strange Interlude* (1932), Gable possibly veers too close to a Leslie Howard–type pose, sitting in a parlor chair and kissing Shearer's hand: "Norma Shearer has realized her ambition and may now be classed with the greatest actresses of the day. . . . So it's no discredit to Clark Gable to say she steals the picture." The *Photoplay* story pleaded with the studios to "give him typical Clark Gable roles" or "his days will be over."

The *Photoplay* articles indicate the value of Clark Gable's masculine attraction to film promotion and how Howard's softer masculinity paled before Gable's. At the end of the decade, these actors would bring to *Gone With the Wind* (1939) the opposing masculine attributes that they brought to *A Free Soul.* Fisher describes the casting: Howard as "Ashley Wilkes, the figure of inadequate, but historically validated, masculinity against which Gable/Rhett's greater power was to be measured" (48). Two masculinities court Scarlett O'Hara and Jan Ashe. The stories of both films pivot around the diversity of heterosexual choices.

Hetero Diversity and Heterotopia

In analyzing the nature of flirtation, Phillips cautions that "no real choices are being made. . . . In flirtation one does not take risks, one only sustains their possibility" (xxi). The flirtation in the promotion for *A Free Soul* goes only so far in terms of gender freedom. Furthermore, posters in the classical Hollywood period do not risk the possibility of homosexual and racially integrated "narratives of self." In fact, film promotion guards against flirtation with racial and sexual diversity.[2] One must ask what "narratives of self" are available to audiences that are not white. The *Chicago Defender*, the African American newspaper, used an ordinary, mundane ad for *A Free Soul*'s run at the Regal, a neighborhood theater in south side Chicago, nearly one month after its first run in downtown Chicago (August 22, 1931). The *Defender* evinced no promotional interest in the spectacle of heterosexual desire, Jan's narrative situation, or the attributes of the men. This ad did not flirt with the viewer except to pay homage to the star system with "SHEARER" in large letters and a medium-shot of Shearer in a basic glamour pose. The ad for *A Free Soul* ran with an ad for Maurice Chevalier, saluting and wearing a kepi, in *The Smiling Lieutenant*, the next feature to play at the Regal. The ad used boilerplate hyperbole: Shearer's film is "beautiful Norma's finest picture with the greatest cast ever assembled!"; Chevalier's is "the picture pleasure of the year."

The *Defender*'s entertainment page did lead with a headline and five-paragraph review of *A Free Soul* followed by a five-paragraph review of *The Smiling Lieutenant.* Both appeared to parrot studio press books with excitement about performance, enthusiasm for production values, and details of story. The column ends with a reminder: "These two outstanding hits of film entertainment will be shown at the Regal's popular reduced prices of 10, 25 and 35 cents." The *Defender*'s perfunctory promotion of *A Free Soul* suggests acceptance of the domination of white film culture yet a resistance to the white gaze of film promotion, exposing both the scope and the limits of flirtation with hetero diversity.

Examining the *Defender*, however, also underlines the intersection between film promotion and the places where film advertising is exhibited. As they are today, 1930s film ads and publicity stories were read in the context of the daily newspaper. One might look for what's playing, sweeping the pages for movie stills and announcements. Film ads are surrounded by ads for products and services. They are embedded in headlines, news stories, and diversions. This larger context can have interesting semiotic relationships to the films being advertised. The daily newspaper as a site for movie ads recalls Kuhn's description of movie theaters as a space of heterotopia. Like movie theaters, daily newspapers "juxtapos[e] in a single real place different spaces and locations that are incompatible with each other" (Kuhn quoting Foucault, 141). The heterotopia in which film promotion is exhibited does not reveal incompatibility as much as the diversity of identities available to readers and filmgoers at the time.

In the *Des Moines Register* during the week of *A Free Soul*'s run in June 1931, front page news was four deaths in a heat wave with temperatures in the 100°Fs and a police raid of a film screening (June 25, 1931); In the raid, "150 taken to jail in raid on obscene movie show . . . the motion picture was unspeakably obscene. Its title and subject matter is unprintable." This film was apparently screened on a program of short films, perhaps at a stag party. The story explained, "Following the Dempsey-Tunney picture [a boxing realite], the undercover agent said a woman danced, clothed as dancers usually are clothed. The obscene picture followed, according to the undercover agent, but only a small portion of it had been shown when raiders burst in the hall." The story continued on an inside page of the newspaper with the headline, "150 arrested at obscene picture show," and two photos, an overhead shot of people being loaded into a paddy wagon and one of a room with several slot machines.

In Cedar Rapids film news the week at the end of June 1931, Lola Lane, "an Iowa girl," was cast in the "new gangfilm," *Little Caesar* (June 25, 1931) and a small-town or rural Iowa eighth grade girl was selected "to represent Iowa at a conference to be held July 6–10 in Washington, D.C., to investigate the value of sound films in rural education work" (June 29, 1931).

In both the *Register* and the *Gazette*, entertainment shared the same space as the women's pages. On these pages during the week of *A Free Soul*'s run in Des Moines, the *Register* ran a "condensed version" of *20,000 Leagues under the Sea* ("strange machines drive huge submarine, tour of vessel reveals") and a romance serial, *Ice Cold Kisses* ("She has Spanish blood in her veins . . . her kisses were ice cold"). On the same page as the movie ads was a photo of a women piloting an "imitation airplane" at Riverview Park, news of the Vanderbilts' separation, and dwarfing the movie ads, a huge ad for Chesterfield cigarettes featuring a switchboard operator, "put in a call for the cigarette . . . it doesn't take a long distance call . . . here's your party—Chesterfield" (June 21, 1931).

Among the regular amusements on the *Gazette*'s film page was "Believe It or Not!": Gandhi, "a little old toothless man weighing but 80 lbs. is the leader of more people than any man on earth" (June 29, 1931). Another day, the film page ran the "Will Rogers Says" column ("all I know is just what I read in the papers") and the item that the aged aunt of Germany's World War I "red ace" Baron Von Richthofen took her first airplane ride (June 28, 1931).

Lurid ads for *A Free Soul* were nestled on pages with domestic advice, such as a "Table Talks" column that surveyed types of refrigerators (mechanical, absorption, compression) and recipes (June 28, 1931); or civic news, including construction bids for the post office; a church concert (June 26, 1931) and an exposé of the gangster menace to society, perhaps a cautionary tale for women who would emulate Jan Ashe: "U.S. Prosecutor who smashed Al Capone ring strips gang chiefs of their Robin Hood glamour; shows them to be merely cowardly criminals" (June 28, 1931).

On one page of the *Gazette* an episode from the serial *What Price Love? The Story of A Girl's Search for Romance* appeared along with Norma Shearer's star face in close-up; and Mary Manners's advice about men's expectations of women ("young love not always permanent, this girl finds") and an unfaithful husband ("there are other girls who have met with disillusionment as you have").

Romance, adultery, gangsters, and domestic appliances: the newspaper heterotopias of Des Moines and Cedar Rapids offered diverse narratives of self to its filmgoing readers. In her study of the couple in

Hollywood films, Wexman cautions critics: "By . . . placing an essentialized conception of sexual normality at the center of every Hollywood film, critics risk obscuring the historical and cultural factors involved in the creation of the couple" (16). A similar caution applies to the study of heterosexuality in film promotion and reception: to be wary of dominating ideologies and univocal notions of audience and meanings in films. As we have seen, the promotion of *A Free Soul* intersects heterosexuality in paradoxical, contradictory, and diverse ways. Although romantic love and companionate marriage may dominate on screen, early 1930s production and reception make room for and enjoy film's erotic attractions.

Notes

1. This chapter elaborates on a portion of my study, *Marked Women: Local Film Promotion of 1930s Scandalous Female Films.* This project examines film advertising and promotion of selected films in newspapers from several U.S. cities: Los Angeles, New York, Chicago, Atlanta, Des Moines Iowa, Cedar Rapids Iowa, and the U.S. African American media. *A Free Soul* and *Blonde Venus* share a chapter in the larger study. For a discussion of the close-up in film advertising as it applies to Marlene Dietrich, see Haralovich 2007.

2. My study of the promotion of *Imitation of Life* (1934) illustrates the power of the segregated market of the time. Louise Beavers, whose performance received accolades in film reviews, would have been a rising star had she been white. She was not given the promotional treatment accorded, for example, Clark Gable for his performances in 1931.

3

David Lugowski

"Pintele" Queer

The Performance of Jewish Male Heterosexuality in Yiddish American Cinema of the Great Depression

Introduction: The Power of the Pintele—Enough to Qualify? Enough to Taint?

Some years ago, while attending Yom Kippur services with my lover at New York City's LGBTQ synagogue, Congregation Beth Simchat Torah (CBST, "House of Joy in the Torah"), I heard the congregation's president, during a pitch for donations, use a Yiddish phrase that does not translate easily into English. She referred to the ways people feel connected with Jewishness. Some, she remarked, were completely observant, keeping kosher, praying regularly, honoring Shabbat, studying the Torah, and more, even down to following Yom Kippur practices such as dressing in all white and not wearing leather. By contrast indeed: One male friend expressed a very different Jewishness by sporting a pair of black leather pants that day! The president kept referring to the "pintele Yid," the bit of the Jew ("Yid") in everyone there, even those not born or raised as Jewish but attending with family, friends, and life partners or who were there out of personal interest. Internet searches yield definitions of "pintele Yid" such as "the Jewish spark" or "the concentrated essence of Jewishness." *Pintele*—quite a phrase, I thought: A sufficient amount, be it a little or a lot, but enough to make one qualify.

In terms of the remarkably diverse community that celebrates the high holy days at CBST, this term was mobilized in a manner at once charmingly inclusive and politically progressive. It carried with it elements of personal choice, as well as pride in making an association and honoring a tradition. Such a phrase, of course, can be distorted to have negative connotations too. One can think of "miscegenation" in this regard; recall the racist ideology that "one drop of Negro blood makes a man a Negro" from U.S. history, as dramatized in *Show Boat*. A broader concept, however, would be that of the hint or the taint. Many scholars have probed anti-Semitic discourses linking Jews for centuries with unhealthy taints ranging from inadequacy and disease to madness, degeneracy, and evil (Gilman 1985, 1991; Mosse). Queer theory, representation and reading practices are surely relevant here as well, from the idea of the "open secret" ("Everybody in town knows, but we can only ever hint that . . .") to stereotypes of queers as weak, predatory, or psychologically underdeveloped, to that of the closet itself (gays and queers cracking open the closet door just a "hint," or perhaps nongay people peeking in, performing camp, and getting "tainted"!). How do queers or as nonqueers read queerness—or heterosexuality? For that matter, how do Jews and Gentiles read Jewishness?

During my years in New York City, I have often seen or heard about people attempting to spot, to "read," the Jew or the gay person. How might these reading positions connect, overlap and affect each other? What does it mean to read race, ethnicity, class, heterosexuality, or queerness across each other, as well as across communities and cultures, and over time? What does it mean to perform these aspects of identity or to stage debates about them? Is such performance necessarily going to lead to the "right" perception, and for which communities, or which outsiders?

In examining the links between representations of Jewishness and those of heterosexuality, I argue that, far from being only an example of how any kind of sexuality relates to ethnicity, race, religion, and other factors, an example interchangeable with any other, Jewishness and heterosexuality have unique, historically specific links that make such a study necessary. Paralleling the invention of the "homosexual" (and its historically constructed "opposite," the "heterosexual"), the late nineteenth century also marks the "invention" of the modern Jew, not only via new Zionist discourses but also via negative categorizations, in "medical" terms, of Jews as a "race" (Boyarin). Of course, we must be careful not to equate "Jew" and "queer," but both labels were bound up with the intolerance of difference and various hegemonic institutional supports. Warren Blumenfeld has helpfully classified hateful representations of queers and Jews into five categories: (1) those to be condemned on religious grounds; (2) the developmentally immature; (3) the immutable biological inferiors; (4) those who recruit and abuse children; and (5) those who dominate or threaten "civilized" society. Queers and Jews are often linked as the "sensitive" but dangerous urban outsiders who seem to wield influence in certain spheres and who can pass for what they are not.

Jewish and queer men are also linked as failures of heterosexual masculinity, as effeminate so as to misogynistically not only denigrate women but also erase them symbolically. Boyarin, Itzkovitz, and Pellegrini write that "anti-Semitic stereotypes of a weak and passive Jewish masculinity were given dangerous new direction when they were grafted onto emerging discourses of race and sexuality" (2). Drawing on the work of Matti Bunzl, they argue, "it is not just that the modern Jew was being secularized and homosexualized—the 'homosexual' . . . was also being 'raced'" (4). As this is taking place, "the male Jew stands in for all Jews"; in other words, if "Jew = woman" is a homology that gains force at this time, then "all Jews are womanly but no women are Jews" (2). Thus are heterosexuality, masculinity, and other markers such as Jewishness reified within patriarchy. And, of course, this time marks the emergence of cinema, a medium central to the dissemination of discourses concerning the very nature and performances of homo- and heterosexuality. Thus, to talk about formations of heterosexuality, we need to talk about homosexuality and queerness, and to do that we must consider the role that Jewishness plays in such discourses.

Pintele American?: The Contexts of Assimilation and Zionism for American Jewry

To grasp the specifically Jewish negotiation of queerness and heterosexuality in cinema during the Great Depression, two key contexts are assimilation and Zionism. Huge waves of Jewish immigrants came to the United States from the 1880s into the 1930s, as was the case with many people. The revival of the Ku Klux Klan in the 1920s was directly tied to immigrant ethnicities, with Jews and Catholics specifically targeted to a greater degree than ever before. Henry Ford could print his anti-Semitic beliefs widely, job listings could specify that applicants should have blonde hair and straight noses, and Jewish women could be denied employment at the New York Telephone Company because it claimed that their arms were too short to work switchboards. Centuries-old ideas that Jews used the blood of Christian children in their services had emigrated as well (Dinnerstein; Feingold, 2–5). And yet the new land "promised" freedom of religion and association. A small but active Jewish minority had long been visible, and indeed Jews, mostly Sephardic (Spanish-Portuguese), aided in the U.S. Revolutionary War. Nonetheless, the 1 million Jews in the United States by 1900, by then mostly Ashkenazic (German-Eastern European), became 3 million before World War I and rose to 5 million by 1940 (Sachar; Stork and Rose, 41–42). Jews themselves were quite diverse, ranging from fairly secular Jews largely identified with an ethnic identity and culture to highly orthodox and religiously observant Chasids. That said, the United States had (and has) an overwhelmingly Christian population, and Jews felt an extra pressure to be good citizens of a country hegemonically deemed to be a "Christian nation." (Think of all the Jewish American film and radio stars from the 1910s until after World War II who had changed their surnames to ones that would sound more "American," which is to say Anglo-Protestant.) Conservative and liberal, radical and anarchistic impulses intermingled as immigrants faced the learning of new languages and a new national culture as well as the sacrifices, gains, and trade-offs that came with assimilation.

Zionism, a form of Jewish nationalism, seen as liberationist by some and as conservative by many others, responded to anti-Semitism by advocating for a "homeland" for Jews ("Zion" being a synonym for Jerusalem in the Bible). Such ideas have ancient roots in religious traditions, but Zionism as a discourse in its modern and often secular, political form solidified at the same time as all this immigration, especially in the work of Theodor Herzl during the 1890s. (Recall, too, the Balfour Doctrine of 1917, in which Great Britain promised aid to the Jewish people in constructing a home in "Palestine.") It became a central discourse in the lobbying for, and the formation of, the current state of Israel in 1948, yet American Jews were very torn on the subject, and Zionism took on a cast different in the United States than elsewhere. Many supported the idea of a nation in Palestine, especially as World War II loomed, while others proposed different locations or vehemently opposed it as bourgeois, nationalist, or racist. Some supported a secular Zionism while others tied it to Judaism and God's "plans" for the Jewish people. Some saw it as dictated in the Torah, while others argued the opposite, that only a Messiah could restore a homeland. Some American Jews even saw the United States, with its many immigrants, as Zion. The rise of

Hitler doubtless convinced many that Jews would never be fully accepted in other countries, which gave added urgency to Zionist debates. Established Jews in the United States feared that anti-Semitism might increase with further waves of immigrants due to World War II. Many, however, were concerned about Arab, Christian, and Muslim reactions; some worried that Jews would be herded all into one small nation while others presciently feared the consequences of forming a Jewish state in Palestine (Avineri; Sachar; Stork and Rose).

The terms of a heterosexual masculinity acquire cultural and historical specificity when considering Jews during the Great Depression, with those born in the United States living among those who had immigrated, and with Zionism on the rise alongside fascism, the Popular Front and the soon-to-erupt World War II. A homeland, either in the United States or Palestine, might be a haven for the traditional, gentle, and scholarly masculinities we will consider, yet it also might require "tough Jews" (gendered as male) who would fight for Jewish nationalism or the American state. New practices, requirements, and ideologies, or the "redemption" or reorientation of old ones, might come into play where the heterosexual reproduction of Jewish children was concerned. Ironically, was an Aryanization of Jewish heterosexuality taking place amid the Zionist struggle for a homeland, and what of the pulls of U.S. nationalism on Jewish American (but still Yiddish-speaking) citizens (Biale; Breines; Mosse 150–53)? As Daniel Boyarin has wittily said, Zionism was, for many Jewish figures such as Sigmund Freud, not only political but also a "sexual and gendered enterprise" and might constitute a man's "return to Phallustine, not to Palestine" (222).

Pintele Hollywood?: Yiddish Cinema's Queerness and Heterosexuality in Comparative Context

Certain examples of Yiddish cinema of the late 1930s illustrate a central point, namely that performances of gender and sexuality within specific areas of Jewish culture could come across as desirably heterosexual but would most likely be misread by the larger Gentile U.S. population as queer if not manifestly gay. I use queer theory, textual analysis, and an ethnic, cultural, and historical studies approach to consider an effeminate masculinity that is sometimes a positive representation of heterosexuality within its own cultural paradigms. This sexuality is, however, also bound up within American and diasporic Jewish culture with questions Zionism, anti-Semitism, and the forces of assimilation raise. Thus another key point emerges: the potential within Jewish communities to critique, stereotype, or alter this performance of a gentle heterosexuality in response to political pressures, to make it conform to other "tougher" models on both the "land" and in the city, also exists.

We also need to keep in mind the contexts regarding sexuality that mainstream cinema, its makers and its audiences faced. Earlier work I have done shows that during the Great Depression, effeminate men and "mannish" women (to use a term of the day) challenged Hollywood's self-imposed Production Code. Sound film, the demand for provocative entertainment to suit post–Jazz Age urban audiences, and new performers, directors, and genres all enabled queer representation to come out of the closet as never before. Yet as the Great Depression lingered, heterosexual masculinity weathered a crisis—men without jobs did not feel very manly. Conservatives found effeminate male florists, dancers, costumers, and interior decorators; butch female lawyers, entertainers, businesswomen, and monarchs; and prison inmates of both sexes to be immoral, distasteful, unpatriotic, and irreligious. Still, even after the studios began to enforce the Code more strongly, Hollywood needed queer gender play as comical entertainment (for example, cross-dressing storylines, ridiculed minor characters, farcical misunderstandings) and an ideological "straw man" (for example, pathologically disturbed villains, lesbian vampires, vanquished sinners, sissies who make the heroes seem macho by comparison) that it tried to contain within film narratives (Benshoff and Griffin 2005; Lugowski 1999, 2006).

Many of Hollywood's gay male stereotypes were coded as "ethnic." African American characters were portrayed as too effeminate, lazy, servile, or frightened to be "suitable" to lead the country from the Great Depression. Italian, French, and Latino characters were comically florid, operatic, and temperamental; Asians were inscrutable, feminized, and "exotic"; the British were too unctuous and effete, obsessed with dress and class status. One of the most common links of queerness and ethnicity came with Jews, the urban, "artistic," leftist minorities who could pass as members of the mainstream. This leaves Aryan Germans and related neighbors, such as certain Scandinavians or at least WASP types, as the most desirably manly; Hollywood racism and that of Nazi Germany do differ in degree and implementation if not entirely in kind (Lugowski 1999, 16, 22; 2006, 45).

Hollywood, however, was not alone in linking gender issues to the economic downturn. Alternative American cinemas—activist and labor documentaries, the avant-garde, independent African American and Italian-language filmmaking—also showed heterosexual masculinity up for grabs and featured diverse (and sometimes ineffectual) masculinities, but specific cultures portrayed and interpreted gender performance differently. One of the richest of these alternatives was independent Jewish filmmaking, which existed during silent days but eventually had the added benefit of the musical language of Yiddish—the vernacular language of many Ashkenazic Jews—or Yiddish-English mixes. Jewish diasporic filmmaking exists in a number of countries, especially Poland and the United States. In the case of American Yiddish-language film, filmed mostly in New York City, New Jersey, and upstate New York, large audiences for such films existed in urban centers with sizable populations of Jewish immigrants and their descendants. A Yiddish literature is imported, but also grows its own examples in the United States, as does an especially influential Yiddish theater (for example, the famous Second Avenue theaters in New York's Greenwich Village). The connections with mainstream cinema were there from the start, ranging from the immigrant nickelodeon owners who eventually became the moguls of the classical Hollywood era to performers such as New York Yiddish theater star Muni Wiesenfreund, who became Hollywood star Paul Muni (Cook, 304–7; Goldman; Hoberman; Paskin).

The period between the two world wars marked the heyday of international Yiddish-language cinema. It did not end with World War II, but the examples afterward are few; the Holocaust in many ways destroyed what was a once-thriving culture, and assimilation also did its share, albeit in a completely different manner. While anti-Semitism is certainly addressed in U.S. Yiddish film, questions of assimilation and Zionism were also central, and such matters impacted the status and the performance of gender and sexuality. The Yiddish theatre tradition, which sometimes included cross-dressing, gender play, and ribald humor about the body, was often translated quite directly to the screen in films shot in both Poland and the United States. To cite a famous dramatic example drawn from Jewish folk legend, consider the male spirit that possesses a young bride in the 1937 Polish *The Dybbuk* (Konigsberg). Comical queerness, however, was more common, and Yiddish American film's discourses on gender and sexuality paralleled those of Hollywood in many ways.

If the social, economic, and political tensions of the Great Depression manifested particular variations of masculinity and heterosexuality in crisis, then modes of *representation* within a culture, modes by which a culture proves its myths to itself, should refract these as well, irrespective of the modes of *production* of these discourses. If queerness was, as I would argue, an important issue during the Great Depression, one should be able to find signs of this, however indirectly, in both Hollywood cinema and in Yiddish American film (and other alternatives as well, of course). Such modes as Yiddish cinema might not manifest queerness or "masculinity in crisis" in quite the same ways that Hollywood production did in response to the economic downturn, but alternative cinemas might follow some of the general trends of such crisis as a result of their placement within certain historical formations.

Also important to keep in mind is that alternatives such as Yiddish-language cinema never exist in complete isolation from Hollywood. Yiddish films were shown in New York City alongside more mainstream English-language films; they were subtitled, and several, including *Grine Felder/Green Fields* (1937), discussed later, were popular. By the same token I do not believe in any monolithic conception of queerness or of heterosexuality that was unchanging and present for all seekers during the Great Depression; my claims are smaller and less problematic than that. Indeed, one use of Yiddish-language cinema of this time is precisely to disprove the idea of a master Zeitgeist. So also with my culturally specific refractory model of interpreting queerness because too many factors influence the relationship of queer representation to a wider culture to justify a simple connection between queerness and heterosexual masculinity in crisis. In what follows I hope to set in contradistinction some opposing tendencies: how these films diverge substantially from Hollywood's renditions of queerness (as with *Green Fields*), and how, perhaps more surprisingly, they are also similar to mainstream cinema's queer discourses in their uses, trends, and limitations (as with *Amerikaner Shadkhn/American Matchmaker* [1940]). That said, I want to emphasize how—in contrast to Hollywood's common use of queerness to mark effeminate comic buffoons, villains, or other "failed" characters as gay (and occasionally to a show good-humored sense of satire, especially on the part of Hollywood's gay and lesbian directors)—these similarities and differences in Yiddish film require an attentiveness to not only the dialogue with Hollywood, but also larger dynamics that Jewish filmmakers, audiences and culture itself were facing.

Before analyzing the two aforementioned films, however, I need to bring up the most famous and analyzed queer Yiddish film of the era. The musical comedy *Yidl mitn Fidl/Yiddle with His Fiddle* (1936) was filmed in Poland but featured some Americans in the crew and cast (especially theater star Molly Picon) and was widely popular in Yiddish-language circuits in the United States. It possesses a picaresque quality as it toys with cross-gendered behavioral codes in telling, to use Chris Straayer's useful generic category, a "temporary transvestite" tale of a woman, Itke (Picon), who dresses as a young man, Yidl, to avoid harassment as she journeys with her father into male territory and male privilege with a group of traveling musicians (Straayer; Sicular 1995, 1999, 2002). Even this short summary suggests how the film is much like George Cukor's *Sylvia Scarlett*, made the same year, with the young "boy" attracted to a "real" man (in this case, the manly Froim, another of the musicians) but unable to "come out" about her feelings.

Part of the film's comedy stems from Yidl's inadequacy at playing her new role. She becomes drunk easily, gets her thumb smacked with a hammer when she tries to help Froim with a bit of carpentry, and cannot swim (which relates to a stereotype that Mark Spitz disproved, that Jews cannot swim). After Froim rescues Yidl and is carrying her to shore, she unthinkingly goes to kiss him, only to have him dump her back in the water. "He's worse than a girl," Froim complains at one point. "What's the matter? Don't you like girls?" he is asked. "Yes, from a distance," comes his reply. Itke/Yidl also cannot compete as a woman with the more girlish Taybele, to whom Froim is attracted after the musicians rescue her from an unwanted marriage and she joins their troupe of street performers as a singer. Michele Aaron has argued that the "feminization" of the Jewish man as "passive, perverse" is both part of anti-Semitic discourses and a stereotypical "self-representation" that "haunts" Jewish culture. Aaron argues that, during the film:

> this stereotype is not avoided but exploited, the "Jew as woman" does not simply haunt the text but determines it. The stereotype

Figure 4. Itke (Molly Picon), in male disguise as Yidl, yearns for athletic Froim (Leon Liebgold) in *Yidl mitn Fidl* (1936). *Photo courtesy of the Archives of YIVO Institute for Jewish Research, New York.*

> is . . . indulged so that it can be undone . . . By enacting the myth of the "Jew as woman," the worst of the character of Yidl differentiates the ideal qualities of Froim. *Yidl mitn Fidl* distances the negative stereotypes of the Jew through two interrelated means: the establishment of the new Jew [Froim] as an ideal man, and the denigration of effeminacy and of womanliness . . . redemption of the Jewish man is achieved through the ridiculing of the Jewish woman and homosexuality. (2004a, 94–95)

As with other films of its period, attempts are made to contain its queerness. At the end of the film Itke steps out onto a stage to replace Taybele, who is frightened of performing in an actual theater and who has been reunited with an old beau. (Thus does heterosexual marriage trump a career for a woman, much like in Depression-era Hollywood film.) Itke comes out both to the audience and to Froim (who is playing in the orchestra pit) as a woman and relates in song and a tearful but comical monologue her story and her unrequited love. The audience only sees and laughs at a performance, but we as spectators are sometimes positioned with them while also occupying a privileged place of reflexivity, as Itke/Yidl/Picon sings a medley of the songs she has introduced throughout the film and describes the comedy of her charade, her adventures, and the film itself.

At the center of this charade is the very issue of queerness, which is explicitly brought up to be disavowed. She poses the question to her diegetic audience (and to us, too, by extension): "'A yingl mit a yingl? Hot epes a tam'/'A man in love with another man?' That doesn't make sense!" This speech near the end of the film is a more obvious and aggressive recuperation than one finds in *Sylvia Scarlett* but it is also done on a stage, suggesting a lingering theatricality to gender performance. Aaron, although critical of how "misogyny and homophobia" work "to dislodge anti-Semitism" (via the film's images of Jews on the land, the collective theater audience, and the formation of several heterosexual couples), notes how the queerness evoked by all this gender play might be "confronting and undermining" the anti-Semitic conventions and stereotypes, and by "illuminating Jewishness . . . might gain [a] defiant edge." (2004a, 90–91) Eve Sicular goes a bit further, arguing that Itke's male drag was not only tolerated, but also encouraged by her father and that the gender play parallels and contributes to the questioning at this time of Old World values about women. This contrasts with the much more explicit punishment of Picon's cross-dressing and assimilated character, a New Yorker who visits Poland with her father in the earlier *Ost und West/East and West* (1923), and becomes a traditional wife to a religious scholar.

Overall, in other words, *Yidl* fits in with some of the things one finds in queer representation in Hollywood cinema of the same period. We can also note the connection to Hollywood material in its having fairly overt queerness in the service of comic entertainment and romantic strategies of complication and delay, only to ideologically deny and contain it. The Hollywood connection is, if anything, made explicit at the finale, as Itke's success leads her and her father to cross the ocean to perform in the United States. Froim, seeing no place for himself amid her professional success, bows out, but the couple is accidentally reunited on board the ship.

That said, as with many Hollywood films, the issues queerness raises are never fully resolved: Will Itke continue to have a career as a cross-dressing performer if or after she marries Froim? And, of course, Hollywood would never address references to some issues confronting Jews at the time. The clarinetist in the band, Isaac, is always boasting of the many cities he has played and begins one story saying, "One day in Tel Aviv . . ." only to be interrupted, "You know you've never been in Tel Aviv." "What's the difference?" he replies, "I'll go there one day." He thus evokes both the "wandering Jew" stereotype that had become such a diasporic reality for many and also a pintele Zionist hope to settle down in Palestine some day. Significantly, his wandering is settled, or perhaps displaced, via one of the film's heterosexual unions.

Pintele Astaire?: A (Jewish) "American Matchmaker" Needs to Find His Match to Play Jewish

While *Yidl mitn Fidl* engages in queer byplay throughout and explicitly raises the relationship between queerness and heterosexuality to recuperate the latter for Jewish audiences, I want to focus on the first of two films made in the United States that are more "pintele queer" and have been less studied vis-à-vis the construction of masculinity and heterosexuality. In Edgar Ulmer's *Amerikaner Shadkhn/American Matchmaker* (1940), made near the very end of the Great Depression, one finds a very different relation to queerness, but again one with remarkable similarities to what Hollywood was doing at the time alongside a specifically Jewish cultural orientation. In this film we have a man who is a composite of some of the types of male queerness one can see in contemporaneous mainstream cinema. Leo Fuchs, a Yiddish star like Molly Picon from New York's Second Avenue Theater district, was known as the "Yiddish Fred Astaire." Invariably garbed in top hat, white tie, and tails and even resembling Astaire slightly, Fuchs here plays the highly successful Nat

Silver, whose only problem is that he is a failed heterosexual who seems doomed to remain unmarried.

As the film opens Nat is making his eighth try at tying the knot; his previous seven fiancées have all called off their weddings at the last second. Gender reversal is hinted at in one song that Fuchs sings, with lyrics including, "Today the bride will lead the groom." During the ceremony, the heartsick childhood sweetheart of Nat's prospective bride appears, threatening to kill himself if Nat marries the woman he loves. Nat, who apparently was being wed only for his money and is accustomed to cancelled weddings, gives her up. Nat is thereby strongly coded much like the ineffectual and often sissified types of the era who were never able to marry the leading lady (for example, Astaire's feminized rivals for Ginger Rogers' hand in several films).

Nat is queerly positioned not only because of his failures at heterosexual marriage, but also because of his class status (as the Great Depression lingered, the wealthy were increasingly mocked), and some of his homosocial relations with other men in the film. Besides his natty dressing style and failures at marriage, Nat is queered as a dandy type by his upper-crust association with his "man's man" butler. Morris, although an engaged man himself and not at all effeminate, is one of many servants, typical of the Great Depression, who shows little regard for his station (much as the queerly coded Eric Blore did in Hollywood films, many of them with Rogers and Astaire).

Nat goes to see his mother, who speaks of his Uncle Shya (whom we see in flashback, also played by Fuchs) who became a matchmaker because he too was never able to marry. Rather like homosexuality, as many theories and much research would have it, this condition seems, she feels, to run in the family. "Family characteristics know no boundaries," as she puts it. The film so far is thus positing a key question: is Nat's queer (hetero)sexuality the product of his Jewishness or does it relate instead to his similarities to American-Hollywood masculinities of the period?

Nat becomes an even greater success in his new career as a matchmaker, changing his surname from Silver to Gold. (While neither name sounds particularly "less Jewish" than the other, the very idea of name changing was a form of assimilation many American Jews felt compelled to do, or which was done for them when they entered U.S. ports. Cultural assimilation is thus displaced onto economic success, signified by the move from Silver to Gold.) For a time, in fact, he alienates the other men in the profession until he offers to employ them. Forever in evening clothes, cheerful and rather asexual, Nat/Fuchs embodies a Jewish version of what Robert Sklar calls the "silly boy" romantic juvenile and the also-queer "Mama's boy" type. (Sklar, 11–28) Nat finally must fail at his business but succeed in love, an interesting switch from Hollywood films where romantic and financial success go hand in hand. A woman named Judith becomes prominent fairly late in the film to play Ginger to Nat's Fred, underlining that Nat's heterosexuality must be resolved for the film to achieve closure. Judith cannot go through with another marriage Nat has been brokering because she herself wants to marry him. She sees his queerness—she knows that he's a "Mama's boy," as she puts it—but the film finally values Nat's success at heterosexual marriage above all else.

In the film's politics we see another difference from Hollywood, an interesting "inversion" (if I might use that psychoanalytic term for gayness) of Hollywood's stigmatizing link of the Jew with the sissy. In *American Matchmaker*, Nat's queerness is linked with his high degree of assimilation. Unlike many of the other men in the film, Nat does not follow observant Jewish tradition and wear a beard and *payos* (sidelocks) and does not keep his head covered with a hat or *kippah* (skullcap or, in Yiddish, *yarmulke*). His clothing does not feature the *tzitzit* (fringes) that the orthodox wear; rather, he is most often in man-about-town garb (à la Astaire). He and Morris also pepper their dialogue with more English, and even American slang, than the other characters. The forces of wealth that push him closer to non-Jewish cultures and a loss of Jewish identity are also what make him queer.

Notably, Nat's sister is an assimilated, wisecracking blonde and a slightly "mannish" type in an Eve Arden (or Ginger Rogers!) vein who speaks even more English than he does. As the film proceeds we hear increasingly more slang from the assimilated queer characters spoken in English, for example, "C'mon, spill it!," "Hold your horses!," and "Don't keep me in suspense." If, in Hollywood films of the period, to be Jewish was sometimes to be queer, here the inversion emerges. In this case, to give up too much of one's Jewishness to become wealthy and assimilated is to lose one's heterosexuality and become pintele queer.

As Nat finally gets married, Morris cries, "You've broken my heart!" responding like all those Hollywood sidekicks who hate to lose "their man" to the love of a woman. The masculine-acting but queerly coded Morris, however, will take over the business with another of the matchmakers. In *Top Hat*, Astaire is glad to sing "No strings / no connections / no ties to my affections." Such is all very well for the opening of a film, but both Fuchs and Astaire must eventually be structured into the heterosexual patriarchy of their respective cultures. What is intriguing, however, is that with Judith, and Rogers in the films with Astaire, the feisty, determined woman, sometimes resisting and sometimes pursuing, is the one who enables the male star to stand apart from his queer friends and successfully perform heterosexuality. For all of the erasure of women and womanliness that occurs in the struggle to defend—or to (re-)establish—Jewish male heterosexuality in its various contested incarnations, women often have to become the central agents, or the ideological props, to make this happen.

Pintele Zionist?: The Jewish Sissy and the Masturbating Farmer

Unlike *American Matchmaker*'s association of queerness with urban New York life and assimilation, Edgar Ulmer and Jacob Ben-Ami's *Grine Felder/Green Fields* has pintele queer markings tied to aspects of European Jewish cultural heritage and the pressures Zionist-influenced discourses of gender and homeland raised. It is a film whose passionate and sincere depiction of pastoral life and religious joy in being an observant Jew would seem to largely preclude overt queerness. Yet it too is pintele queer in a culturally specific way, one that also involves a range of reading positions vis-à-vis its protagonist's heterosexuality. The character of Levy (Michael Goldstein) is a classic example of what Daniel Boyarin, in a move to explicitly reclaim an "oppositional" masculinity within a long-standing culture of rabbinic Judaism, calls a "Jewish sissy" (Boyarin). Levy is a seemingly asexual, nerdy young man, extremely shy, intensely devoted to prayer and the study of Torah and the Talmud. Historically, his "soft" masculinity might have provided a positive alternative for Jews living under the "hard" masculinity of ancient Roman martial law. That said, he realizes that valuing male effeminacy potentially problematizes, undervalues, or ignores women. "[T]he cultural value rabbinic Judaism placed on soft masculinity was in no way a rebuff of patriarchy and male privilege" (Boyarin, Itzkovitz, and Pellegrini, 2). Women do, however, play potent feminine roles in *Green Fields*, as I will argue.

The relevant term for Levy is "yeshiva bocher," which translates as "yeshiva boy student," and yet this term is applied even to young adult alumni of the yeshiva education tradition, men who should be past the stage of being called boys. As a student and scholar, Levy has none of the manly attributes such as strength that the film identifies with the land. In staging issues at stake relevant to masculinity and heterosexuality, therefore, I would characterize the film as being perhaps more conflicted and complex than Noah Eisenberg's description of it as a "simple romance of a semiutopian pastoral ethnic enclave." In discussing the film's production and historical contexts, J. Hoberman agrees (as do I) that the film does have its lyrical, hopeful aspects, but he also sees a richer interplay at work: "[T]he film evokes a host of Jewish utopian traditions, mixing an inchoate Zionism with a displaced Chasidism, Bundist communalism with childhood nostalgia" (251).

At the film's opening Levy is wondering about his role in life and his studies at the yeshiva, and so decides to scour the countryside in search of what he feels are "true Jews." Eventually he is taken in by farmer Dovid-Noich and indeed is fought over by two families, Dovid's and Elkone's, who value him for his learning. The awkward, fey Levy, afraid of women, and complete with a dithering manner and limp wrists, is contrasted with the strapping eldest son of Dovid's house, Hersh-Ber, and his closest bond is with the sensitive youngest son, Avrom-Yankov (played by a young Herschel Bernardi). Levy is slender and pale, does no manual labor himself, and rarely ventures outside from his days filled with prayer; he even worries about his usefulness vis-à-vis his manhood, quoting the Talmud in which the Rabbi Eliezer taught, "A man without land is not a man." Talmudic reference or not, such a statement had particular resonance in the United States during the Great Depression, linking masculine heterosexuality with labor, capital, property, and Zionism. Politically, the film has what Hoberman states is a "Popular Front inflection," which includes "a discussion on 'the union of Labor and Torah'" (Hoberman, 252).

At first one might read Levy only as an ineffectual and dysfunctional homosexual sissy—the "Jew as sexual schlemiel" in the terms David Biale discusses character types from Yiddish theater to Woody Allen—especially in comparison with the men who work the land (Biale, 204–7). But this would be to some extent what one might call a "Gentile" reading. One also might see it as a possible reading internalized by assimilated American Jews unfamiliar with this performance of heteromasculinity, or even Zionists who would feel that strong farmers and soldiers would be more desirable in the future homeland of Israel. The film indeed considers the issue of whether the "true Jew" (presumed to be male) is the manly (presumed to be male) Jew. And yet we see a positive side to Levi's femininity as represented in that his learning is deemed worthy of respect. The masculine Jews of the land are embarrassed that they do not study Torah like Levy, who could teach the rural children to read, write, and pray.

The long-standing rabbinic and Talmudic traditions of Judaism, Boyarin argues, have a place for such a pintele queer heterosexual, a "Jewish sissy" who is respected by the community as such, and indeed is presented as sexually desirable by the women of the community. The older men who want him to stay admire him and the younger, less educated men are either jealous of him or want to emulate and learn from him. In one of the film's intriguing and culturally specific reversals, Levy is finally seduced into staying and marrying the daughter of Dovid-Noich's family, Tsine, who has pursued him quite aggressively. "Such a gentle face," she notes admiringly to her friend Stera, who replies, "City people are that way." Levy is not homosexual except if one is culturally positioned to read (or misread) him as such. Rather, his is a positive and yet also pintele queer performance of heterosexuality. Indeed, Boyarin argues, as does George Mosse, that the Zionist movement was in some ways a betrayal of this "alternative" tradition of masculinity insofar as it aided in the development of the so-called muscle Jew, aiming to win (back) the "homeland" at any cost. These scholars see this nineteenth- and twentieth-century model of macho hetero-masculinity as having appropriated, ironically, the very Aryan models of manhood that were oppressing European Jews so cruelly.

A scene late in the film throws many of these issues into relief, while calling into play concerns, which sharpened during the Great Depression, about "aggressive" and "knowledgeable" women and their own performances of heterosexuality. Tsine shows Levy that she has learned how to write—gender issues are galore in such a premise alone. Several generations of immigrant women had not been well-educated before coming to the United States. During the Great Depression, many men were concerned that women not get "too much" education lest it upset gender roles and take jobs away from them. At their most extreme, such discourses contended that educated women would become less feminine (losing the ability to have children, growing extra body hair!) and "turn" lesbian. In 1939 a male writer had a "solution," which reflected the gender dynamics of the era far more than it made any kind of sense: "There are approximately 10 million people out of work in the United States today. There are also 10 million or more women, married or single, who are job holders. Simply fire the women, who shouldn't be working anyway, and hire the men. Presto! No unemployment. No relief rolls. No depression" (Cousins). While *Green Fields* does not suggest that women who can write will threaten men as farmers, Tsine does link their education with issues of gender, thereby causing turmoil for Levy's heterosexuality.

Not believing that Tsine can write, Levy erases his portable blackboard and asks her to demonstrate her new prowess again. She agrees to do so but only if he closes his eyes, whereupon she begins to write but suddenly sneaks a kiss and then runs off, to a crash in the film's musical score. (Women are feminine but forthright, dominant, and romantically aggressive in this film. Earlier Stera, Elkone's daughter, also had sneaked a kiss with Hersh-Ber.) Levy is nonplussed by Tsine's writing and especially her kiss; the film's score again underlines this as he throws away his writing slate—one of the tools of his scholarly ways that have been, to this point, the mainstay of his masculinity. He wanders around, unable to cope with this act of (hetero)sexual aggression in his heretofore asexual life. Finally, he sits down next to a churn and, in a way that cannot help but hilariously evoke masturbation, begins to pump idly at the phallic handle. Being kissed by the farm girl is threatening to turn him from a yeshiva bocher, a queerly masculine man, into a person who can actually do farm chores. When asked what he is doing, he notes with some surprise, "I can also churn butter." That said, churning was a kind of farm work often associated with women, so Levy's hetero-masculinity is still in a queer space or, because he is now both scholar and farmer, he has been maneuvered into giving a more in-between and hence more queer performance of his masculinity than ever before. The masturbatory look of his gesture signifies that this is very much a question of gender, labor, and sexuality, and one not solely based in reproductive impulses, yet his masculinity is one that has been *hetero*sexualized by Tsine's kiss.

An example such as this throws into relief how queerness and heterosexuality alike can be read, or not read, depending on specific parameters of textuality and culturally positioned spectatorship. Furthermore, the codes of queerness, and of heterosexuality, are not immutable but take on conflicted meanings amid social and political pressure. Also important to reiterate is that performances readable as queer in some manner are not necessarily negative (or gay, or nongay, whether positively or negatively perceived) within specific reading communities; here it is a case of heterosexuality taking them on, or at least considering them, in a manner seemingly approved by the community! The broader issues in play—the increasingly Zionist and, especially for *Yidl mitn Fidl*, the diasporic audiences; the manifest assimilation and city life explored in *Amerikaner Shadkhn;* the old-fashioned longing for both redemption by the land and an observant, traditional masculinity in *Grine Felder*—stage vital debates for Jewish audiences during the Great Depression as the storm clouds of war grew over Europe.

Indeed, for all of the good-humored gender play in these largely comic films, the growth of the macho Zionist image and the longing to recuperate pintele queer "Jewish sissies" into modern marriage and possession of the land might themselves have been influenced by an assimilated appropriation of Aryan masculinity and American heterosexuality. The images in these films, with their links to folk tales, Yiddish theater and long-standing character types, might seem unexceptional from a Jewish old-country perspective, but could seem increasingly queer from an assimilated American one.

The existence of such perspectives has repercussions for a greater possible diversity of readers and interpretations of queerness and Jewishness in Yiddish film, mainstream Hollywood, and international cinema, and even today's news media, beyond the homophobic or anti-Semitic seeker of stereotypes. One sees points of contact with which to respond to writers in developing countries who see homosexuality as a Western invention imposed on them imperialistically. So too with neo-Nazi, anti-Semitic, and anti-Arab beliefs, practices, and institutions in Europe and the United States once again trying to scapegoat Jews, Arabs, and Muslims amid the tribulations in today's Middle East, rather than develop a fully rounded critique of reactionary Zionist, Israeli, American, European, Palestinian, and larger Arab mistakes in policy. Raz Yosef has begun work along these lines; he sees in Israeli cinema since the formation of the country Zionist discourses that, by marginalizing queerness, build up orthodox, narrow conceptions of Ashkenazic Jewry as the heterosexual male breeder, soldier, and nation builder while stigmatizing both Palestinian citizens and the *Mizrahim* "Oriental" Jews.

Such work is ever necessary as certain world leaders wage macho-posturing wars unnecessarily on peoples within their own borders or far abroad. One can witness the globalization of culturally specific Western concepts of sexuality, democracy, and nationalism, as well as the failure to critique, or to even understand, the formation or reorientation of cultures and nation-states, as these are grounded in ahistorical and heterosexist discourses. The images we find in film do not necessarily try to hide their pintele queerness as heterosexuality, but rather give us contextualized insight into how concepts of sexuality (including the ever elusive but omnipresent heterosexuality) are culturally learned, understood, and debated by peoples facing dislocation, altered national identities, globalized capital, and political oppression.

4

LOUISE WALLENBERG

Straight Heroes with Queer Inclinations

Male Film Stars in the Swedish 1930s

"So, tell me grandma, what made him so special? Why Ekman?"

"Well, how should I put it . . . (and she smiles), he was not like other men, if you know what I mean."

IN THE 1910s AND EARLY 1920s, THE SWEDISH film industry held an international reputation, successfully exporting much of its film to other European countries and, to some extent, to North America. Within film history, this period has become known as the Golden Age of early Swedish cinema. By the mid-1920s, however, the Swedish film industry had stagnated, having lost not only its two founding fathers (Victor Sjöström, in Hollywood known as Victor Seastrom, and his longtime working partner, Maurtiz Stiller), but also two of its most important film stars (that is, Greta Gustavsson, later to become Greta Garbo, and Lars Hansson) to Hollywood. In addition, mass unemployment and the worldwide economic crises of the early 1930s helped bury the Swedish film industry.

The mid-1930s, however, would experience a sudden explosion in filmmaking. New directors, new stars, new audiences, and new businesses resurrected the industry. Crucial to this dramatic transformation was the introduction of talkies and with them, Swedish film went from its slumbering state to a prosperous industry. This was manifested in the building of new movie theaters, in the production of numerous films, as well as with the rise of various ancillaries including film journals, film related contests, and various fashion and beauty products film stars endorsed.

Being the second most prosperous period in Swedish film history (after the Golden Age of Swedish silent film), we should not be surprised that it has been focused on and explored by several Swedish film scholars (Furhammar 1979, 1991; Jerselius; Qvist). These previous studies, which have been carried out since the early 1980s, however, have tended to take a rather mainstream—and male-centric—perspective on this era and show little attention to the representation of gender and sexuality. Tytti Soila's dissertation *Kvinnors ansikte: stereotyper och kvinnlig identitet i trettiotalets svenska filmmelodram* (*Women's Face: Stereotypes and Female Identity in the 1930s Swedish Melodrama*) from 1991, and the more recent dissertation by Ylva Habel, *Modern Media, Modern Audiences: Mass Media and Social Engineering in the 1930s Swedish Welfare State*, paved a new direction within this field of study, opening up for more transgressive readings regarding (1) the representation of gender, and (2) gendered audiences.

This chapter follows a similar path, investigating the apparent inconsistency and ambivalence of gender representations in the 1930s. And, because gender and sexuality often are understood to be intimately connected, especially in discussions of gender ambivalence, representations of sexuality will also be contemplated. I contend that the Swedish popular films of the 1930s, perhaps more than films of any other decade, offered its audience an inescapable queerness: a gender queerness that was presented explicitly on the silver screen and conferred implicitly in many of the secondary texts relating to popular cinema, from chronicles, film journals, and film magazines to fan letters and memoirs. And, as the title of this chapter indicates, it was distinctively *male* film stars that offered potentially gender queer images in their representations of ideal men.

For anyone interested in queer images on film, and for anyone slightly knowledgeable of Western film history, Rudolph Valentino will come to mind as an equivalent figure: he too, as American film scholars

Miriam Hansen and Gaylyn Studlar so convincingly have pointed out, presented a slightly different version of masculinity on-screen, while never entirely deviating from the demands on gender that were distinctive of his era. In fact, various national film industries of the late 1920s and the early 1930s displayed images of nonconventional masculinity (representations that have been understood as symbols for struggles between patriarchal values and women's new freedom that were characteristic of the era).[1] In France, stars such as Louis Jouvet and Pierre Brausseur who often appeared in makeup and presented lean features, were highly popular, and in Finland, exotic and beautiful Teuvo Tulio (also know as Theodor Tugai) was considered to be an attractive male idea, especially for the female audience.

Yet clear and unavoidable differences exist between these queer stars: whereas Valentino and the other stars slightly deviated from traditional masculinity through their supposed exotic origin, the Swedish film stars would never diverge in their masculinity in terms of exoticism. Culturally and ethnically they were symbols of unquestioned Swedishness, and as such, they incorporated the national ideal that was dominant at the time. Sweden, as a nation and as a society, went through a significant social change at this time, overtly involving issues of gender and sexuality.

By transgressing gender boundaries and consistently moving toward the feminine, these three stars—Ekman, Lagerwall, and Westergren—embodied or constituted male ideals that were clearly nonpartriarchal and that in turn opened up for a certain sexual ambivalence. In retrospect, these star personas and the characters they played on stage (and, in Ekman's case, the characters he also played off-stage) offer the present-day spectator an almost inevitable queering of the then-dominant Swedish masculinity, which dominant sociopolitical discourses of the era nonetheless promoted and marketed as unquestionably manly and as undeniably straight.

Paradoxical Ideals

Swedish historians, political scientists, and gender theorists, among others, have for the past thirty years emphasized the 1930s and the rise of Social Democracy and its focus on social engineering as crucial and fundamental for any understanding of a more contemporary Sweden. The various studies emerging from these disciplines, have all accentuated the 1930s as indeed the most central decade for the development of a new society, a new Sweden. The politics and the social movement of 1930s, these scholars argue, came to form modern Sweden and its foundation in terms of values, rules, and social and economic structures. Within gender studies, one has developed a theoretical model for understanding the gender relations developed during this era. Historian Yvonne Hirdman coined the term *genussystem*, that is, gender system (1989; 1994; 2003), arguing that during the 1930s the modern gender system by which we live today came into being. With this she refers to symmetrically formed gender positions within both a more social (public) and a more family-oriented (private) system. Her analysis has laid bare women's subjugation within its patriarchal structure, and it has offered models with which we can question these traditional gender roles as well as the system. However, her analysis does not leave room for any asymmetries, nor deviances from or within the system. The symmetry, with women as subjugated and dominated, has become naturalized, as have women and men in their respective roles. No system can be totally rigid and congealed in its structure: counterpowers, counterdiscourses, and counterdesires always threaten to blur the steadiness of rigidity. Within any system, a certain mobility, and in this specific system, a mobility of fluid genders, sexualities, and desires, exists. As the next section shows, the dominating discourse emanating from Social Democracy might have been unquestionably symmetric in terms of gender dichotomies, and a few of its popular texts followed this line. Yet, other discourses also emanate from popular culture, in this case from popular film, which openly demonstrated and made possible several asymmetries.

Just such an asymmetry can be found in the "ideal paradox" of male images. On the one hand, we see a clear focus on the traditionally masculine man, promoted by political, economic, and social discursive forces as an archetype and who was indisputably straight. On the other hand, we see an emphasis on a more effeminate, if not "girly," man who promoted as an ideal man in various popular and high cultural texts was also regarded as straight (although perhaps not so indisputably).

This ideal paradox exemplifies issues discussed in queer studies, in particular the phenomena of queer stardom and of specific star bodies read through the philosophical and cultural oppositions of inside and outside. As Diane Fuss convincingly argues, the opposition between masculine and feminine may not be as rigid as first thought: the outside does not have to be an absolute outside, nor the inside a waterproof inside. The outside, we may assume, "is also an alongside; the distance and proximity is sometimes no distance at all" (5), and the image of the feminine male, within the specific setting that popular culture of the 1930s actually presented, is very much an inside figure, becoming in some ways more "real" than the male ideals promoted by political dominant ideology.

Before moving onto a discussion of a few specific films and film stars in trying to make visible the fluidity and the asymmetry, I wish to describe briefly the transformation that Swedish society went through during this specific time. For readers with little or no familiarity with this era in Swedish history, this description will serve as a broadening framing within which the following discussion will become more understandable.

Essentialism in Times of Construction

Sweden went through a fundamental change in the 1930s when the Social Democrats came to power: the prevalent and faddish idea of a Swedish *folk home* (also known as the "people's home") and a Swedish model, required a reorganization of society to build a new classless society that would make the working class—as a homogenous body—the dominant class. The building of such a "classless" society where everyone was included involved goal-oriented construction on all levels. The mechanistic aspects of this otherwise apparently humane cultural endeavor were crucial: the social transformation was seen as a matter of social engineering. The new folk home needed both intellect and technology: economists, social scientists, architects, designers, and politicians.

Most central to this transformation of Swedish society, as a whole, was the smaller microunit, that is, the family. Many felt that Swedish families needed to become healthier, happier, more productive, and, most important, more *re-productive*. Due to various factors, the national birthrate was very low in the early 1930s. Continuous emigration to the United States since the mid–nineteenth century had led to a noticeable decrease in the reproductive part of the population. An increase in illegal abortions and the recent emancipation of women were also regarded as factors. The latter meant that young, mostly urban, women could choose to postpone, or even reject, marriage and childbearing in favor of a career and a certain degree of personal (and sexual) freedom. Sociologists, economists, and Social Democrats Alva and Gunnar Myrdal published their book *Kris i befolkningsfrågan* (*The Population Crisis*) in 1934 as a response to the low birthrate. In this study, which became enormously influential, they described the causes and origins of the "crisis" as well as offering solutions. They perceived the low birthrate as a problem, arguing that only the good, reproductive family could constitute the center and backbone of a healthy, working society.

The ideal family, as promoted by the new dominant ideology of Social Democracy, was young, healthy, and indeed very "Swedish." Swedish nationalism, characterized by a certain xenophobia, flourished. The ideal family also now had its mother and its father positioned as equal in terms of private and public: the emphasis was on men being more supportive of their wives working outside the private sphere, and hence, a greater call for men to take a more active part in child rearing and—to a certain extent—in the activities that were connected to the home, which earlier had belonged to woman's role and duty. The new family man, then, was to be a present father, a man who saw his private, personal role to be as important as his public, more professional role. But even though traditional gender roles were being slightly subverted within political, social, and cultural discourse, the notion of gender (and sex) as biological truths was as rigid as before. Hegemonic negotiations thus asserted that Swedish men could (and should) be present and proud fathers and still be regarded as authentically masculine.

In fact, the notions of gender differences as essential, universal, and natural were reinforced during this era. While the 1920s had seen, at least in Sweden's bigger urban cities, a certain opening of the feminine role with suffragettes, flappers, and other types of emancipated women refusing the traditional female role as mother and wife, the political and sociocultural discourses of the 1930s emphasized an inescapable, essential femininity associated with motherhood more than anything else. The ideal woman was suddenly in a unique position, on a pedestal as the nation's and the new society's savior and backbone. She became the most important figure in this reproductive machinery: her body was to give birth to new generations of Swedes. Although men were encouraged to be more involved in child rearing, she was still given the prime responsibility for upbringing and nurturing.

The new folk home as a collective concept, as an imaginary structure for Swedishness and national character, served to reinforce sexual difference as natural and universal, and was repeatedly rehearsed in speeches, posters, popular songs and literature, and (of course) motion pictures. Many of the popular films produced during this era meticulously followed the folk home–manifesto by presenting fictions with happy straight endings, with blonde men and women coming together, creating perfect couples with baby-making on their mind. Such propagandistic fiction celebrated a democratic and equal state in which (what would eventually be termed) the nuclear family took center position. In Gustaf Edgren's *Valborgsmässoafton* (*Walpurgis Night*, 1935), the contemporary political discourse on the national need for massive reproduction is overtly and conspicuously translated and reframed within a romantic fiction.[2] Within its narrative, the national problem of low birthrates is smoothly solved by naturalizing heterosexual love as an incontestable desire for children. The film portrays a patriarch and a widower, Frederik Bergström, who as the chief editor for a big daily newspaper is well aware of the problem of the population crisis and wants his paper to participate in the debate. (This part is played by Victor Sjöström, who had returned from Hollywood in the late 1920s and who developed his acting career, rather than his directing career, once back in Sweden.) The problem, he proclaims in an early scene, is due to the "lovelessness" that characterizes the new times and the younger generation. Having lived in a happy marriage, and having fathered plenty of children himself, and now being the grandfather of even more, he believes he has the solution to the crisis: traditional love, with traditional gender roles, and traditional family structures that make woman into mother and man into father. Parenthood, according to him, is a blessed state. In an early scene in the film, Bergström's parental and child-rearing expertise is emphasized to leave no doubt about his excellence as a loving father: celebrating his sixtieth birthday surrounded by his extended family (his own adult children, his in-laws, and a handful of blonde, blue-eyed grandchildren), and being the very center of attention, he cares as much for his children as he does for his grandchildren, taking time talking to them and explaining things to them. Apparently no one is excluded from his care and love.

However, not all of his off-spring has managed to reach that consecrated state of marriage and reproduction, and this is unsurprisingly the problem or obstacle that has to be solved within the story. Bergström's youngest daughter, Lena Bergström (played by a young Ingrid Bergman), is single, but carries a secret: she is in love with her boss, Johan Borg (Lars Hansson), who is an unhappily married man. His wife, Clary Borg (Karin Kavli), is a shallow and luxurious woman seduced by the good life who does not want to have any children. This, of course, is the source of the unhappiness of her good husband. She has her secret too: pregnant (supposedly with her husband's child, although of this we cannot be sure), she decides to have an illegal abortion. So, the contrast between the two female characters is presented starkly: a single woman, in love with a good, but taken, man, dreams of having his children and to live happily ever after with him, and a married woman, having it all, but refusing her marital duties, choosing to live life rather than to procreate. Their difference is also reinforced explicitly in terms of appearance: Bergman's character, who is blonde and wears simple, girly clothes, is presented as sweet and loving toward her father and family members, always ready to help out and care for her nieces and nephews, and Kavli's character, who is dark-haired and wears somewhat extravagant clothes, is presented as coldhearted and selfish.

After many troubles and many more sorrows, including blackmail, a murder, a divorce, a father distancing himself from his daughter (old

Bergström believes that Lena has had sexual liaisons with the married Borg, which of course, she has not), the good woman gets the good man, they get married and have a baby—and the old patriarch is delighted, getting to prove what he had known all along: that the crisis in population can only be solved by love. The liberated woman Clary Borg is the problem here—not the men. The good woman finds happiness as a mother and wife, and the bad woman, more or less, goes to hell. Within this narrative, she commits suicide once she realizes her loss. The film ends with one patriarch giving away his youngest daughter to another: manly, virile, and potent men who love their women and the children they will give them. Parenthood is blessed, and both sexes are shown their place and role within this constitution, both within the smaller unit, as well as within the larger social structure, that is, the nation. The film's last scene shows parental joy and heterosexual happiness. In a medium close-up with Johan slightly with his back to the camera and Lena and the baby facing it, the happy and fertile Borgs hold the baby, a son, between them. As Johan lifts the baby up, yet holding him rather close to his chest, Lena looks lovingly at him with great admiration and tenderness. The film leaves us with no doubt that this father is going to be as good and as caring as Lena's own father.

Yet, while the folk home concept attempted to assimilate previously considered women's work into masculinity, Swedish screens saw other male images that blended gender expectations. Arguably, Swedish cinema during this period actually presented more queer masculinities than ever before (or after). Two ideals of manhood were allowed to occupy the scene simultaneously: on one hand, the manly, heterosexual, and working-class (or, preferably under Social Democracy, classless) man with work, marriage, and child rearing on his agenda; on the other, the effeminate, often upper-class man with heterosexual romance and pleasure on his agenda. Discursively connecting male effeminacy to upper-class status is important—only the upper-class man is allowed to show gender deviance (as if expected of him), hence both romanticizing and estranging him. From a Social Democratic view (which sought to break down class barriers and uphold traditional masculinity), effeminacy and the upper classes were unwanted and undesired. Thus, by linking effeminacy to the upper class, class distinctions are potentially held up for critique. Yet, for audiences, both female and male, that yearned for stars that played such characters, effeminacy and upper-class manners were indeed wanted and desired. A different life, a different desire, a different identification and notion of self, all made possible through—however short and temporary—the engagement between spectator and film text.

Effeminacy

While some of this specific period's most famous and popular actors were straight acting and manly in appearance (always appearing in certain genres such as the *pilsner*-film, that is, simple comedies often taking place in the Swedish countryside with scenes depicting joyous beer-drinking as the standing ingredient, or in more propagandistic films such as *Valpurgis Night*), the biggest male stars of Swedish cinema all seemed to reach beyond traditional masculinity. Effeminate and pretty indeed, they presented themselves, as well as their characters on-screen, without any traditional masculine features, attributes, or manners. However, they were the ones playing the more serious roles, that is, the roles that that were closely linked to the dominant ideological discourses on the family and the building of a new society. No matter their effeminacy, they were the ones who came to constitute the image, the ideal, of a new generation of good men, fathers, and husbands. Gösta Ekman, for example, ends up both as possible baby-maker and good husband in most of his romantic comedies, and he does so despite his lack of traditional masculine traits. Sture Lagerwall and Håkan Westergren, too, embodied romantic ideals with rather typically feminine attributes and would within most narratives end up as husbands and possible fathers. The male femininity of Lagerwall's characters was, we should note, closely connected to his physical features: he was rather short and slim, had golden curls, long eyelashes, and voluptuous lips, which made him resemble a doll. Westergren, on the other hand, was tall and dark with sharp yet feminine features, looking almost like a wax figure. He, too, had very long eyelashes, and these would—as in the case of both Ekman and Lagerwall—be highlighted through excessive makeup and through cinematic devices such as lighting and camera framing.

Lagerwall appears in *Valpurgis Night* as the old chief editor Bergström's young, ambitious, and rather insensitive colleague. His character stands out in relation to the more traditionally manly and controlled calmness of both Bergström and Borg. Youthful, obstinate, and self-assured in his new job, he is also newly wedded and has decided to wait before having children (purely for economic reasons, he assures his boss). His selfishness and his "irresponsibility" in relation to the nation in crisis can, within the film's discourse, be understood as an incapacity to become a real (that is, a heteronormative) man: by avoiding fatherly duties, he can still live his life as a single man. His youth is being equated with nonmasculinity; in fact, youth was one of Lagerwall's characteristics in many films. However, by the end of the film, he has succumbed to the pressure, and happily proclaims that he is the father of twins. Westergren, on the other side, appeared as more adult in his roles. Yet his nonmasculinity was also connected to a certain refusal to marry, to take responsibility, and hence to become a grown-up. In Paul Merzbach's *För hennes skull* (*For Her Sake*, 1930), Westergren's character is a selfish and not very loving man who is not willing to commit, and who, in the end, loses his girlfriend to another man, suitably played by the effeminate Ekman. But in most of the films he appeared in, Westergren plays the effeminate lover, just like Ekman, and hence, the two share many similarities (although Ekman would take his androgyny and effeminacy further than would Westergren or Lagerwall).

Figure 5. Gosta Ekman as Sigge Wulf in *Brokiga blad (Colorful Leaves*, 1931). *Author's personal collection.*

Ekman, on whom I have chosen to focus, seemingly swayed among a variety of identity positions throughout his career. As a cultural icon, in his public performances, and through his personal tales, he constituted a paradox that inevitably brings to mind the Nietzschean dual, paradoxical self: he embodied all oppositions, those between genders, sexualities, working class and aristocracy, popular and high culture, youth and decay, life and death. Performing young, healthy romantic ideals on stage up until his death in 1938 (at age forty-seven), he would lead a busy life on and off stage, being both a workaholic and a drug addict. Busy acting both for the cinema and for the theater, he was even a theater director with his own theater company.[3] To keep himself and his many occupations together, his addiction to cocaine and amphetamines—which began when starring in F. W. Murnau's *Faust* in Berlin in 1925—grew heavier over the years, slowly exhausting his body. Injecting the drugs intramuscularly, his body would disintegrate but he would be able to keep his mind clear. Consequently, it was a scorched body that incorporated the romantic and healthy young ideals on-screen. Innocent yet temptingly decadent, he radiated virginity, while also exuding a certain promiscuity.

Most important, at least for this chapter, he was obviously a man, yet he could also be read as "womanly." The audience, as well as the media, was spellbound by his gender deviance, which was a large part of his charisma. For example, in 1919, journalist and chronicler Guido Valentin wrote a short notice on having seen Ekman on horseback with a woman (and Valentin is very alert to point out that this woman is not Ekman's wife), and he marvels both over the makeup Ekman is wearing, as well as over his exceptional beauty (Valentin). Nonetheless, he expresses great relief when he realizes that he is witnessing a performance. Ekman, with his nameless coactress, was shooting a scene, and hence, Valentin feels "no cause for alarm!" Obviously writing for a majority of female readers, addressing his readers as such, Valentin positions himself in a feminine point of view when telling about his adventure. He thereby creates an imaginary bonding with other admiring women, positioning himself in their place by expressing to his readers the jealousy and the love that he—as a she—has experienced when seeing Ekman with another woman. Beyond acknowledging female sexual desire, his notice also can be, of course, read in terms of closeted gay desires: as soon as Valentin finds out that he is indeed watching a performance, Ekman's ample makeup and beauty, and the desire they obviously invoke in Valentin, are no longer threatening: it is only an act (and a heterosexual one at that); there is no cause for alarm.

Ekman's queerness and the response it evoked (and still evokes) in his admirers is much in line with Michele Aaron's definition of "queer" ("New Queer Cinema" 2004, 5). She ascribes to the term a critical edge that serves to upset the dualism of both gender and sexuality: "Queer represents the resistance to, primarily, the normative codes of gender and sexual expression—that masculine men sleep with feminine women" (5). Furthermore, she describes queer as representing the resistance "to the restrictive potential of gay and lesbian sexuality—that only men sleep with men and women sleep with women" (5). Queer, then, is a critical concept that "encompasses the non-fixity of gender expression and the non-fixity of both straight and gay sexuality" (5).

The King

Ekman, who unquestionably is the most famous of these straight heroes with queer inclinations, started his film career in 1911 and during the late 1920s and early 1930s came to set the structures for a "new" male ideal. He became an icon for both female and male audiences, and, we can assume, for straight and nonstraight audiences.[4] The male ideal that he represented and embodied (together with Lagerwall and Westergren) played up his androgyny, feminine features, and exceptional beauty. The epigraph at this chapter's beginning is from a conversation with my own grandmother, an enthusiastic Ekman fan as a young, urban, and middle-class woman, who would—whenever the subject came up—let me know for sure that Ekman was indeed "special," that is, "not like other men."

However, because of the apparent straightness of the romantic narratives in which he often appeared, he must be considered a heteronormative ideal, no matter how queer he may have seemed. Evidence suggests that many women found effeminacy, especially with regard to Ekman, a valued and desirable trait in a man. Among such expressions of appreciation and infatuation with him are these words from the young Ingrid Bergman, who starred with Ekman in Gustaf Molander's *Swedenhielms* (1935) and *Intermezzo* (1936):

> My admiration for Gösta is soon unbearable to myself and to the people around me. To me he is like God himself—within the profession! He gave me an enormous bouquet with forty carnations because he said I had been so good. . . . After having finished the film I would embrace and kiss him and then we would say goodbye. I write this in a very expressive manner because I am so filled with him and I do want to remember everything he told me. I do not want to work with other people any more. I only want to work with him. Thank you God for your kindness in letting me getting to know him. (Forslund, 117; my translation)

A 1930s' saying explicitly conveys Ekman's affiliation with and impact on women: "When Ekman entered the room, the ladies would faint." His friend and coactress Birgit Tengroth explained his impact on people, saying "everywhere he would spread encouraging words around him as a king would throw gold. . . . That's what it was like to work with Gösta. Everyone would fall in love, not with each other, nor with him, they would just fall in love" (Forslund, 116. My translation).

Like Lagerwall and Westergren, Ekman tended to play feminine men who were nonetheless heterosexual. In Merzbach's *For Her Sake* (1930) and in Gustaf Molander's *Kära släkten* (*Dear Relatives*, 1933), although he is positioned as an object of desire, a traditionally female position, his romantic partners are female. In the already-mentioned *Intermezzo*, he is a feminine, tragic, genius maestro, but one who is having an extramarital affair with Ingrid Bergman's ingénue (thus implicitly having sexual relations with two women). At least once, however, in Edwin Adolphson's *Brokiga blad* (*Colorful Leaves*, 1931), he steps off the tightrope and acts overtly, invitingly, and flamboyantly gay.

In one scene in the latter film (which is a compilation film consisting of scenes taken from various stage performances by actors, singers, and artists), Ekman plays the part of real-life entertainer Sigge Wulff who during the latter part of the mid–nineteenth century was famous for his singing and for his charm. As Wulff, Ekman is strutting around on stage singing a song about a certain Kalle P, a fictive character, who—the song informs us—"catches the King's eye" as he passes him in the parade. Throughout this song, Ekman repeatedly implies that the King has had gay liaisons. Although the scene takes place in the 1800s, inferring that this is Ekman (not Sigge Wulff) singing about King Gustav V, who was king in 1931 and who was rumored to be gay in various circles, is not difficult.[5] Making this already quite explicit "outing" of the king even more unambiguous, one should note, is the introductory inserts of newsreel footage of Gustav V as he hands over a prize to a male athlete at some athletic ceremony: this footage is followed by the scene with Ekman singing, clearly indicating that he is referring to Gustav V.

This scene offers a triple queerness in all its campiness, and it is one that easily lends itself to being read as gay. First, Ekman performs as Wulff, obviously queering both Wulff and himself through his very extravagant and effeminate body movements. Second, the song about Kalle P has lyrics that present him (Kalle) as a man of great erotic attraction to others. The lyrics explain how he walks and moves "like no other man" and how he attracts everybody's looks, regardless of gender and social class (although he appears, according to the lyrics, to be more attractive to the male gazes). The king, who is a real and living person (in comparison to Kalle who we may assume is a fictional character, and to Wulff, who is long since dead), is being outed as attracted to Kalle (and to Ekman?), which together with the already existing rumors outs him as most likely gay.

Because Gustav was the last Swedish monarch to exert any sort of direct power over the government, this sort of outing could be seen as a strategic shift from the older class structure to the model the Social Democrats espoused: the aristocracy's masculinity is problematized. Yet by positioning Ekman as somehow connected to the king, such potential criticism is complicated. Given that audiences often referred to Ekman as "king Gösta," an apparent playfulness and awareness is at stake that Ekman willingly exposes. Whereas the real King is made fun of because of his supposed closeted gayness, Ekman proudly reveals his queer persona in absurdum. The joke may be on King Gustav V, but *not* on King Gösta.

(De)Sexualized Erotic Object

In his other films, films with clear narratives in which Ekman plays a romantic hero, the flamboyant queerness is expressed in relation to the female other. Appearing in straight sagas with the heterosexual coupling as the only possible ending, Ekman's queerness serves to question the other male ideals occupying other film texts, as well as other kinds of cultural and political texts of the time. His femininity and conscious lack of masculine traits helps to deconstruct those other ideals. Because he (almost) always gets the girl in the end, he is positioned as a heteronormative ideal man, but an alternative one (in his gender deviance, and through his own intentional positioning as star and icon).

By voluntarily occupying an object position on-screen, offering himself as a desired object for our gaze as well as an object for the gazing that goes on within the narrative, that is, on-screen, Ekman not only deviates from the gender role that cinema as a gender technology assigns to him, but he also manages to upset the laws of sexual difference with the male as acting subject and the female as passive object that cinema so often relies on. Through his performed effeminacy and through his own objectification in frame, he takes a conventionally feminine position. And he does so together with his coactress. Yet, because both occupy a feminine position in frame, the question of advancing the story becomes crucial. Most often, as in *For Her Sake* or in *Dear Relatives*, the female character leads the story forward and makes choices, whereas Ekman's character only seems to follow (when he actually takes the lead, he only does so unconsciously). Yet, the changing of positions is not a total reversal of the active male/passive female equation: the queer straight couple is presented as equal, and (queering these representations even more) in ways that may to some resemble female friendship, whereas to others, the coupling even lends itself to a lesbian reading. By deviating in terms of gender and by explicitly showing sexual and romantic interest in women, Ekman becomes doubly queer: he becomes a proto-lesbian or a version of a "chick with a dick."

In Molander's *Dear Relatives*, Ekman's character aristocrat Clas af Lejionstam and his wife Lilli af Lejionstam (played by famous actress and singer Tutta Berntzen Rolf) pass as a sexually undifferentiated couple (what I prefer to read as a lesbian couple). Not until the very end, when the wife's father (played by Carl Barcklind) demands that the two youngsters fulfill their marital duty and make him a granddad, do they become sexually differentiated. What makes it possible for the father-in-law to convince, or force, the couple to procreate, is financial. Lejionstam, although an aristocrat, has lost most of his family fortune and needs money to keep his family manison. In exchange for financial security, the young couple gives in to the baby-making that the older generation requires. This fact unsettles and invalidates the very heteronormativity that the text tries to establish and confirm: the sexual differentiation between the two lovers that must follow, a differentiation that the film applauds by its conventional ending, can therefore be understood as a purely extrinsic need or demand. Desire for sexual differentiation and for steady gender and parental roles is not intrinsic to our characters, but something forced on them from outside.

Within all of Ekman's films, sexual difference is constantly being defied and refused: the laws of attraction between genders are much guided by their similarity, rather than their difference. Sexual difference officially works as organizing principle: the romance these films bring forward is one with outspoken heterosexual frames (that is, marriage—straight copulation—that will lead to reproduction, as in *Dear Relatives*). On a symbolic level, however, the spectator can often enjoy a relative absence of the phallic regime in the romantic relationships between Ekman and his leading lady. This becomes apparent in several scenes in *Dear Relatives*. One of these is with the Lejionstams still in their bedroom. Although late morning, they are both in their pajamas; Clas is in no hurry to get up, and Lilli is by the end of the bed. Clas, who is laying flat on his belly on his elbows with feet in the air, talking to his mansion manager, is placed as the object of Lilli's and our desire presented in a classic female pose. Lilli, happy to be the one who desires and not merely the one who expects to be desired, is in control here, although she remains silent throughout most of the scene. Due to her position as the one who holds the gaze, she takes on a subject position in relation to Clas as object. A sudden cut and she is now sitting next to him, holding him, and the scene transforms itself into a romantic scenario. Sexual difference however appears to be nonexistent. Perhaps because of this he apparently becomes even more desirable to her. They are equal, managing to minimize sexual difference. If anything, their similarities are precisely what draws each to the other (and the audience to them).

Floating In-Between: Queerness and Its Audiences

To focus on these representations and to disclose the queerness they possess, welcomes, if not requires, the structural framing or method of making explicit how queer elements continuously make themselves visible and heard in an otherwise strict straight context, a society rigidly formed by a straight matrix that wishes to leave little room for alternatives. Following the poststructuralist path, one could say that dominant culture needs its opposite to constitute itself as such, as dominant, as center. What this positioning implies, however, is that the dominant center cannot fully distance itself from the periphery surrounding it: the two have no watertight boundaries between them. Queer representations and queer elements float around in straight culture, regardless how it tries to repress them (see Doty). Hence, following a Derridean line, we need to think of the division as a membrane and not as a border. The membrane metaphor opens up for conceiving these two spaces as inseparable from one another. Such a view questions any notion of culture as universal and monolithic and opens up for the diverse, the heterogeneous.

The heterogeneity of culture makes queer heroes possible in a straight universe and constitutive of culture is its audiences and their desires. The queer heroes of the Swedish 1930s must be seen in relation to their audience: During the 1930s the female audience came to constitute a powerful majority and desired stars such as Ekman, Lagerwall, and Westergren, creating a space for gender-bending male ideals. The new film culture, which was intrinsically connected to both female emancipation and consumerism, was a female culture with women both consuming and negotiating various gendered images (Habel). Connecting the female audience and the male ideal personas on-screen in this case refuses a strictly heteronormative structure, not only because of the queerness implied in these ideal representations, but also because, as Eve Kosofsky Sedgwick (1990) has argued, any analysis of male and female, of feminine and masculine, must include an analysis of homo and hetero. This latter opposition structures society as forcefully as does the former; in fact, the opposition between male and female may very well be understood as a difference built or based on the homo/hetero divide.

This does not mean that the actual sexual predilection of these three stars is crucial (no matter how tempting dwelling on their private sexuality is). Rather, it is of no greater importance here. As far as we know, these screen heroes were openly "straight" (if straightness is taken to equal marriage and children, and it usually is).[6] Yet, their on-screen queer qualities made them antistraight in their capacity to blur the boundary between hetero and homo, as well as between feminine and masculine. The representations of gender deviance they offer, that is, their very roles on-screen as well as their public persona that contribute to an inevitable queerness. A queerness that somehow becomes detached from their private persona and transformed into a cultural and social quality, a new masculinity made possible within Swedish culture that and women (and men) could desire as ultimate ideals. Hence, these individuals, in their performances, opened up for a larger cultural acceptance and acknowledging of queer masculinities broadening the otherwise rigid dichotomous spectra for genders and sexualities.

Conclusion

One must of course be careful when ascribing a contemporary understanding and interpretation of stars as signs (and personas) and of their audiences' response, both of which belong to an earlier period. While we today may have a certain way of reading gendered images, looking for the queering potential that all cultural images may have, the audience of the 1930s most probably did not dwell on the queerness (no less, the possible homosexuality) of these stars. Yet, we may assume that it was quite aware of the possible meanings that gender transgression on-screen had, and of certain "different" desires expressed and put into play through these stars. The quote that opened this article from a conversation with my grandmother on her love for Ekman during her younger days suggests as much. Ekman´s effeminate persona apparently opened up desires that other men could not incite in her.

Negotiating patriarchal masculinity, lending themselves to a blurring of dichotomies and to a possibility for a certain similarity in terms of sex and gender, these male ideals must be understood as important contributions to the development of a new Swedish "classless" society. If gender is to be connoted to, or equalized with, class and, ultimately, with classification, then the gender transgressions that these male stars offered can be understood as a questioning of class, and, in its extension, as an opening up for multiple desires and pleasures that reach outside of its very compartmentalizing. The queer outside constitutes itself, through the response it gets both from the inside and its own outside, as an alongside, and, to quote Fuss once more, the distance and proximity is sometimes no distance at all.

Notes

1. Hansen describes how the crisis in gender relations in the United States arose as women started to work outside of their homes. She positions Valentino in the midst of this crisis, arguing that he emerged within an ongoing battle between "traditional patriarchal ideology on the one hand and the recognition of female experience, needs and fantasies on the other" (7).

2. For a dynamic reading of this film, see Soila 1991, 1992.

3. Some of his later films were actually filmed during the night. Busy with his other occupations at the theater (rehearsals in the morning, teaching young actors midday, performing in the afternoon and evenings), and devoid of all need to sleep, Ekman requested that his scenes should be shot during the night, a demand that few colleagues would deny him. See Forslund.

4. His rise to stardom came early in his career, but it was not without obstacles. Some critics, such as novelist and Nobel Prize–winner Pär Lagerquist, regarded both his early acting and his beautiful looks as being too exaggerated. Other critics loved him: the novelist and Nobel Prize–winner Selma Lagerlöf (who more recently has been outed as a lesbian) wrote in 1913 that his performance was "irresistible. He was beautiful, he moved on stage with terrific elegance . . . , he presented his lines with such an emphasis that he made the entire audience look at him, and at him alone" (Forslund, 28–29, my translation).

5. These rumors were widely spread within Swedish society during the 1930s but not until 1950 would they transform into a most unwelcome and itching political affair: the royal family was being blackmailed by a man who threatened to go public with the erotic liaison he claimed he had once had with the king during the 1930s. Between 1936 and 1947, it was revealed, this man had, because of blackmail, received a large amount of money to keep quiet, but when King Gustav V died in 1950, he once again started his blackmailing, which led to his imprisonment.

6. Ekman's best friends who were out as gay or bisexual (for example, writer Hjalmar Bergman, painter Nils Dardel, entertainer Karl Gerhard, film director Mauritz Stiller, and writer Noel Coward) are sometimes mentioned as proof of Ekman's bisexuality. His gay friendships do not make him one thing or the other, however. In fact, he had also many straight friends (and what do they make him, if anything?).

5

Adrienne L. McLean

Putting 'Em Down Like a Man

Eleanor Powell and the Spectacle of Competence

In his 1959 autobiography *Steps in Time*, Fred Astaire famously characterized the virtuosic tap dancing of Eleanor Powell, with whom he had starred in MGM's *Broadway Melody of 1940* (1940), as follows, "She 'put 'em down' like a man, no ricky-ticky-sissy stuff with Ellie" (242). Without irony, Astaire also calls Powell "one of the all-time great dancing girls" (241–242). Eleanor Powell, who made ten film musicals for MGM between 1936 and 1943, was more than a screen dancer, however; like Astaire, she choreographed her own film numbers and, in many cases, supervised their staging as well. When Hedda Hopper asked her in the 1950s why she continued to practice and to dance even though she had retired from the screen after marrying Glenn Ford in 1943, Powell replied, "The dance routines I created are like children to me. I don't want to forget them" (Hopper 1951).

These quotations taken together map out a rich but relatively undeveloped area in film studies and, more obviously, classical Hollywood cinema itself: the relationship of creativity and virtuosity to gender, or the problems created for Hollywood's generic systems of representation—and, de facto, the scholarship examining those systems—when the virtuosic and creative performer is also a woman, a "showgirl" (in Laura Mulvey's well-known formulation). Eleanor Powell (1912–1982) serves as a useful locus for considering the ways in which competent labor and creativity, and or as the virtuosic film(ed) performance, interact both with Hollywood's Production Code–mandated narrative valorization of heterosexual romance and film theory's notions of spectacle as a "feminizing" realm wherein sexual difference is constructed and maintained. Although significant work has been done on the effects of such feminization and spectacularization in relation to song-and-dance men such as Fred Astaire and Gene Kelly (for example, Cohan 1993, 2005; Farmer; Tinkcom), less attention has been paid to the effects of what might be called an aesthetics of competence, the physical practices of virtuosity and skill, on the showgirl herself, much less one who puts 'em down like a man.

This is not to say that unconventional showgirls have not already been the subject of scholarly attention. In his 2005 discussion of the camp star turn in the MGM musical, Steven Cohan argues that Judy Garland "personified a gender problem ready-made for camp in her numbers: her talent made her extraordinary, perfectly suitable for the musical genre, yet did not translate into the 'pinup girl' or 'cheesecake girl' movie-star standard" (Cohan 2005, 133–34). Stars such as Garland therefore enact "a camp's recognition of the incongruities arising from glamour's operation as a cultural mechanism of heterosexualization" (93). Cohan also notes that Garland often "was paired with a male lead who did not sing or dance with her," and that her star numbers in these films allowed her to cut loose to revel in both what she had and what she lacked: "too much intensity, too much physicality, too little glamour, too little heterosexual rapport with the dancing boys" (134). Although other female stars at MGM, Cohan writes, also had a "problematic relation to glamour" (for example, Debbie Reynolds and Ann Miller), he lays the studio's "understanding of a star's unconventional value with respect to both showgirl glamour and the male chorus" at the figurative, if not literal, feet of Eleanor Powell (137).

Powell was attractive to MGM because of the fame she had acquired as a tap dancer on Broadway and the success of her first-billed appearance in the Fox film *George White's 1935 Scandals* (1935), where she danced in one number and played a brief role as a woman trying to steal star Alice Faye's boyfriend. Despite the short duration of her time on-screen in the Fox film, Powell received rave press reviews. *Vanity Fair* wrote, she was "the best thing about the whole film," and according to the *New York Times*, she was a "genuinely stirring novelty . . . who brings you actively awake during the minute or two when she is performing her miraculous tap-dance routine" (Schultz, 100). MGM was impressed enough with Powell and her talent to revive the title of its first big musical, *Broadway Melody* (1929), for a series that would star her (beginning with *Broadway Melody of 1936* [1935] and running through *Broadway Melody of 1938* [1937] and *Broadway Melody of 1940*). But Cohan writes that even her first star vehicle, *Broadway Melody of 1936*, "evinces signs of MGM's uncertainty about how to showcase its new star because of her nonconformity"; the studio tried "to make the star's dancing conform to a femininity more consistent with star glamour" by putting her in an Albertina Rasch dream ballet, a "mistake MGM did not repeat again on so grand a scale" (139).[1] In the same film, however, the big production number in which Powell "goes solo" (and which she choreographed herself) gives her the "freedom" missing from the earlier number, and her "'masculine' physical moves . . . disrupt the heterosexual binary" (140) that otherwise structures it (and most other numbers in Hollywood musicals). Especially when she "performs with the boys in the chorus," Powell's numbers (along with those of Garland, Reynolds, and Miller) "resist the norms of glamorous stardom to imply a stance which recognizes its incongruities as a mechanism of gender regulation" (144). Yet by 1941, Powell's box-office appeal had diminished so much that properties originally intended for her were being redesigned and given to other up-and-coming stars, such as Garland (137). If MGM was willing to take a chance with yet another performer (Garland reportedly replaced Powell in *Ziegfeld Girl*, 1941) who was also going to present problems involving her "nonconformity with the glamorous protocols of female stardom" (137), the question remains as to why Powell was not able to remain a star.

Of course no one is suggesting that Garland and Powell are actually similar, beyond the sheer magnitude of their performing talent and except for their problems with glamour and their concomitant status as camp stars. In other words, Powell had too much intensity, too much physicality, too little glamour, too little heterosexual rapport with the dancing boys, and so on. But even if the comparison is limited to the "camp dynamic," critical differences still exist between Garland and Powell—that Powell does not exhibit the same relationship as Garland even to what Shari Roberts calls "the artificiality of the concept of femininity" (in Cohan 2005, 138). As is well known, much of Garland's nonconformity and lack of glamour was located in her body—her "stubby, barrel-shaped" physique, her "unfortunate proportions," her "top-heaviness," her "short neck" (see McLean 2002, 6–7). Garland was always remarkable, as critics were in the habit of pointing out from her earliest appearances in show business, for singing—for "belting"—with the voice of an adult. That voice emanated at first literally from the body of a child and later from someone whose height (Garland was less than five feet tall), stance, and physique continued to embody the childlike and, at least partly therefore, the ambiguously feminine. Moreover, one of the most famous and enduring elements of Garland's continuing appeal over time has been her fragility and insecurity in the face of her physical shortcomings, her well-publicized suicide attempts signaling, despite her equally well-publicized sense of irony and bitter humor, an *in*competence in relation to facing the trials of life without the help of drugs or alcohol or a string of unsuitable husbands.

Eleanor Powell, on the other hand, had few problems with her performing body, which conformed easily enough to ideals of feminine pulchritude in its contours and size and which also served her well as the source of her subjectivity as a dancer. Shari Roberts claims that MGM forced Powell "to undergo a series of beauty treatments" to make her more conventionally glamorous (in Cohan 2005, 137–38), but all that these treatments entailed were capping her teeth, minimizing her freckles, and curling and styling her hair. There is virtually no female star (or male, for that matter) who did not undergo some sort of physical "improvement" along these lines when signed to studio contracts. Powell, like Garland, began as a "youngster" in show business, but she did not make her first film until she was in her early twenties. Powell, too, came from a broken home where money was hard to come by, and she rose through the ranks with hard work and determination. And from her earliest appearances in film, she was noticed, and lauded, for her competence and skill in many forms of dance—ballet, acrobatics, ballroom, and tap (she reputedly learned to tap in only ten lessons)—as well as for her forthrightness, simplicity, freshness, and beauty. As a fan magazine writer characterized her at the time of the release of *Broadway Melody of 1936*, Powell was "one of the minor mysteries" to Hollywood because she "is simple and unaffected and unspoiled," "nothing is too much trouble in order to perfect her work," and she "never attempts to take credit for what she hasn't accomplished" (Cannon). Powell and Garland differ most, then, in their attitudes toward their stardom, as well as the sorts of talents they possessed; Powell was portrayed as being able to handle anything life threw at her with a minimum of fuss and bother, and her nonconformity, if it was that, lay in her extreme competence and, or in spite of, the fact that she was also unutterably normal and healthy.

And feminine. Although of course my contentions here (like most of those I have been citing) are less demonstrable fact than informed interpretation, ultimately I do not feel that Powell ever displays or inhabits what Cohan calls a "camp subjectivity" that finds "humor, not [only] pain, in the balancing act required of femininity" (Cohan 2005, 105). Indeed, while I largely agree with Cohan's broader analysis of the camp dimensions of the MGM musical and many of its star turns, the lack of apparent irony or "knowing" camp subjectivity in Powell's persona or her film performances is most significant to me. What made Powell special was, and remains, virtually unmatched in Hollywood history; she was a dancer whose prowess and sheer proficiency at the control and exhibition of her body and its virtuosic abilities were recognized for a time as being of inestimable value, both in some amorphous ideological sense and, more practically, at the box office. But ultimately Powell was simply too comfortable in her own competence and abilities to succeed for long as a female star in Hollywood. She ignores her own deficiencies, in acting, in singing (MGM made no secret of the fact that Powell's singing voice was dubbed, usually by Marjorie Lane; Schultz, 8), and concentrates on her strengths, the only alteration in her relationship to her art coming from the new skills she learns to exhibit it: dancing while skipping rope in *Honolulu* (1939), studying and mastering the moves of a matador fighting a bull for a number in *Ship Ahoy* (1942), learning cowboy roping for an intricate routine in *I Dood It* (1943).

That dancing in a man's tuxedo, or in pants, or manipulating a lariat like a rodeo champion, or being able to keep up with Fred Astaire or any other man on the dance floor would necessarily alter her relationship with her femininity just does not seem to occur to her. Nor does she appear to be uncomfortable in sequins, spangles, frills, skirts, shorts, or high heels. She is a great tap dancer—"a percussion instrument with [her] feet," as she called herself (Kobal 1985, 221)—and she is a very feminine woman. In fact, Powell's male drag was, in most if not all of her films, fully integrated with a spectacular femininity, such that she was always recognizably a talented woman performing, in her own words, "difficult things easily" (Schultz, 1). In *Broadway Melody of 1938* Powell disguises herself briefly as a stable boy, and in *Rosalie* (1937) she plays a Balkan princess who pretends to be a West Point cadet for a bit and who leads a formation of soldiers and performs a Sousa number in the same getup. But despite the cross-dressing, she never truly masquerades as a man, nor do I believe we are meant to take her as one, or to think that the other characters in the diegesis really would either.[2]

An Alternative Style of Femininity

Virginia Wright Wexman writes of musicals, "although women actors are more likely than men to sing and dance onscreen, their roles are less likely to 'spill over' in a way that could endow their off-screen personas with the status of musical professionals. Thus, Fred Astaire is known primarily as a dancer-star of the movies, Ginger Rogers as a movie star who danced with Astaire" (143–44). Eleanor Powell's name appears nowhere in Wexman's book. But Powell's star image was clearly based, perhaps even more than that of Astaire, on her status as a "musical professional." Moreover, Wexman believes that "by representing its leading actresses as singers and dancers, Hollywood has been able to focus on aspects of their bodies and faces that expressed their desirability as romantic companions" (145). But that is precisely what is at question, according to Cohan, Roberts, and others, in Powell's image.

Paradoxically, of course, because Fred Astaire and Gene Kelly are also singers and dancers they function a bit oddly both in Hollywood's systems of representation and in film theory's elucidations of those systems as always being structured according to binary notions of gender. Hollywood's promotion and publicity machinery spent a lot of time and effort laboring to prove that what Astaire and Kelly did was not just work but hard work and that their own spectacular status as singing and dancing "boys" did not automatically make them sissies (see, for example, Cohan 1993; 2005, 149–99). There is considerable ambiguity and complexity in both Astaire's and Kelly's star images for these reasons. On the one hand, they are nominally straight males so what they do on-screen will most likely be automatically characterized as "productive labor," as Wexman puts it (143). On the other hand, when they sing and, especially, dance for public consumption, they invoke a whole register of associations in American culture of the male dancer with problematic or uncertain masculinity.

Ramsay Burt, in his 1995 study of the male dancer, suggests that the primary basis for U.S. and European attitudes toward the dancing male in the nineteenth and twentieth centuries that were at least tinged by homophobia was that "the male dancer displayed himself, and thus was in danger of infringing the conventions which circumscribed the way men could be looked at" (22). But Cohan suggests that the film musicals of Astaire and Kelly "imagined an alternative style of masculinity, one grounded in spectacle and spectatorship" (Cohan 1993, 66). Astaire's colorful clothing and dance moves, for example, are substantially mediated by his professional prowess and abilities; Astaire is not feminized as much as he represents a different mode of self-presentation tied to well-known theatrical and show-business values. Unlike John Wayne or Cary Grant, say, who can also be forms of male bodily spectacle, Fred Astaire is a "highly theatricalized representation of maleness onscreen, which oscillates between, on the one hand, a fictional character grounded in the static and reductive binarism of traditional gender roles and, on the other, a musical persona whose energy choreographs a libidinal force that revises conventional masculinity and linear desire" (63–64). Again, much the same could be, and was, said of Eleanor Powell: reviews of her star vehicles mark the plots as "weak," "formula," "typical," "dull," full of "stock patterns," and "lacking freshness," while Powell's dancing is "magical," "dextrous," "excellent," "winning," "flawless," "exquisite," "superlative," "incomparable," full of "warmth and beauty," able to "tap you into admiration and amusement," and so on.[3] Just as men who dance on-screen are not all "feminized," women who dance on-screen are not all "showgirls" whose activities are unproductive, not construed as labor, and whose meaning resides only in their desirability as romantic companions. Powell's films, in short, imagine an alternative style of femininity.

And Now I Pronounce You Man and Wife

Powell's male costars themselves are not known as paragons of virile masculinity—Robert Taylor (*Broadway Melody of 1936* and *Broadway Melody of 1938*), James Stewart (*Born to Dance*, 1936), Nelson Eddy (*Rosalie*), and Red Skelton (*Ship Ahoy* and *I Dood It*). In *Lady Be Good* (1941), she barely has a romantic partner at all. With the exception of *Broadway Melody of 1940*, which stars George Murphy and Fred Astaire, Powell does not dance with any of her romantic leads, although she sometimes dances around them as they stand there, as happens to Stewart in *Born to Dance*. In *Broadway Melody of 1938* Powell and Murphy perform two dance duets that seem romantic—they are very much in the style of Fred Astaire and Ginger Rogers, the first an incidental number in a park in the rain, the second a ballroom dance performed on a stage—but Murphy is not Powell's love interest in the plot. Powell always has a nominal male suitor, however, and she usually ends up paired with him in a film's final shot; thus her vehicles can be made to fit prevalent definitions of the genre's syntactic structure as constituted by the overdetermined male-female couple that "*is the plot*," Rick Altman claims, of the classical Hollywood musical (35, emphasis in original). But even in her more populated films, especially the *Broadway Melody* series, many of the featured women, no less than the men, do *not* end up even visually paired in this way. Moreover, frequently the couples that do occur are otherwise, and noticeably, far from normative—the diminutive Judy Garland, playing a child, paired with thirty-something beanpole Buddy Ebsen in *Broadway Melody of 1938*, to use one relatively famous example. And poor George Murphy, despite being one of the very few male costars who actually dances with Powell in romantic ballroom style, never ends up with a girl of his own.

Heterosexuality, in other words, seems a bit rote in the narratives of Powell's films, granted lip-service but not with much energy—and never with as much energy as is expended in her films' numbers. Perhaps because its normativity is built not on conviction but on convention, heterosexuality in a Powell film varies widely, and sometimes wildly, in its contours, resulting in a range of represented and often spectacular sexualities that are much more interesting (even if occasionally disturbing, as in the case of Garland and Ebsen) than a mere recounting of any "love plot" would suggest. In *Born to Dance*, to use one typical example, several sailors are seeking women, and one of them is in fact already married but has only spent one night with his wife and has not seen her in four years. Unbeknownst to him, he is the father of a child; but his wife, Jenny (Una Merkel), is neither particularly interested in reuniting with him nor able to recognize him when he does appear (she rushes toward and kisses Jimmy Stewart's character, Ted, instead). Eleanor Powell's character, Nora, first meets Jenny at the Lonely Hearts Club where Jenny works; within minutes, Jenny asks Nora to move in with her, which Nora does. Subsequently we see as many scenes featuring the happy and fully self-supporting family of Jenny, the child, and "Aunt Nora" as we do of any of the film's heterosexual couples.

Nevertheless, although Stewart and Powell bear a disconcerting resemblance to one another physically—it has something to do with their jawlines—they do engage in several romantic clinches and are convincingly besotted with one another. And the more Nora dances, the more Ted loves her. But Ted also spends a lot of time with the guys and, in one exceedingly odd scene, is taken to bed by a gay man, a department store employee played by Barnett Parker. On Nora and Ted's first date, they appear, through framing and editing, to be getting married in front of a large group of people. We hear a voiceover proclaiming, "And now I pronounce you man and wife." We find out that they are in a department store (for reasons that are never explained) at the demonstration of a prototype "honeymoon cottage." Parker's character, who speaks with a lisping British accent, shows off the decorations and fabrics, the patterned chintzes, the accent pillows, and so on. When the trio reaches the cottage's bedroom, Ted asks, "Where's the other bed?" The "floorwalker" (as he is listed in most credit lists) responds, "Other *bed*, Sir? We believe in the double bed and a lasting marriage!" Ted protests that the bed is "too short" for him. The floorwalker urges him to try it out, and then gets in bed with Ted: "It's *awfully* comfortable, isn't it, Sir!" They begin to bounce together, testing out the mattress. The bed collapses and the two men are buried under its canopy, the one "with ball fringe." Nora, who has not said a word during any of this, points and giggles. End of scene.

The episodic nature of many of the plots of Powell's films, then, makes them resemble revues as much as narrative features. They not only devote little screen time to the formation of their couples, but they are also full of other idiosyncratic and spectacular performers whose abilities make them very difficult to integrate into a "dual-focus narrative," as Altman calls it, in which male and female characters structure the film through their participation in parallel scenes and numbers. The floorwalker, the wacky conductor who appears in the park in *Born to Dance*, the wild-haired man with the pack of dogs in *Broadway Melody of 1938* (not to mention its racehorse subplot), the crazy soprano and the ball-juggling (sometimes by mouth) Trixie Firschke in *Broadway Melody of 1940*, and myriad other specialty acts, performance set pieces, or comic interludes that appear, take place, and then disappear (from narrative concerns if not from the audience's consciousness) all help to fragment and decenter the couple-producing proclivities of such musicals. The male characters cannot do much, if anything, that the women cannot do except what is granted to men as privilege merely by virtue of their gender (being in the Navy, for instance). And in all of Powell's films the men do desire her; her dancing ability is part of her attraction, not something that is in any way meant to be taken as threatening—not even when she dances in top hat, white tie, and tails. So given her films' construction of heterosexuality in their narratives, the paucity of romantic duets in a Powell film does not seem intended to highlight either her nonconformity or her "masculinity," as Roberts calls it (Cohan 2005, 138), unless extreme competence, and the ability to be comfortable exhibiting that competence, is itself taken to be a masculine trait. That this may in fact be the case is one of the most disconcerting aspects of the trajectory of Powell's career and deserves further exploration.

Lady, Be Good

Cohan's study of the MGM musical and its stars offers excellent descriptions of many of Powell's best-known films, particularly the *Broadway Melody* series (Cohan 2005, 137–44). And, thankfully, most of Powell's films are now regularly shown on cable television and have become available in various commercial home-video formats (producing new reception contexts for Powell's work, an issue to which I return later). One film that is not as easily obtainable as the others as of this writing is *Lady Be Good*. Because it encapsulates many of the problems that Powell's stardom presented to Hollywood, to the generic requirements of the musical and musical stardom, to her contemporary audiences, and to theoretical considerations of all of these, I examine it in some detail. Like all of Powell's star vehicles, *Lady Be Good* is in black and white. It features some songs from the George and Ira Gershwin songbook (including the title song), and others by Jerome Kern and Roger Edens.

Powell receives top billing in *Lady Be Good* but has very little to do in or with the narrative, where the heterosexual couple that "is the plot" comprises nondancing Ann Sothern and Robert Young as an estranged married songwriting team. Powell plays Sothern's best friend, a Broadway dancer, who helps scheme to get the couple back together again. There is a guy, appropriately named "Buddy" (John Carroll), hanging around for Powell, but they share no romantic scenes alone nor do they perform together in any musical numbers. Powell appears in only two numbers in *Lady Be Good*, but they are among her best and are carefully and, in the second instance, lavishly produced (Busby Berkeley is the film's named dance director). Despite her marginality in the story, Powell still had substantial control over the mise-en-scène and staging of her own performances, both showstoppers. The first is an "incidental" number that takes place in her character's living room, the second a lush multisectioned Broadway finale that, in addition to Powell, features singer Connie Russell; African American "flash" dancers the Berry Brothers; and "five pianos [and their players], a sixty-five-foot chiffon curtain, eighty chorus boys, and a two-thousand-foot soundstage" (Schultz, 134).

The setting for the first number, performed to "Lady Be Good," is Powell's character's apartment, where she is shown thinking about and choreographing a number for her Broadway show. After some plot patter with Sothern's character, Powell is left alone in her living room with a record player, a tiny model of her stage set, and a spotted terrier mix named Buttons. Powell is dressed in what passes for casual clothing in the average 1940s Hollywood musical, a tailored white top and patterned bloomer-style pants that are fitted at the ankle. As she begins to noodle around with some tap steps, Buttons joins in and becomes her partner for most of the number. He walks on his hind legs around her, weaves in and out of her legs as she taps, leaps through her encircled arms and over her extended leg, and even performs a little bit of hula dancing before the tempo of the dance increases spectacularly for the finish, which includes Buttons running up and over Powell's back and leaping across the length of the room to end in her arms. They collapse in a laughing heap on the couch as the scene fades out (Powell is laughing, not Buttons, although Buttons also seems to be having a pretty good time).

Some have argued that the number with Buttons is a sure sign of Powell's impossible gender status in Hollywood. According to this line of reasoning, Powell is so unassimilable into any heterosexual partnership, so problematic because of her lack of glamour, that she is reduced to dancing with a dog, as though no one else would have her, or as though the studio had run out of men who would allow themselves to be paired with her. But the publicity about Powell and Buttons paints a less depressing story. As Margie Schultz summarizes the information circulated in various mass-media sources, Powell auditioned "hundreds of canines" and had settled on a poodle (134). But the poodle would not perform before the cameras, and Powell ended up with Buttons, who belonged to Powell's prop man. Powell herself trained Buttons to dance, and the dog proved so talented (and was so devoted to Powell, and she to him) that he was given a bigger role in the film. The number was Powell's idea, her creation, and is shot in relatively long takes—spectacularly long takes if one considers the difficulties of getting a dog to perform his tricks perfectly and on time and in the right spot. Like most of Powell's numbers, it is brisk, cheerful, and lively. If one wishes to use the number to argue that Powell has been reduced to dancing with a dog, one certainly may; but the number received raves, and of all Powell's dancing partners, Buttons is the one with which I would most like to dance.[4]

The final number in *Lady Be Good*, "Fascinating Rhythm," is presented as a flashback recounted to judge Lionel Barrymore in a divorce courtroom. As mentioned, Connie Russell initially sings the song. Trick photography makes silhouettes of male orchestra members grow behind her as individual instruments are named, and eventually Russell is in close-up, shot from a high angle, singing into the camera. Although she has a round, somewhat chubby face that makes her seem too young and wholesome to be singing in torch and scat fashion as she does here, she is dressed in a long sequined gown and easily represents structurally the sort of static, fetishized spectacle with which the showgirl is associated as a theoretical construct. The action of the sequence comes from the special effects, and as Russell's final high note ends two more silhouettes appear, this time of dancing men in tails, and grow to gigantic proportions; they turn out to be two of the three Berry Brothers.

The Berry Brothers were an African American team as legendary in dance circles as Bill Robinson or the Nicholas Brothers; *Lady Be Good* was the first of the two films in which they appear as themselves. Although their dancing is carelessly shot and edited, the pyrotechnics—the "flash"—of the virtuosic and acrobatic number remain startlingly entertaining and effective. But what the segment also underscores, no less than Powell's number with Buttons, is the marked absence of the heterosexual couple as the locus either of *Lady Be Good*'s musical entertainment values or really of its syntactic structure. Pairs or groups perform together (the Berry Brothers have appeared earlier in the film too, where they also sang), but not in the service of romance or sex. In "Fascinating Rhythm," in fact, the heterosexual couple has thus far been rendered structurally "impossible" because of Hollywood's own Code-regulated racist sexual politics. The woman who sings is white, the men who dance are African American, and therefore no romantic interaction can take place.

Eleanor Powell's appearance immediately following the Berry Brothers—through a shot of their feet, then to a moving shot of a piano player's hands, then down to a match shot of Powell's feet dancing to a soft-shoe rhythm—continues the film's emphasis on virtuosity and performance values rather than heterosexual romance. It is also obviously the result of meticulous consideration of how best to present the dance as a film sequence and of tremendous amounts of blocking and rehearsal. After the pullback from the shot of Powell's tapping feet, the first three minutes of her dance are performed in one long, unbroken tracking shot. Facing front, in silver-gray pants, modified tuxedo jacket, white shirt with bow tie, and top hat, Powell addresses us directly as spectators, while dancing backward through shifting rows of five African American jazz piano players (they smile admiringly at her as they play). The technical difficulty of the dancing is extraordinary: near the end of the three-minute sequence, for example, she executes multiple turns that, had they been flubbed, would have necessitated refilming the number from the beginning. But, as is true of the Berry Brothers, the difficulty is something she handles easily, cheerfully, and professionally.

Berkeley's influence during this three-minute shot seems confined to the use of a gigantic curtain to mask areas of the action, to the smoothly patterned movements of the pianos, and to the final crane pullback to a long shot of the all-male orchestra that Powell directs to rise to its feet. It becomes more prominent during what Martin Rubin calls the "final mass tap dance" at the end, with its frequent close-ups, overhead shots, and montage-style editing (153). But while Berkeley sets up what Rubin describes as a "labyrinthine, amorphous, slippery space that casts itself loose from narrative space and moves into the realms of abstraction and spectacle," Rubin also notes that because of its "individualized, foregrounded performers" the number never makes the "final leap to abstraction and sheer spectacle" (153). We do not see much precedence in Berkeley's other work, in other words, for extremely long tracking shots that remain focused on a single dancer's body and that showcase her dancing rather than fragmenting that body or turning it into one element of an abstract design. The integrity given to her opening dance was Powell's doing, as is the number's degree of difficulty and risk. Jerome Delamater is wrong when he refers to Astaire's and Powell's dance to "Begin the Beguine" in *Broadway Melody of 1940* as being shot in a "typically Astaire/atypically Powell long take with frontal camera" (77); Powell frequently, indeed usually, employed long takes and a frontal camera for her own numbers throughout her MGM career. The Berkeleyesque ending of "Fascinating Rhythm" also features a male top-hatted chorus that does not dance but supports Powell in a series of throws down their ranked rows, to end with her in cheerful grinning close-up after a sequence of rapid turns as canes move in to the shot from all sides.

Steven Cohan refers to other of Powell's tuxedo dances, as it were, with male chorus boys as amounting to "a female's passing as male" and displaying her comfort at dancing as "one of the boys," and doing so "effortlessly" (Cohan 2005, 142). In contrast, in some of her partnered ballroom-style dances, as with George Murphy in *Broadway Melody of 1938*, Cohan writes that Powell's face is "stern, forsaking her usual big toothy smile," and that the choreographed pairing "makes Powell's glamorous demeanor register as an artifice imposed on her body, despite the effort to link her, as the feminine half of the ballroom duo, with the elegantly dressed showgirls" who populate the set while the couple dances (141). Powell does not look so much stern as serious; the number in question is more like a ballet piece than a ballroom dance in its choreography. And her smile when it does appear after the completion of a particularly tricky sequence or at the dance's end is all the more affecting for being unforced, the result of a quiet satisfaction and pleasure. (Murphy, in contrast, wears a plastered-on grin throughout.) Moreover, this demeanor is part of any Powell dance that is performed to ballad-like or adagio music rather than jazz or swing or even blues—and the same could be said of Ginger Rogers doing a romantic ballroom dance with Fred Astaire in any of their films, too. I suggested earlier that Powell's cross-dressing would serve to highlight her nonconformity or her "masculinity" only if masculinity is itself defined as the locus of competence, and this is indeed what I believe Powell's stardom "means" most profoundly—not only that she is showing up the artifice of gender, but regardless of what she did or did not wear, regardless of the expression on her face, regardless of whom she did or did not dance with, she would always have been caught in a bind because there was no other model for being a superbly competent unpassive female performer in a musical that could be read as anything other than "drag."

She's a Bit too Powerful for Me

Although musicals remained popular throughout the 1940s and into the 1950s, the sorts of spectacle that MGM began to valorize in the 1940s also had little to do with the expression of female competence except as something that needed to be sublimated to the "ideal" of romantic and narrative integration ritualized by the couple dance that symbolizes sexual as well as marital union—but that increasingly ends up being more costly to the female half of the couple than the male half. As Richard Dyer puts it, later "integrated" musicals depended on "subordination within heterosexuality" in couple-dance choreography, and the strongest female stars ceased to be dancing stars (63). Regardless of Powell's distinctiveness, then, her very inability to become something other than herself—a virtuoso dancer who did not need male partners for support, for pleasure, or for inspiration—ultimately reduced her value. In 1952 Hedda Hopper asked Fred Astaire, who was still making musicals as a romantic lead even though he was at least twice the age of most of his leading ladies, to name his favorite dancing partners. Astaire's response is nothing so much as a testament to his own masculine insecurities, but Hollywood in the 1950s was even more of a man's town than it had been in the 1930s and 1940s: "I love to watch Rita Hayworth dance. But being Spanish, her style is different from mine. And she's too big for me. Eleanor Powell, one of our greatest talents, is a bit too powerful for me, too. She has a mannish style, but is very easy to work with" (Hopper 1952–1953).

Indeed, the returns on Powell's and Astaire's only film together, *Broadway Melody of 1940*, were disappointing to MGM, which had hoped that Powell would become the next Ginger Rogers (although the last few Astaire-Rogers films had not done so well at the box office either). *Broadway Melody of 1940* was not a failure, but one of the most frequent critical responses was that it had too much dancing, and "too much dancing," as *Silver Screen* put it, "no matter how good, gets on your nerves" (Schultz, 131). No one seemed to know what to do with a woman who was not just the partner but the equal, in technical terms, of a Fred Astaire—if she was as good as a man at what she did, she must also be "mannish," regardless of how little this actually defines her in all other respects. By the early 1940s audiences, too, according to Gallup research on *Broadway Melody of 1940*, were getting more uncomfortable with Powell and her prowess ("Report XI"). MGM had apparently assumed that Astaire (then forty-one) was the drag on *Broadway Melody of 1940*'s profits. But Gallup's audience surveys indicated that while 33 percent liked Fred Astaire, only 25 percent liked Eleanor Powell (the same percentage, however, as liked

Figure 6. Fred Astaire and Eleanor Powell dance to "Begin to Beguine" in *Broadway Melody of 1940. Author's personal collection.*

"musical dancing pictures" as a group). When asked whether they would prefer to see a musical with Astaire and Powell or a musical with Astaire and Rogers, 68 percent voted for Astaire and Rogers and only 32 percent for Astaire and Powell. (The survey was equally hard on Ginger Rogers's solo career prospects; audiences wanted her back as a partner for Astaire rather than in her own films with other actors.)

Unfortunately, Gallup did not ask anyone why they did or did not like Powell (or Astaire, for that matter). But coming up with plausible reasons for the gradual decline in her popularity in the 1940s was not difficult, among them her insufficiencies as an actress, her "advancing age" (Powell turned thirty in 1942), the lack of attention paid to the stories of her films, and so on. The fact that MGM began to recycle Powell numbers from film to film also undoubtedly contributed to audience ennui, and it is unfortunate that the ones that ended up repeated also tended to be the most expensive and (if not therefore) tasteless. Parts of her "Hawaiian" hula dance from *Honolulu*, which is performed in a silver lamé hula skirt (partly in bare feet, partly in tap shoes), later shows up as a Red Skelton dream sequence in *I Dood It*, as does a section of "Swingin' the Jinx Away," from *Born to Dance*, with different music. Roger Edens, who was a musical arranger at MGM in the mid-1930s and later became Arthur Freed's assistant, referred to "Swingin' the Jinx Away," in which Powell dances with "several thousand dancers and singing sailors" on a battleship with "sequined cannons," as a "really monstrous epitome of nonsense" that "haunt[ed him] as an embarrassment of bad taste" (Kobal 1972, 133).[5] The effect of seeing the same numbers, and similar signature moves from number to number, too, over an extended period of time can sometimes make Powell seem mechanical as well as competent; *Time*'s review of *Rosalie* called her legs "beautiful" but "sexless, superhuman, and morbidly adept, as if animated by a baleful intelligence of their own" (Schultz, 121). And any blackface number, even when intended to be a respectful homage, cannot help but make us cringe today (in *Honolulu* Powell impersonates Bill Robinson, even performing his famous "stair dance").

Overcoming Diversity

But the increasing production of the new Broadway-style musical that demanded integration of dance, story, and character and became ubiquitous following *Oklahoma!*'s success in 1943 is arguably by far the most significant development in the lowering of Powell's status in Hollywood. As Mark Grant writes, "beginning with the Broadway ballets of Agnes de Mille and Jerome Robbins in the 1940s, choreographers [rather than performers or producers] began to ascend the chain of command." Grant continues:

> It was de Mille's discovery [in *Oklahoma!*] that tap, ballroom, and acrobatics were too expressively limited to open up the form, to convey subtext and character, to reveal that there could be meaty depths. . . . To achieve this, she refashioned ballet for Broadway into an eclectic theatrical language, narrative-driven and character-interpreting, that combined elements of classical ballet, interpretive modern dance, and occasional hoofing. She understood that tap couldn't subsume ballet, but ballet could subsume tap. (259)

Although Powell was trained in ballet, she was apparently not interested in using, or not given the chance to use, dance to "convey subtext and character," other than the pleasure felt in dancing itself. What Martin Rubin calls the "aggregate musical" remained a part of Hollywood's generic arsenal through the end of the studio era, but Powell's anomalous status in musical history is most obvious in studies that point to the integrated musical as the apotheosis of the film musical as work of art, as the ideal toward which the genre had been striving since the introduction of sound. Jerome Delamater calls the integrated musical of the 1940s and 1950s the "integrated dance musical" because that is when dance, he argues, became "as essential a cinematic code as music, lighting, and camerawork, rather than an isolated display of a particular skill or an intrusion into the combined codes otherwise working to make a unified cinematic experience" (48). Delamater's analysis of the integrated musical's rise, then, has to slight Powell's contributions to the musical genre because his frame of reference is so wedded to integration as the "key word in analyzing dance in the musical" (185). Powell did not make dances that served the narrative; Powell's dances did not "become signs of courtship and love, joy and sadness—exterior manifestations of a character's interior feelings" (164). Rather, any Powell number "could have been transferred among the various films without destroying the sense of the film's plot nor of what the dance was attempting to do" (76). Powell's "stylistic consistency"—a consistency that Delamater otherwise applauds in the work of *auteurs* such as Astaire or Kelly—thus is downgraded because her persona was the same in "all her roles." And finally, he concludes, "conventional costuming concealed neither the persona nor the style" (78)—an argument that also could certainly be made about Astaire or Kelly.

Delamater acknowledges, if not with much approbation, the fact that Powell did her own choreography; to wit, she "evidently imposed her own material on to" that given to her by her dance directors, and this kind of "diversity" was "one of the things which Gene Kelly and others would shortly attempt to overcome" (90). Delamater points out that her dancing style was "unusual" because the "training in several dance disciplines" that Powell exemplified and "which would characterize work in the later forties and fifties had not yet begun to manifest itself on the screen" (76). Except that it had begun to manifest itself on-screen in the work of Eleanor Powell (and therefore could not have been the "exclusively male territory" that Delamater claims it became later). The essential point, however, is that Powell practically could never have been the star of an integrated musical because her dances "represented an aggressive individuality which *was* the Powell persona" (78, emphasis in original).

Powell was already breaking down one barrier by having star vehicles built around her professional abilities as a virtuoso dancer. But this does not mean that she might not have yearned to do different things with her films had she had the power to do so—even with her degree of autonomy at the studio, she sometimes felt her best dancing bits ended up on the cutting room floor—and she was not ignorant of what others were doing in the field of film dance. Her numbers, as *choreography*, certainly meant as much to her as Astaire's or Kelly's did to them ("The dance routines I created are like children to me . . ."). True, the conventional heterosexual dance duets are usually the least interesting things in a Powell film, primarily because there she has often to subsume her own skills to those of her less able partners. But to say that we do not have access to Powell's interior life through her numbers does not mean that they are not expressive. Her dances may do little to illuminate her characters' interior feelings, romantic longings, or dreams of heterosexual marriage, but what they are expressing is no less important, even now: a more generalized, and still valuable, sense of kinetic possibilities and the joys of professional, dedicated, self-disciplined competence.[6]

The only way, on these terms, that Powell could have remained prominent given the musical's generic development was as a specialty, which is in fact the role she played in her final few films. Powell's last film under her MGM contract (and the only one in Technicolor) was as a "guest star" in *Thousands Cheer* (1943), an all-star "troop show" starring Gene Kelly and Kathryn Grayson. After her marriage to Ford in 1943, she made one more film, another all-star vehicle—albeit a low-budget one—for United Artists called *Sensations of 1945* (1945), which is chiefly remembered today as W. C. Fields's last movie. But while Powell kept dancing—for hours each day, for a decade or more, in a bungalow MGM made available to her on the studio lot—she essentially left the filmmaking business after 1945, becoming instead one of Hollywood's best-known mothers (to her and Ford's son, Peter), and her marriage, at least until it was dissolved by divorce in 1959, was regularly pointed to as one of Hollywood's happiest and most secure. Powell did not disappear entirely from the public eye, then, but her brand of musical stardom did. No other female musical dancing stars achieved the heights that Powell reached, although Esther Williams's career, with its basis in the sport of competitive swimming, forms an interesting comparison to Powell's (see Williamson).[7]

I Just Discovered Eleanor Powell Last Night . . .

Despite her anomalous status in musical history, Eleanor Powell and her dancing are not, or rather are no longer, obscure or forgotten. I remember well the release of the first MGM compilation film, *That's Entertainment!*, in 1974, in which Powell's and Astaire's tap dance to "Begin the Beguine" is featured. That number was the highlight of the film, producing waves of applause and cheers at its end, a reception unmatched by any of the film's other manifold musical treasures of which, to paraphrase the film, we "would never see the likes again." Powell solos were featured in other numbers throughout the *That's Entertainment!* series, and in *That's Dancing!* too (which differed in not limiting itself to MGM films). *That's Entertainment! III* includes a split-screen segment that shows the filming of a bit of Powell's dance in the "Fascinating Rhythm" section of *Lady Be Good* (another applause-getter), with the filming on one side and its result on the other. While the segment certainly serves as, in Steven Cohan's words, "a documentary record of the hard physical labor of anonymous studio employees behind the scenes during filming," it also reveals the astonishing difficulty of Powell's job in producing what Cohan calls the "apparent visual seamlessness" of her number (Cohan 2005, 268).

As Cohan also points out, by the time of the release of *That's Entertainment! III* in 1994, we *could* all see "the likes of it again," should we choose to, because huge numbers of classical Hollywood musicals were now available not only on network and cable television but for purchase and ownership. The rise of the Internet has also provided a place for audience members to gather metaphorically in time if not space to discuss all sorts of issues invoked by the free movement and availability of film and star texts cut loose from the contexts in which they originally acquired and produced meaning. Eleanor Powell has her own fan--generated sites and message boards, and recent postings to the 114-page guestbook linked to her site at <www.classicmoviefavorites.com/powell> (note that the site does not feel it necessary to indicate that the star in question is Eleanor rather than William, Dick, or Jane) serve well to underscore not only Powell's continuing appeal but also some fans' consternation that they had to "discover" her accidentally.

For example, one "aspiring dancer" writes that he or she "just discovered Eleanor Powell last night while watching *That's Entertainment!* I thought she was an incredible dancer! I'll make sure I watch every movie she's made." Another (male) writes, "I just discovered Eleanor Powell today. . . . I was . . . mesmerized by this beautiful dancing angel. . . . Her smile is breathtaking and her dancing is electrifying. I feel ashamed at having never been aware of this megatalent." An older fan writes that she has "admired her since I was a little girl, and often thought her every bit as skilled as Fred Astaire, if not more so. . . . She always seemed to me to be the image of a strong, smart, successful, independent, talented woman!" Another female fan wrote after watching Powell films "all day": "What a beauty! What a dancer! I always thought Ann Miller was my favorite dancer but not after today!" Many writers compare her to "male tap dancers of her era including Astaire and Kelly," and find Powell as good or better. A sixteen-year-old girl wonders why she "had never heard of Eleanor Powell," even though she had been studying dance "since the age of three. Now [that] I know her background and all of her achievements, she is just an idol to me." I give the last word here to another male respondent, who writes, "I think I've fallen in love with her. In rewatching *That's Entertainment!*, she struck me, REALLY struck me, for the first time. Weird."

Back when she was first being written about in fan magazines in the mid-1930s, some attempted to make Eleanor Powell's competence seem natural, easy, and effortless, rather than the result of her own productive labor: "Why, it was so easy," writes *Modern Screen* (Cannon). "The music played and somehow you just danced. You simply couldn't help it. All the drudgery of the Russian Ballet, bar [*sic*] work and the floor turns suddenly emerged into a beautiful routine. Eleanor, herself, was surprised at what a cinch it was! Surely, this was *the* thing to do. It was far pleasanter than being a school teacher. Anyone could tell you that!" But at the same time, the writer notes that Powell's abilities matter in registers far away from those of glamour and appearance: "She's won the very stiff [tap] contest for five years in succession, a contest in which the judges sit *under* the stage and where perfect taps, shading and rhythm count. The contestants are never seen while in action, so beauty, personality and smart clothes are of no avail. You've gotta tap, sister, or you don't win." In the end, though, however fresh, youthful, and natural Powell is, her labor has to be acknowledged too, albeit in equivocal ways: "Endless rehearsals, striving for new effects, bouncing out of bed at 2 A.M. to try a new step that has suddenly, out of nowhere, occurred to her. . . . Yes, when people see Miss Powell, so tall and so expert in her profession, they forget she's only a kid." Powell was not a kid; she was a young woman of twenty-four.

If there are any tragic dimensions, if tragic is the right word, to Powell's story they would lie here, in the fact that her prodigious talent was enormously attractive to audiences, but also became in her short Hollywood career the only thing that made her valuable. By the 1950s and 1960s, writes Richard Dyer (1993), it was as if, in the Hollywood musical, "it was no longer possible to imagine in bodily terms a heterosexual happiness for which the star woman did not have to pay too high a price in terms of subordination" (63). Across her films, Powell's dancing prowess was increasingly compartmentalized into an arena separate from her romantically defined femininity. But Powell as a star was constructed, and constructed herself, as at once extremely and conventionally feminine but also unique and prodigiously able, and for a time she functioned, no less than an Astaire or a Kelly, as one of the musical's prime *auteurs*. Moreover, Powell clearly succeeded not only at being a star for her individuality and professional prowess, but also for her femininity. Hollywood's failure ultimately to sustain and to develop the promise of such a complex model of femininity in the film musical as a genre was its loss—and ours.

Notes

1. But both Powell *and* Fred Astaire (who looks none too comfortable in his Pierrot costume) dance in a lavish ballet sequence in *Broadway Melody of 1940*, although they do have taps on their ballet shoes.

2. Brett Farmer notes, the "figure of the androgynous female performer in male tuxedo and tie" is "seemingly ubiquitous" in the Hollywood musical generally (87).

3. All quotations are from the reviews of each of Powell's films reproduced chronologically in Schultz, who also is the best source for a detailed Powell filmography (see also Powell's entry on the Internet Movie Database, <http://imdb.com/name/nm0007224>). Moreover, as Arlene Croce points out, while emphasizing the director as *auteur* makes many movie musicals (such as Powell's, presumably) "look very bad indeed," this does not alter the fact that it was the musical's *performers* that "most audiences wanted to see" at the time (444).

4. For example, "Eleanor Powell sets a new high in her dancing career in a timed routine performed with a dog which cooperates as if trained from puppyhood for no other destiny. Much later on Miss Powell leads, with one of the longest single-take tap routines on record, a production number as big as MGM's biggest stage and packed with audience value" (*Motion Picture Herald* July 19, 1941, n.p. Production Code Administration files, Margaret Herrick Library, Academy of Motion Picture Arts and Sciences, Los Angeles). Also worth noting is the similarity in the names of "Buttons" and "Buddy," Powell's other male "love interest" (and pet?) in *Lady Be Good.*

5. For more on the influence of Edens, a gay man, on the MGM musical, see Cohan 2005; Tinkcom.

6. For more on the importance of dance to women's subjectivity in the musical, see McLean 2004, esp. chap. 3.

7. Although Ann Miller (1923–2004) was also an MGM "queen of tap" from the early 1940s through the 1950s, her persona was very different from Powell's. As Cohan describes it, Miller "sends up" glamour through hyperbole, through "relishing the sexual exchange motivating showgirl glamour" (Cohan 2005, 135) rather than cross-dressing or drag. Moreover, Miller is flatly not as good a dancer as Powell; while a trained dancer can match virtually every tap on the soundtrack with the steps and motions of Eleanor Powell's feet on-screen,

this is often impossible with Miller. But Miller's career, too, as a dancing woman whose "stock in trade," as Dyer puts it, "was guts, wit and self-assertion" (63), suffered from the musical's increasing insistence on female subordination and gender polarity in couple-dance choreography in the 1950s, and she most often performs alone as a specialty, rather than as a headlining star.

6

DAVID A. GERSTNER

Turned Inside/Out

Violent Inversions of Heterosexuality in Vincente Minnelli's *Home from the Hill*

ARGUABLY *HOME FROM THE HILL* (1960) was not a production that necessarily catered to Vincente Minnelli's sophisticated modernist sensibilities. The film, however, offered the director a provocative challenge in which to explore one of his long-standing cultural interests: the terms for heterosexual masculinity. If Minnelli often transgressed heteromasculinist traditions of the Hollywood-American home through the use of what I have elsewhere called a "queer modernist" mise-en-scène, in the family melodrama *Home from the Hill* he strategized an aesthetic that did more than express repressed desire to follow Thomas Elsaesser's concept of the genre (Elsaesser 1992; 1995; Gerstner 2000). Indeed, Minnelli drowns the film's male characters in the androcentric excess that decorates the "man's castle."[1] Minnelli's Cold War "Superwestern," visually occupies, on the one hand, the traditional manly frontier of cowboys and hunting while, on the other, reveals a visceral ripping apart, a rebirthing, of the very aesthetic and corporeality that identifies itself as such.[2] Perhaps more startling, Minnelli reveals the privileged station of ideal heteromasculinity through a perverse inversion of heterosexual reproduction. If, as Diane Fuss argues, the logic of "inside/outside functions as the very figure for signification and the mechanisms of meaning production," Minnelli portrays the violence of heteromasculinity as a virile undoing of the very ideal "functions" it purportedly seeks to uphold.

Noted for its "baroque" mise-en-scène and highly charged Oedipal narrative, *Home from the Hill*'s décor makes visible the overvaluation of masculine cultural re-production itself (Elsaesser 1992; 1995; French; Harvey; Klinger; Lang). Minnelli never made a secret about his distaste for what he viewed as supermasculinized culture (45). Indeed, his cinematic aesthetic often trips up or confuses his male characters and their presumption that they may freely move through the usual order of the Hollywood frame (consider *Father of the Bride* [1950], *Tea and Sympathy* [1956], or *Meet Me in St. Louis* [1944]). What makes *Home from the Hill* especially provocative is Minnelli's turn to an aestheticized violence of masculinity that ultimately disembowels itself. In *Home from the Hill*, the aesthetic disembowelment, portrayed through the rituals of hunting, quite literally extirpates while regenerating the entrails of masculine culture.

Released in 1960, *Home from the Hill* rode the coattails of the melodramatic "adult" fare that Hollywood dished out in the late 1950s (*Picnic* [1955], *Peyton Place* [1957], and *Cat on a Hot Tin Roof* [1958]). Arthur Knight remarked at the time of film's release that *Home from the Hill* was "*Peyton Place South*—another cross section of a seemingly respectable community caught with its pants down." Being caught with their pants down was the least of their worries, though the metaphor Knight raises is certainly not insignificant.[3]

To the extent that the film's landscape imagery wanders between dream and reality, *Home from the Hill* evokes Minnelli's aesthetic relish for the debauchery of surrealism and detailed use of color. Shot through with Minnellian reds that puncture and saturate the virile (but drab) browns and olive greens of the family home where the ideals of heterosexuality are thought to occur, Minnelli's vision of the masculine, familial place is one in which its cultural logic of inside and outside is grotesquely toyed (Polan 1986, 258–60). That is, Minnelli creates a world in which the reaffirming signposts of heterosexuality and homosociailty, marked by their necessary relationship to difference (male/female; masculine/feminine), are dismantled and less easy to navigate. If the tradition of the Hollywood mode of production neatly organizes the artificial (heteromasculinist) assertion that maintains a logic of masculine and feminine, inside and outside, Minnelli's mise-en-scène muddies such comfortable boundaries.

Staging the Hunter and His Home

By the time William Humphrey published his successful novel *Home from the Hill* in 1957, the well-worn theories of masculinity Theodore Roosevelt popularized had become inextricably stitched into the fabric of American culture; the rite of passage from boyhood (effeminate/passive) to patriarchal manhood (masculine/aggressive) through activities such as hunting appeared natural. The following passage from the Humphrey's novel is cited in its entirety because it brings together and highlights important fictions (landscape and body) relevant to the concerns of the place of American masculinity and fatherhood. Here, the novel's young male protagonist, Theron, reflects on his place in the world of the hunter:

> For he knew, had always known, that it was not just being able to line up the front sight in the rear one, not just the meat you brought home for the table. It was to learn to be a man, the only kind of man, to learn it in and from the woods themselves and from the woodsmen, the hunters, who had learned it as boys from their fathers there—and so back through the generations, making you a link in the long strong chain of men of courage and endurance, of cunning and fairness, of humility as well as becoming pride. It was not to be confused with sportsmanship. He knew that too without being told. They were not sportsmen, those men in whose midst his father reigned there on the corner of the square on Saturday afternoons; they were hunters. He had a scorn for sportsmen. For among the hunters, he knew without ever sitting amongst them, was a bond of fellowship which no mere sportsman could ever know or share in, since for him hunting could at best be the thing he enjoyed most in life, while for the hunters it was life itself. (50)

Humphrey's woodsmen/hunters embody Hunting. Immersed in the masculine arena of Nature, hunters gather to prove their dominance of and freedom to move within the landscape where the primitive and barbaric are necessarily contained. In Humphrey's novel "[the hunter] could walk in the woods in no other way except as noiselessly as ever, seeming *to glide* across the clearings like the shadow of a bird overhead and to melt into the shadow of the trees"(61, emphasis added). Minnelli's *Home from the Hill* commingles Nature and Body, where virile men "glide across the clearings," mired in the bloody aesthetic of American masculinity.

While the novel focuses on the virtues of "good" and "bad" manliness (hunting is not a conflict for Theron because it is the "natural" thing for a man to do),[4] the film explores Theron's (George Hamilton) troubled manhood because of his absent, lustful, and dominant father Wade—read here animalistic, savage, yet civilized (that is, successful landowner, Robert Mitchum). Theron's overdoting mother (Eleanor Parker) does not help matters. Unlike the novel, Wade must encourage Theron to pursue those things that men must do.

The film's screenplay is different from Humphrey's novel in some other important ways. Because of its complex interactions and melodramatic highs and lows, recounting the film's narrative is useful here. With Minnelli's rich mise-en-scène providing the landscape for these complexities to unravel, the excess of middle-class masculine production visually explodes in this family melodrama.

Although Humphrey was recognized as a modern-day Faulkner, the Hollywood melodrama is more Faulknerian than the novel with its complicated and troubled genealogical bloodlines.[5] The Harriet Frank Jr. and Irving Ravetch script includes and gives prominence to one of Wade's bastard sons, Rafe (George Peppard). This treats Wade's lustful savagery as, at least, virtuous insofar as his conduct toward Rafe is riddled with guilt-ridden paternalism. Wade gives Rafe a place to live, supplies him with work, and shelters him from the town's vicious gossip about his paternity. Wade, however, refuses to recognize him as a legitimate son. Rafe's character is thus the catalyst for the uneasy fraternal doubling that occurs between the legitimate son (Theron) and bastard son. Rafe's common sense and hard-working values substitute for Theron's spoiled, rich-boy manliness. Rafe is a pure hunter of the earth (he must hunt for, among other things, his father's love); he was not, like Theron, born to wealth and privilege. Nonetheless, as blood rivals, Rafe acts as Theron's big brother. Rafe teaches, protects, and picks up the messy pieces that the oversensitive Theron leaves behind in acting out against his father.[6]

Moreover, Rafe remains by Wade's side on all hunting excursions, picks him up when lying drunk in the "town whore's" apartment, and keeps quiet (to both Theron and the town) about his own paternal ancestry. Theron (although living for seventeen years in the same town and home) never once hears any suspicious talk about his father or Rafe. Even when Rafe saves Wade's life from the shot of a jealous husband, the family secret remains guarded by a manly code of honor. Rafe's wish to be recognized is not fulfilled, as we will see, until the film's conclusion.

The most important rewrite from novel to screenplay is the emphasis on Theron's troubled masculinity. In the Frank and Ravetch script Theron becomes an ideal candidate for Minnelli's treatment of sensitive men. Unlike the novel, Frank and Ravetch introduce Theron's at-risk-masculinity—the awkward "mama's boy"—precisely through and because of the heterosexuality that delimits the family unit. In *Home from the Hill* the structured absence that serves this configuration in which Theron is caught is the violence of the oedipal trauma.[7]

The film's story also focuses on the father's anxieties over his son's passage into manhood. After Theron's birth seventeen years ago, Hannah shut Wade out of her life (doors are slammed shut on Wade, especially the bedroom door) because of his well-known but unspoken indiscretions. She agreed to stay in the marriage to maintain the appearance of husband and wife. The family secrets (their separate bedrooms, the bastard son, Wade's days-long sex and drinking escapades) are tightly kept by both parents so that Theron will not know the truth. As part of her husband's punishment, Hannah demands that Wade give up his paternal responsibilities to his son and leave his upbringing to her (hence Wade's displaced relationship with Rafe and Theron's moniker, "mama's boy"). To avoid a town scandal and divorce Wade agrees. The key to the melodramatic suspense, of course, is the gymnastics performed to keep the nonsecrets secret.

As Theron grows older, however, he wants to be a part of Wade's manly world of hunters. He cannot understand why his father consistently absents himself from his eager pleas to spend time with him. The local hunters are aware of Theron's familial troubles and take advantage of the less-than-manly sensibilities that he exhibits (presumably because of his mother). One evening when Theron is in town, the hunters gathered in the square decide to help Theron acquire a dose of manliness. As they see it, the time has come that he no longer be "Hannah's boy": instead, he now must join the "Captain's" manly world. Hence, the hunters use Theron's youthful naiveté to humiliate him as part of a practical joke where the boy enthusiastically agrees to hold the empty bag (as it were) for the hunter's feigned snipe-hunting excursion.[8] When Wade sees his son caught thus he realizes quick action is needed to rescue his son from the mark of eternal sissiness. Any past promises made to his wife are now null and void.

To prove his manhood to both his father and local hunters, Theron sets out to hunt down the wild boar terrorizing Wade's tenant's land. With his hunting skills (genetically inherited, apparently, by his father and refined by Rafe's shooting lessons), Theron eagerly hopes to catch a boar's head to hang proudly along the head of the boar his father killed. Successful on the hunt, Theron's fresh manhood is celebrated at a barbecue given by his father where the hunted wild beast is roasted and its bloody meat ingested by invited guests.[9] Once successfully inside the hunter's world, Theron soon realizes, however, that the ethics of homosocial manliness foreclose the more tender attributes his mother inculcated. For Theron to move inside the world of masculinity thus forgoes movement outside or back into his mother's feminized world. The cultural binaries associated with heterosexuality and gender appear rigidly set. Like other Minnelli sensitive characters, Theron's quest for manhood is presented as the struggle to balance masculine and feminine traits, to move ambiguously, yet freely, through the social regulations of gender and heterosexuality. In *Home from the Hill*, Theron finds himself in an either/or place and, like the rest of the film's men, caught within the Minnellian hysterical mise-en-scène that desperately frames a heteromasculine world ready to burst at its seams.

Hence, the disadvantages of assuming his father's legacy of virility outpace the advantages. Although Theron's newfound manhood helps to identify his primal instincts, his gentle civilized humanity is forsaken, a form of humanity his father long ago relinquished. This human essence in the film is equated with the ability to love—heterosexually, of course. Just as Theron recognizes the need to be gentle and kind, he confronts another father figure who thwarts his manly, yet romantic, desires. The evening of the barbecue Theron picks up Libby Halstead (Luana Patten) as his guest. Her father, Albert (Everett Sloane), refuses him entry into their house. The Hunnicutt family secret, still unbeknownst to Theron, bubbles to the surface in Albert's mind, especially now that his daughter may get involved. He fears that Theron will simply follow his father's adulterous footsteps and Libby will be his prey.

Soon after, Hannah tells Theron about his legacy. He becomes distraught and unable to maintain any sort of intimate relationship with his parents or Libby. Once again, Theron is left holding the empty bag (Wade later comments to Theron that his mother must have been the one "to let the cat out of the bag" about his indiscretions). Hannah, seeking to rub salt in the bloody family wounds (blood red wounds, as we shall see, are treacherously spread throughout Minnelli's mise-en-scène), informs Theron that Rafe is his illegitimate half-brother. To make matters worse, Theron learns this immediately following his first sexual experience with Libby where, it turns out, she becomes pregnant (another piece of information about which Theron will know nothing). After his mother drops these familial bombs, Theron flees to Rafe's cabin in the woods to make emotional and financial retribution over his father's savage behavior. Theron is disgusted with both his father's and mother's lives—long deceptions leave him cold and empty.

Albert, realizing that Libby is in a dilemma now that she is pregnant, goes to see Wade about bringing Theron and Libby back together. Wade reminds Albert that he once closed his door on Theron and firmly tells Albert that crawling on all fours is humiliating and will not change matters. In fact, as Wade sees it, why should Theron take responsibility for Libby's accident? Wade suggests that because Albert is a good local businessman he should know better than to dump his "damaged goods" on a loyal customer. Albert, "damaged goods" himself because he is not manly enough to make it in Wade's virile world and take responsibility for his own family, has a nervous breakdown.

As the complex narrative unwinds (taking 150 minutes to do so), the melodramatic deus ex machina is set in motion. In yet another act of desperate fraternal bonding, Rafe marries Libby to prevent another town scandal around the Hunnicutts. At first a marriage to save face (after all Rafe understands the debilitating effects of not being recognized as legitimate), the couple fall in love. But the marital subterfuge to hide their child's true father fails. At the baby's christening Albert overhears the hunters' ladylike gossip (another bit of Minnelli irony) that Libby's child actually belongs to Wade. Considering Albert's anxiety about Wade's reputation, he believes the news to be true.

Now hysterical, Albert dregs up the remnants of his long-repressed primal instincts to hunt down his own wild boar: Wade. For Albert, Wade symbolizes the beastly remains of man's barbaric past. Wade has overstepped the boundaries between masculine savagery and civilization. Albert's feminized, male hysterics (all the more dangerous with gun in hand), come toe-to-toe with Wade's hyperbolic truculence. This scene of masculine excess foregrounds the instability and artificial lines that demarcate heterosexuality and homosociality, masculinity and femininity, savagery and civilization. Indeed, Albert's hysteria and Wade's overdetermined masculinity collapse the boundaries between inside/outside that the masculinist order of things defines. Recalling Fuss's remarks, if "inside/outside functions as the very figure for signification and the mechanisms of meaning production," then Albert and Wade's gender excess reveals the deceit that is the cultural determinations of manhood. (1) The delicate balance of inside and outside (savage and civilized) so carefully procured under homosociality and heterosexuality is blurred and confused here in the face of masculine hysteria.

Given these corroded boundaries and their inability to balance their masculine and feminine traits, both Wade and Albert are destined to die. Albert finally shoots Wade in the sanctity of his den. When Albert flees the scene (again unable to face his manly responsibility for his actions), Rafe and Theron fight to see who will have the right to hunt down their father's killer. In a series of unusual wide-screen close-ups, Minnelli shows only the torsos of the two young men engaged in the brawl. In this montage sequence, we see only shoulder to waist and the arm of one brother slugging the stomach of the other. Through this cinematic doubling and blurring of faceless bodies, Rafe and Theron are finally rendered one and the same, blood brothers. Theron, of course, wins the fight to hunt down his father's killer.

Theron hunts Albert through the woods just as he had earlier tracked the wild pig. When he finally catches up with his prey, Albert is weakened and passed out from exhaustion. Theron aims to shoot, but does not fire. He has learned to be not like his father and to recognize the necessary balance between civilized and savage manhood. Albert, now a freak of masculinity, sits up to shoot Theron. With one hand and a single shot, Theron fires and kills Albert. In a final fraternal exchange, Rafe (who has since caught up with Theron), asks Theron how he plans to survive because he's just a "colt" in this still untamed world. Theron respectfully tells him, "the same way you did, Rafe." With musical crescendo, Theron escapes against the backdrop of Minnelli's yellow smoke-filled quicksand (called "Sulphur Bottom"), and Rafe proceeds home to his family.

In the final scene of the film Rafe meets Hannah at the cemetery where she has erected a "handsome" red-stone marker for Wade. There she shows Rafe his name listed as one of Wade's sons. Hannah accepts Rafe's offer to move in with his new family and become a doting grandmother. With her promise to "spoil" her grandson, the film presents a genealogically confused male child named Albert T(h)ere(o)nce Hunnicutt. Minnelli's Hollywood happy ending thus delivers the new postwar American family: the bastard (Rafe), the impure wife (Libby), and the illegitimate child.

The Old In and Out

In what way do heterosexual men move freely and "glide" in and out of (cinematic) space and time? What acts of idealized violence must occur to secure this privilege of androcentric-defined heterosexuality? In Wade's perceived world of pure and aggressive masculinity, his bodily presence (the strong, silent type) speaks all there is to say. He carries no identification, no keys, no money, and no watch. True manhood is the only key needed to manage time and place efficiently. I would like to consider both Minnelli's visual rendering and displacement of the places in which inside and outside, the masculine and the feminine collapse.

During the barbecue festivities described earlier, Theron (as we have seen) sets out to pick up Libby as his guest for the party. He boyishly leaps onto the Halstead porch and knocks on the front door. And, as we have seen, Albert refuses Theron entry into his house. In this scene, we see Albert approach the screen door that separates Theron and himself. Divided by the screen door, Theron shyly and awkwardly requests

Libby's presence: "They're throwing a little dance for me tonight . . . I don't know how . . . I guess Libby is going to have to teach me." Given the sexually charged metaphor of "learning how to dance" in a 1950s family melodrama, Albert appears uneasy. "Oh yeah," Albert stiffly responds, "what are *you* going to teach her." Theron, confused by these remarks because he is still unaware of his father's dalliances, is taken aback by Albert's unexpected outbursts. Albert tells Theron that Libby is sick and cannot attend the party. Flustered, Theron tells him that he hopes that she is feeling better, and he will call on her tomorrow at which point he attempts to open the screen door to at least deliver his corsage to Libby. Albert again resists Theron's entry, yanking the door from Theron's hands. He frantically tells him to get out and never to call on Libby again. Stunned, Theron glances through the screen door where he sees Libby in her party dress ascending the staircase. Insuring that Theron will not be able to enter, Albert shuts all doors to the house. Theron is refused a comforting and stable place in the family home putting again his heteromasculinity at risk.

From the Halstead porch Minnelli cuts to the Hunnicutt porch on the evening of the party where Wade, filled with patriarchal pride, approaches Hannah.[10] Wade's rapprochement, however, does not convince Hannah that his overture is sincere. He tells her that we "need to have more parties. Open our doors. I like having people over. It makes me feel good." Laying on the charm, Wade recalls the first time they met and danced at a party. Feeling proud, Wade's husbandly desire is aroused, and he seeks to move back into the hearth. Hannah tells him (uttered in Eleanor Parker's fabulously overwrought Southern accent) what he is feeling is "liquor and nostalgia." To prove his sincerity, he boldly grabs her and kisses her to which she refuses to respond. "Even when you freeze up," he tells her, "you're still the most—" (Hannah interjects) "beautiful of them all?"

Cut short by Hannah's retort, Wade's fury is unleashed. Seeking to "open doors" at any price he admits to Hannah that certainly "there have been others. But you can put an end to that. *You* just unlock your door . . . tonight if you want to . . . right now if you want to." Obviously, because Hannah has heard this before, she concludes that Wade only "finds [her] attractive because [he] can't have [her]." Because his heteromanly prerogative presumes that no keys are needed to enter any room he wishes in his castle, Hannah makes sure her bedroom door is locked.

In a world of closed family doors, Theron (in the shadow of the patriarchy and the duplicity of heterosexual standards of morality) sees no way out. He is locked in and reduced to "playing chess" as the pawn of his parents where he is forced either into the feminized world of his mother or the masculine sphere of his father. Rafe, on the other hand, gets an out by marrying Libby. The same doors that prevented Theron from dancing with Libby are later opened for Rafe when Albert urgently concedes to let the bastard son in his home for the good name of the family. As Albert hands over the house keys to Rafe (unlike Wade, Rafe and Albert always need a key), Albert finds the front door jammed and cannot leave. Trapped inside, Rafe (assuming his new patriarchal role in the realm of genteel domesticity) assures his father-in-law that he can fix the jammed front door, thereby freeing his movement. Indeed he does, and Albert can move again.

Door after door is slammed shut while new and troubling ports of entry appear on the scene. *Home from the Hill* is layered with painful transitions, psychical exchanges, and short-circuited penetrations that are visibly played out (or not) from room to room. Characters shuffle between places framed by a disintegrating logic of inside and outside: Wade's masculinist travels cast him outside Hannah's feminine home; once Theron is in the world of his father's hypermasculinity, he is shunned by the emasculated patriarchy of the Halsteads. *Home from the Hill* displays the forces that entrap desire under the rigid demands that define heterosexual difference. Minnelli's perverse aestheticization of masculinity pervades the rooms in which the inside/outside transitions revolve by specularly probing the male bodies that occupy those rooms. His use of color, especially red, splatters in and out of both these places and these bodies. Significantly, Minnelli's *Home from the Hill* finds its most discomfiting and violent aesthetic realization in the family man's den.

Natura Simulare

"Make [the den] a place," writes Christine Terhune Herrick in 1902, "where [the man] can lie and growl over his bones when he feels like it. . . . One lucky man of my acquaintance has such a den, which is to him as a cave to a primitive man" (889). In such a place, man communes with his prizes of domination, contemplates and reenacts his primitive oneness within his evolutionary place in nature. The privatized home is thus constructed here to support the manly desire to maintain his tightly woven relationship between nature and body, between the primitive and the civilized, between inside and outside. Through sensible bourgeois décor chosen by the good wife, the outdoors is brought indoors without disturbing the interior comforts of the family home. Indeed, the vital securing of heterosexual appearances depends on the at once unified presence of the home and the divided spaces where the gendered interests of the individual are enabled.

Herrick's interior design concepts are noteworthy because they call attention to the way a primitive den should be marked off, made separate from the civilized portion of the home. Although separated, the den's cavelike place allows for man's savage instincts while enabling close ties with his modern family. The den in *Home from the Hill*, however, looms large and reaches far beyond, indeed collapses, the domestic boundaries Herrick identified. Minnelli's den is thus borderless; its masculine aura seeps throughout the homeplace. The space is inundated with leather, wood, and painted in Minnellian browns and deep blood reds. Taxidermic trophies and Wade's other assorted hunting conquests line the thick redwood panels. Shotguns line the walls and are proudly encased behind glass doors. Animal hides and bearskin rugs drape the furniture and cover the floors where Wade's hunting dogs defensively lie in wait. An enormous stone fireplace displays the patriarch's prized boar's head trophy over its mantel. The violence of Theron's birth and historical dissemination into manhood will occur here.

Importantly, the ubiquity of the den's saturation stains while it displaces any trace of feminine décor in the Hunnicutt home. Minnelli's masculine browns and fading yellows taint the remnants of what bright colors were once present. Floral flocked wallpaper looks dingy in this home from which Hannah divorced herself seventeen years earlier. The browns, olive greens, and fading yellows suffocate the more genteel

Figure 7. Hannah (Eleanor Parker) and son Theron (George Hamilton) square off among the manly accoutrements in the den of Wade Hunnicutt (Robert Mitchum) in *Home from the Hill.*

ambiance of the family home. Minnelli's usually bright bouquet of cinematic flowers is instead positioned here as an assortment of pale yellow and orange roses drearily placed in the foyer. Low-key lighting indicates that no, or very little, natural sunlight permeates this dank castle.

If this manly décor pervades the home, one room initially opposes the masculinist dissemination: Theron's boyhood bedroom. Wade sees the room as a threat to his son's masculinity. After Theron's humiliation on the "snipe" hunt, father and son have their first manly heart-to-heart in the boy's room. Although flooded with the browns and greens oozing out of the den, Theron's room is peppered with boyhood memorabilia: stamp-collecting books, wall maps, a boy's captain's chair, a telescope, and a butterfly collection (an addition that Minnelli's favored dandy, John McNeill Whistler, would have been proud because the butterfly was a centerpiece of the artist's signature). Significantly, Hannah helped build this room with Theron. As Wade sees it, Theron must move out of this place to become a man. "This is a boy's room," Wade tells Theron while gently fondling the boy's telescope, "come on downstairs and I'll show you how a man lives."

Lured into Wade's den, a place always already everywhere, Wade shows off his manly wares. This room, like his imposing body, needs no explanation. Wade introduces the wide-eyed Theron to the trophies of the hunter that represent the man. "You're going to be either known as a man or a mama's boy," Wade firmly tells him. Situated within this lionized arena of manly props, Minnelli's excessive manly mise-en-scène ironically undercuts Wade's virile proposition to his son: "You can take those rocks and butterflies and stamps and whatever toys you have been occupying yourself with and just throw them in the [tr]ash can." Wade's directive to Theron to replace one set of "toys" with another set is similar to Minnelli's parody of men teaching one another how to "walk like a man" in the baroque music room of *Tea and Sympathy* (Gerstner 1997).

In the den, a place that Lee Edelman might identify as a site of normative "male hysteria" (40), Wade's labor involved in dispensing with his son's effeminacy is so overwrought that it calls attention to its own hyperproduction. To be sure, identifying Wade's work as "labor" in the process of inculcating the terms of masculinity into his son is tantalizingly suggestive. Not only is the den the domesticized simulacrum of primitive nature where Wade "growls over his own bones" and passes on his legacy to his legitimate firstborn, but also it is the interiorized place where the father's labor gives birth to his manly son. The bloodied violence of this red-soaked room evokes not merely the congratulatory site of primal murder, it is, at the same time, the place of heteromasculine reproduction: the bloodied male womb.[11]

From the father's den/womb—a masculine construct delivered through man's primitive oneness with Nature—Wade tells his son that he will "send him to the woods to confront his own courage" because "*what everyman hunts out there is himself*." If difference between inside and outside is collapsed here, it is so to the extent that ideals of masculinity not only control difference and sameness on the outside but also simultaneously reproduce those ideals from the inside. It is an exhaustive exercise to be a man. The hunter, who both gives life (and the cultural logic that defines it) and takes it away, continually wards off and contains the excesses of inside and outside worlds. If the hunter, as Wade makes clear to Theron, is endlessly hunting himself, there is indeed no way to escape the deceit of the ideals that define one's heteromasculinist self.

Blood Simple

"It's not blood, it's red."[12]

The wild boar to be hunted in *Home from the Hill* is, as the hunter sees it, the evolutionary, residual past of himself. This grotesque trace of manly self that persistently returns to threaten civilization is the insidious embodiment of the merged Other and Self revealed as disfigured beast. In a perverse inversion, the bodily functions of this man/beast circulate between inside and outside. "[W]hen he [the boar] come into the clearin' he was red, solid red, all over," the African American servant tells us in the novel, "cause he couldn' find hisself no mud to waller in an he was covered with tiny drops of blood coming outa ever' pore stead of sweat" (Humphrey, 54). This incredibly defiled and uncivilized living thing has no control over the corporeal barriers that protect the exterior from the interior. The animal's entrails and the mixing of blood and sweat ooze out of its pores. The boar literally wears its own excrement and blood causing it to smell "like burnt flesh an' feathers" drawing gnats and flies around him driving him "half crazy they was aggravatin' him so." This wild pig is the vile representative of savagery that must be contained, but, importantly, never fully discarded so as to solidify manly essence.

Thus, Minnelli's hunt begins in search of the hunter's residual past from where the heteromasculinist ideals emanate. Using long tracking shots through the woods of Mississippi, Minnelli follows Theron and Rafe (sent along by Wade to protect Theron) along the edges of "Sulphur Bottom." Yellow gaseous smoke billows from this place where, according to Rafe, "once men enter they never return." Combined with the smell of the wild beast and the flatulent sulfuric odor of the landscape,

Minnelli's mise-en-scène evokes the novel's emphasis on manly smells of nature.[13] If indeed Nature is the mythic manly world it is reported to be it certainly reeks of the aromas of primitive man that civilized man's chthonic instincts find so alluring.

During the hunt, the violence of the beast's inverted bodily functions raise the specter of a similar violence that potentially puts the hunter's body at risk. Yet the hunter's fear provides for his pleasure. To track down and contain the uncontrollable Other/Self is to invigorate the rigorous demands of civilized masculinity. For Theron, however, this corporeal violence becomes a bit too much when the boar butchers a hunting dog. Minnelli, rather than hide the body's entrails, emphasizes it.[14] The bloodied and ripped carcass is displayed in full view. But the blood and entrails, the insides of the beast, are heightened in a Minnellian red that aestheticizes the violence enacted in this manly game. If the uncivilized beast displays its bloody excrement on its body, Minnelli plays with the concerns to stuff away and hide the shit of the civilized body. While they examine the hound "whose guts spilled out onto the ground," Rafe, conjuring the heteromasculine desire to penetrate deep within his truculent past, tells Theron that "[the dog's] chest [has been] ripped from throat to belly to the depth of a man's hand." Theron, sickened but undaunted, continues.[15]

When Theron finally shoots the boar in a direct aim that moves straight through the animal's snout into its heart (he only has one opportunity to do this), red shoots from the boar's nose as the beast tumbles into muddy slop. Relieved and satisfied, Theron (splashed with the same muddy and bloody slop) collapses against a tree. For the time being, Theron, mirroring the oozing animal, has conquered the beast, an image of his past and threat to his future, by purging its fetid blood.

With red the only primary color of significance in the film, Minnelli disperses it throughout the film in his own aestheticized game of inside and outside. In this Minnellian terrain, the interiorized red blood of the beast is exposed precisely as the violence of masculine decorative sensibilities. He takes his cues from Humphrey's novel where red blood is akin to the violence of homosocial activity and the impurity of this small town's genealogical ties. Indeed, Minnelli's aestheticized red saturates the everyday of the Hunnicutt home (and the "cut" in Hunni<u>cutt</u> is worth a nod here). When Rafe is in a grocery store, for example, a mother with a grocery cart with twin brothers dressed in matching crimson shirts passes him. The mother stops the cart directly in front of Rafe while she looks for additional items. Rafe, uncertain how to react to these doubled brothers who are obviously blood related (they wear it on their sleeve after all), momentarily stares at them holding two cans of vegetables. Confronted this way by a distorted reflection of his world, Rafe (enacting what amounts to his daily routine) performs a juggling act with the cans. Soon after, he encounters Libby in the store (distraught and pregnant with Theron's child) where he will accept the role of father in yet another obligatory (juggled) fraternal transference. The tragic banality of heterosexuality is made no more clear than in a Minnellian grocery store.

And because Wade teeters between civilized and uncivilized, Minnelli dresses him like the ambiguous creature he is: half beast, half man. Minnelli equates Wade with the boar by exposing Wade's insides, like the boar, on the outside; the impure bloodlines of his savage past pour through his body and home. Wade's brown hunting jacket, for example, is lined in a quilted red silk; his cowboy hat is similarly lined. When he walks, the red lining spills out from the inside of his coat. The excreted color of excrement and blood, like that of the boar, is matched by the everyday objects around which Wade is surrounded. At home, his red leather chairs, red walls, and brown walls engulf him in his den where he reproduces himself through the rebirth of his son. When Albert later kills Wade, the patriarch's insides are splattered on the walls and sofa; his blood is "unbelievable red, phosphorescent, vibrant, as if pulsating, alive . . ." (Humphrey, 302).

Like the hunted boar, Wade's impurities of a primitive past are simultaneously disseminated and contained. Wade's death only confirms this flood of masculinist corporeality and aesthetics that are pushed inward and outward. Humphrey's description of the boar's barbecue, in fact, anticipates Wade's gravesite. Mimicking the dimensions of a grave. "eight feet long, three wide, and six feet deep" (Humphrey, 97), the barbecue pit marks the final site for both the boar and Wade. Death, however, does not finalize the eternal conflict between beast and man. Doused in barbecue sauce, the beast continues to ooze red from its pores just as Wade does when he is slaughtered in his place of primitive and perverse return—the den. But the red does not stop there.

In this small Texas town, the cemetery (as everything else) is divided by those on the inside and those on the outside. In an earlier scene, Hannah meets Rafe at the cemetery while tending their family gravesites. Hannah notices Rafe across the road that divides the inside from the outside. Hannah asks why the side on which Rafe's family is buried is so unkempt. Rafe tells her that this is "Reprobate's Field" and lying there is his mother Ann Copley—a woman Hannah knew quite well given Wade's exploits. Hannah remarks on this hypocrisy of who is in and who is out because many of those who are lying where the Hunnicutt family rest should certainly be resting on the outside.

In the final moment of the film, against the backdrop of the new (impure) American family—the Hunnicutt suzerain now defeated and the Rafe Copley-Hunnicutt's middle-class mockery of heterosexuality in place—Hannah and Rafe once again meet at the cemetery. She has erected for Wade an enormous red stone. And like the boar again, Wade spills red from the inside. On the enormous stone, Hannah, in a gesture to rid the boundary between inside and outside, has engraved Rafe's name alongside Theron's. The final resting place of manly excess (that which is tainted by impure savage blood) is now entombed in stone.

But Minnelli's red stone that thrusts out from the fragile security of the inside is marked by a red that continues to ooze outward. The masculine violence that controls inside and outside does not end at the gravesite. Minnelli's mise-en-scène, rather, floods this masculine sensibility—this place of control—with its own decorative violence. We see no pure inside or outside to this Minnellian place of heteromasculine aggressiveness because such artificial divides are its very deceit that report to know the pure essence of Nature. The putrid blood and entrails—family secrets—invariably seep through the crevices (the den, the town, the grave) by way of the pressure applied to contain them. The browns, drab greens, and fading yellows that remain in *Home from the Hill* are always interrupted by the blood red that surges out from the mise-en-scène's rancid interior. This interior—that which the hunter furiously and continuously seeks to hunt—is nothing other than himself. The stench and rot of the inside (the excess the middle-class hopes to hide, but never quite succeeds) is precisely what Minnelli makes visible in these places of heteromasculinity.

Notes

I dedicate this chapter to Stephen Mamber.

1. De Cordova argues that the bourgeois home here masks the residue of a feudal state. In "*Home from the Hill* the real parents actually represent the feudal order and the ideal is elsewhere—in the values of the privatised bourgeois family" (259).

2. Considering *Home from the Hill* within André Bazin's notion of the "Superwestern" may be advisable. For Bazin, the perfect "balance" of the classical Hollywood Western found its apotheosis before 1940. The "Superwestern, which is almost always intellectual," loses its mythic/heroic quality in the face of world conflict. The Western is no longer "itself." The intellectualizing of "aesthetic, sociological, moral, psychological, political, or erotic interest" has tainted the purity of the classical genre.

3. For a description of Minnelli's work on male melodrama, see Naremore, 30–33.

4. Brief concern surfaces in the novel when Wade thinks Theron may be a "mama's boy" because of his close relationship to his mother. It does not, however, take on the weight that the film gives this anxiety (see Humphrey, 36).

5. After all, Faulkner's novels are rife with a colorful melodramatic imagination. In fact, Faulkner originally wanted the text of *The Sound and the Fury* to be color-coded to identify the temporal shifts in the novel. The French, great admirers of Faulkner, first noted *Home from the Hill*'s similarity to, especially, the paternal angst in *Absalom, Absalom* (see Guérif, 106; Lang also refers to this, 216).

6. Rafe speaks of the women with "doe eyes" that he "hunts in the town square." Later, he steps in for the timid Theron (one of the several times Rafe assumes responsibility for his half-brother) to ask a girl out on a date. Rafe tells her that he has come "to put salt on [her] tail."

7. The threat of castration by the doting mother in the era of "momism" was accepted without question and considered a real psychological barrier to masculine civilization. Based on the wacky and extremely popular Freudian/Jungian theory in Philip Wylie's *Generation of Vipers*, the United States was in the throes of a "mother-problem."

8. "Snipe-hunting" plays on the cowardly act of shooting at small wading birds (a snipe) from a concealed location (a sniper) as well as the speech act (to snipe) of making malicious charges.

9. From the novel, "Chauncey [the family servant] punctured the ham with the long skewer and slowly pushed it all the way in. He drew it out and a trickle of red juice followed it. He straightened, took off his apron and folded it up, took of his chef's hat and yelled: 'Come and git it!' "(Humphrey, 109).

10. The heavy breath needed to articulate all the names that begin with the letter H and dwell in *Home from the Hill* is worth noting. Indeed, one is left short of breath through the miasmic articulation the narration of the film undertakes.

11. I'd like to thank Sean Griffin for bringing this provocative reading of the den to my attention.

12. Jean-Luc Godard quoted in Deleuze. That Deleuze, on the same page in his discussion of Godard's "colour image," evokes Minnelli's "colourism" is noteworthy. For Deleuze:

> "[i]n opposition to a simply coloured image, the colour-image does not refer to a particular object, but absorbs all that it can: it is the power which seizes all that happens within its range, or the quality common to completely different objects. There *is* a symbolism of colours, but it does not consist in a correspondence between a colour and an affect (green and hope . . .). Colour is on the contrary the affect itself, that is, the virtual conjunction of all objects which it picks up.

Deleuze points out that "from the beginning of a total cinema of colour, Minnelli had made absorption the properly cinematographic power of this new dimension of the image" (118–19). That Deleuze negates the possibility of "correspondence between a colour" is curious because the relationship between affect, absorption, and "correspondence" is another turn of analysis, another line of flight.

13. Many passages in the novel evoke the odors of manhood. The den, for example, is rich with "the manly smells of leather and steel and gun oil and boot grease, the smells his father brought in, of the woods, damp and mouldering, the strong hot, rutty reek of game, and the odor of dogs, for there were always three of four dogs there . . ." (Humphrey, 47).

14. Minnelli's image here echoes Francis Bacon's painting *Dog* (1952). Bacon's painterly imbruing of the figure in red also recalls Deleuze's consideration of Minnelli's absorption of color.

15. This moment in the film closely recalls Minnelli's own experience as a young boy on a cattle ranch. One day on a farm where he had a summer job, the owner approached Minnelli with a steer and asked him to keep him still. Minnelli "looked into the animal's soulful brown eyes. From out of nowhere, a sledgehammer came swinging over the farmer's head, hitting the steer right between the eyes. It let out this horrible painful sound, and blood trickled down its face. The front legs buckled, and the steer collapsed and died. Maggots immediately began to form. The farmer made me hold a hose on the carcass as he proceeded to butcher it. I managed to control my nausea, but when I returned home at the end of the day, I was violently sick" (Minnelli, 41).

7

MICHAEL DEANGELIS

Mispronouncing "Man and Wife"

The Fate of Marriage in Hollywood's Sexual Revolution

The route that takes Katherine Ross from almost-bride, wedding-dressed Elaine Robinson at the back of a bus heading nowhere, exchanging troubled glances with her savior-abductor Benjamin Braddock (Dustin Hoffman) at the end of *The Graduate* (1967), to the place of a once-independent and resistant but now complacent and very married housewife automaton Joanna Eberhart at the end of *The Stepford Wives* (1975), provides a revealing trace of the development of Hollywood's perspective on female gender roles in committed relationships during and immediately following the sexual revolution. According to the signposts marking this path, to end up with the man you love is to risk losing yourself, if not to him then to the abstract yet legally and ideologically constraining concept of "marriage." And if for women the marriage contract harbors the threat of a loss of individuality and identity, for male protagonists of this era the risk inherent in marital commitment manifests itself as the curtailing of pleasures earned and seemingly guaranteed by the sexual revolution—foremost among these, the pleasure of performing the sexual act with whichever woman one wishes, or if not to perform it, at least to be free to fantasize about doing so without guilt or other imposed restrictions.

For Hollywood cinema in the sexual revolution, the complications involved in maintaining individual identity and performing sexual freedom, and in either preserving or forfeiting such rights in legally bound committed relationships, play out as problems of difference—of both gender and sexuality—whose ultimate stake is repeatedly posited as the stability of "heterosexuality" itself. These seemingly irreconcilable dichotomies of freedom and commitment in opposite-sex relationships unfold on the stage of two popular and interconnected generic cycles of the era. The historical backdrop of the "campus" film is the national and international campus political unrest in the late 1960s in the final years of the Vietnam War—a politics that emphasized an ever-widening generation gap, entitlement to (hetero)sexual freedom, the outmoded nature of prevailing social and political institutions, and a heightened sociopolitical awareness the civil rights movement fueled. The primary films of this cycle include *Three in the Attic* (1968), *Getting Straight* (1970), *The Revolutionary* (1970), *R.P.M.* (1970), *The Strawberry Statement* (1970), and *Carnal Knowledge* (1971). Capitalizing on the proven success of countercultural youth films such as *The Graduate* (a campus film minus the unrest), *Easy Rider* (1969), and *Medium Cool* (1969), political unrest and student protest appear to take center stage in many of the "campus" films, yet the campus narratives more often focus on the more personal and seemingly universal male problem of how best to manage the sexual freedoms that come with living away from home without the constraints parents or other representatives of a "square" generation that has not been enlightened by the sexual revolution imposed. If the maintenance of sexual freedom is wrought with its own anxieties, the prospect of indefinitely suspending such freedom in more committed relationships only exacerbates the problem, especially because such narratives are invariably anchored to a male perspective.

The second set of films, which might be termed the marriage-as-problem cycle, manifests itself as a logical extension of the first set. Signaled by the phenomenal success of *Bob & Carol & Ted & Alice* (1969), the comedies (*Lovers and Other Strangers* and *I Love My Wife*, both released in 1970), and domestic melodramas (*Diary of a Mad Housewife* [1970], *Doctors' Wives* [1971], *The Marriage of a Young Stockbroker* [1971], and *Such Good Friends* [1971] struggle with a post–freedom era of commitment in which spouses test the constraints and explore the flexibilities of the marriage contract, never entirely able to shake off the memory of what it meant to be "free"—or at least free to be "themselves." Reaching its heyday in the early 1970s, the marriage cycle was undoubtedly fueled by issues of sexual freedom and relationship commitment that were inflecting the incipient discourse of the women's liberation movement with its development of a new language for confronting alienation problems and identity politics. With divorce rates quickly rising to a crisis point, the marriage cycle also drew on a national therapeutic discourse of marital "healing" that emerged to inspire the collective national heterosexual consciousness that marriage was worth preserving and fighting for and that it remained immanently possible to attain a sense of individuality in a legally binding committed relationship.

As this chapter demonstrates, the intersection of these discourses of sexual freedom and commitment failed to mark a coherent, navigable path by which opposite sex couples might ensure successful relationships and secure an integral sense of self; instead, in the realm of contemporary Hollywood cinema, this intersection manifested itself as a collision of disparate cultural voices that exposed the tenuous and precarious nature of "heterosexuality" as both a practice and an identity.

Heterosexuality in the Campus Film

In a 1970 article on sex as a form of "salvation," *Time* magazine reports that as a result of the sexual revolution, "the American male has succumbed to the widely advertised notion that he should be the super-performer in what has been called the decade of orgasmic pre-occupation. . . " ("Repairing the Conjugal Bed" 49). Beginning in the late 1960s and unofficially concluding by the year in which this article appeared, Hollywood's campus protest cycle comprises a set of films that render sexual freedom as an earned privilege that demands to be enjoyed, as long as self-avowed heterosexual men experience and define the limits of such pleasures. Sexual free agents such as fraternity brother and celebrated womanizer Paxton Quigley (Christopher Jones) in the campus drama *Three in the Attic* and revolutionary-turned-English graduate student Harry Bailey (Elliott Gould) in *Getting Straight* have earned a reputation for a prowess sustainable only by the repeated performance of sexual acts with multiple female partners. Each man harbors anxiety over his inability to maintain the level of sexual performance required to sustain his identity as campus stud, and each is ultimately punished or compelled to reform for failing to maintain the delicate balance between expression of sexual freedom and sexual commitment. "You've heard of the sexual revolution?" Paxton exclaims at the start of *Three in the Attic*. "Well, I'm its first casualty."

Certainly not all campus films of the cycle are defined by this male sexual anxiety. Some of the films retain a significant revolutionary force in large part because they manage to establish a version of political action that is not measured by their male protagonist's sexual performance. With grace and humor, fifty-two-year-old sociology professor-turned-university-president F. W. J. Paco Perez (Anthony Quinn) in Stanley Kramer's *R.P.M.* endures the jokes about being past his sexual prime that are launched by his twenty-five-year-old live-in mistress Rhoda (Ann Margret) as well as the undergraduate revolutionaries occupying the campus administration building. Although *The Strawberry Statement* connects its central undergraduate protagonist Simon's (Bruce Davison) transformation from jock to activist to the onset of first love with fellow activist Linda (Kim Darby), Simon's political awakening and enlightenment are never presented as merely an effective way to "score." More often, however, the phenomenon of the late-1960s college campus film demonstrates Hollywood's determination to capture contemporary political affairs and social movements while subordinating sociopolitical concerns to the more personal, sexual stakes of individual male protagonists, and even in these two more politically responsible films the male perspective clearly dominates. In *Three in the Attic*, *Getting Straight*, and *Carnal Knowledge*, the concept of a sexual revolution translates cinematically and ideologically as a classic battle of the sexes in which men struggle to maintain the status of free agents, reaping the benefits of new freedoms of sexual expression while being confronted with demanding female sexual partners, some casual and others all too eager for the opportunity to entrap their men in relationships of commitment. The paradigm remains intimately familiar as a carry-over from the castration anxiety plaguing the white male consciousness in the 1950s in such seemingly disparate genres as film noir and the romantic comedy, except that by the end of the 1960s, with new representational liberties following the demise of the Production Code and the inception of the movie rating system, studios were obligated to employ a much less restrained sexual discourse in dramatizing this battle.

With or without the narrative seasoning offered by a sit-in, a protest, or a riot, the college campus provides the ideal setting for dramatizing challenges to the upholding of heterosexual masculine identities of the late 1960s. The proximity and accessibility of so many eligible young female coeds nurture male fantasies of multiple female sexual partners even in situations such as Paxton Quigley's where three of his "dates" happen to be rooming in the same dormitory of a small Vermont women's college. Paxton's envious roommate Jake (John Beck) develops such a fascination with Paxton's multiple date "problem," and such a determination to see his roommate succeed in his orchestrated serial deception, that he devises elaborate tactical quizzes—complete with detailed dormitory maps—to train Paxton to perfect his strategies of seduction and evasion of the "enemy." In *Getting Straight*, Harry has sex with another woman almost immediately after each time he and his graduate student partner Jan (Candice Bergen) argue, but the prospect of Jan's dating the stuffy, socially inept intellectual Dr. Greengrass (Richard Anders) is enough to arouse Harry's jealousy, scorn, and invective. In a darkly satirical vein, *Carnal Knowledge* takes the male obsession with multiple partners to its logical extreme through the character of business major Jonathan (Jack Nicholson), who not only must have every woman he wants, but even those whom his roommate Sandy (Art Garfunkel) desires. When, by Jonathan's own strategy, Sandy's girlfriend Susan (Candice Bergen again) finds herself maintaining sexual relations with both roommates at once (and feeling terribly guilty about a deception that she claims as her own) Jonathan relentlessly imposes on her the necessity of deciding between the men, or more exactly, of carrying out the only decision that he perceives as correct—for her to dump Sandy and stay with him. In the environment of free intellectual exchange that these films envision, "commitment" is reserved primarily for the discourse of social protest; it is also what men should reasonably expect from their women with the tacit understanding that these same women refrain from becoming so demanding that they begin to expect their men to follow their own rules.

If, in Hollywood's version of the sexual revolution, straight men want more sex with straight women, and straight women just seem to want more of everything, the college campus environment only exacerbates the demands on an already strained heterosexual identity by adding intellectual acumen to the expanding list of requirements that form the composite virile stud. In *Getting Straight*, Harry is depicted as an "experienced" and therefore desirable man not only because he has been a protest organizer (and perhaps even a Vietnam veteran), but also, more importantly, because he is now a graduate student who knows how to transform knowledge into sexual and intellectual power. This transformation insidiously sustains white male heterosexual privilege by rather curious means: the tenured professoriate of Harry's English department is depicted as a largely over-the-hill group of rarified aesthetes and ivory tower intellectuals who have greedily consumed knowledge for its own sake rather than using it as an instrument of social change. Their disconnection from the contemporary political climate and the needs of their alienated students signals hang-ups coded as forms of emasculation, as is the case when a professor finds himself unable to relieve himself after catching a glimpse of Harry's penis at the urinal. As the professor retreats in shame into a closed stall, Harry smirks, "sometimes running a little water helps." We, however, do not need to see Harry's penis to confirm its size because evidence of its grandeur is implicit everywhere in his naturally cool and hip integration with the student body. Unlike his more academically accomplished colleagues, Harry aspires to become a high-school teacher and the "dumbbell English" undergraduate students he is assigned to teach inspire him.

As so often occurs in Hollywood's late 1960s campus environment, Harry readily assumes the spirit of a revolutionary brotherhood that plays as a sexual politics: both he and Paxton in *Three in the Attic* best demonstrate their enlightenment about race relations by their desire to have sex with black women. In fact, *Getting Straight*'s insistence on its own enlightened perspectives on racial integration and equality play out as conspicuous extensions of normative racial and gender power relations. In a scene depicting a student group discussing the possible formation of a black studies department, Harry's black revolutionary friend Ellis (Max Julien) becomes the new scion of the movement after Ellis intimates that Harry's has already copped-out through his desire to become part of the establishment. Immediately after this confrontation, however, the two men engage in private homosocial bonding with requisite misogynist

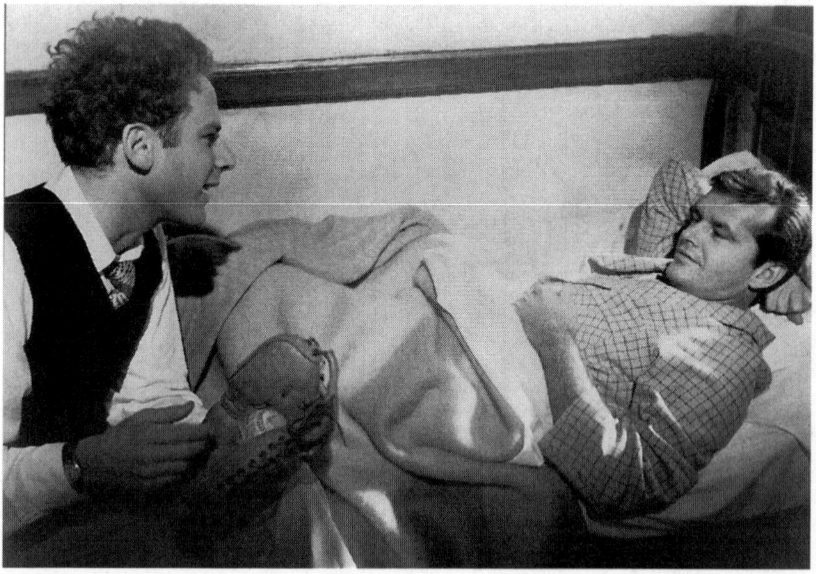

Figure 8. Sandy (Art Garfunkel) and Jonathan (Jack Nicholson) in *Carnal Knowledge* (1971). *Photo courtesy of Springer/Photofest.*

humor regarding Harry's sexually repressed sister, whom he would be happy for Ellis to enlighten, adding a few stereotyped quips about the magnitude of the black male's "equipment."

To play big man on campus convincingly in the late 1960s, the male student must navigate the troubled waters conjoining a sexual-intellectual power coded as masculine and a sensitivity coded as "something else." In *Carnal Knowledge*, not long after he starts having sex with his best friend Sandy's girlfriend Susan, Jonathan expresses resentment over Susan's suggestion that Sandy is more sensitive than he, especially given that Jonathan's initial seduction of Sandy required his "playing" sensitive against his more rugged masculine type, and Jonathan initially told Sandy to "tell her about your unhappy childhood" as a strategy of seduction-by-sensitivity. Susan, Sandy explains, has read many books and inspires him to read more as well. This observation incites Jonathan to engage Sandy in rivalry, expressed in his outburst, "I read more than you, so who's the one that's more sensitive, you or me?" In *Three in the Attic*, Paxton is much more adept at negotiating women's perception of his image: Tobey (Yvette Mimieux) meets him while sitting alone at a bar during a fraternity mixer, and although she initially pegs him as a typical womanizer because he's staring at her behind, she falls for him seconds later once he starts quoting Kierkegaard (on the institution of marriage) and Simone de Beauvoir. Only when Tobey discovers Paxton's simultaneous affairs with Eulice (Judy Pace) and Jan (Maggie Thrett) does she come to perceive this sensitivity as only a ruse; herself betrayed, Paxton becomes just another conniving, sex-starved college boy, so what better punishment than to conspire with the other two women to force him to keep having sex until he dies?

The path from commitment to marriage registers as a pathetic, entirely "square" reiteration of only what these young radicals' parents may have settled for, given their unawareness of alternatives. In *Three in the Attic*, the suggestion that Paxton is prepared to commit to an exclusive sexual relationship with Tobey (Yvette Mimieux) is enough to drive Jake to paint a horrifying scenario of Paxton's future: "Do you want to get hung up on a split-level with automatic sprinklers?" When Tobey carries out her father's suggestion of testing Paxton's devotion by pretending to have rented an apartment for them to live together, Paxton freaks out and considers this test as a duplicitous, unforgivable humiliation. In *Getting Straight*, Jan's frequent insistences on Harry's exclusive commitment to her become the basis for arguments and excuse additional insistences of "infidelity" that drives them further apart.

Of all films of this campus cycle, however, male anxiety and solipsism take their most severe beating in *Carnal Knowledge*. If the first section of the film centers on the two 1950s college roommates' competitive efforts to "score" with women, in the subsequent section the 30-year-old version of Jonathan only extends the commitment anxieties of his former on-campus self, abruptly fleeing the bedroom in fear and rage each time that unfulfilled Bobbie (Ann Margret) mentions marriage or children. Not even when Jonathan's mistreatment of Bobbie drives her to a suicide attempt does he consider her as anything but a manipulative shrew hell-bent on destroying the sexual freedoms that he has so insistently maintained. The disturbing final section of the film—which takes place in present-day 1970s New York City—darkly depicts the consequences of a life dedicated to avoiding commitment. Here, in his cold, sterile, contemporary Manhattan high-rise apartment, a middle-aged Jonathan entertains Sandy and his girlfriend Jennifer (Carol Kane) with an elaborate, chronologically arranged slide show entitled "Ballbusters on Parade," depicting a narrated history of his sexual conquests from adolescence to present. Bobbie has earned a central presence in this chronology by the path that her character takes, from the first months of their relationship, evolving from shapely, self-assured sex goddess, to a case study in excess: eating, sleeping, and whining too much about the lack of fulfillment in her life.

Although Jonathan's self-proclaimed battle of the sexes provides for some stimulating sexual foreplay, it more emphatically demonstrates with overt misogyny how from a male perspective women have all too often become obstacles to the same pleasure that they have been commissioned to elicit. After intimating to Sandy that he has recently been "having a little trouble" in bed and has consequently had to endure some "very nasty innuendos" from women, Jonathan's ultimate fantasy motivates the disturbing final sequence of *Carnal Knowledge*. Orchestrated by the prostitute Louise (Rita Moreno), who after multiple sessions has clearly become proficient in arranging the intricacies of the only routine to which her client will respond with the desired "attention," the fantasy unfolds as a narrative of ultimate male control and solipsism, portraying its subject as "a man who inspires worship, because he has no need for any woman, because he has himself and is better, more beautiful, more powerful, more perfect, more masculine. . . ." In Jonathan's perfect world—the only one left that can still turn him on—he gets to experience sexual pleasure while altogether eliminating the problem of ballbusting, emasculating women. All he needs to be cured is a good mouth and the properly narrated biography.

Getting Married but Staying Single

Carnal Knowledge is certainly one of the key films marking the transition between Hollywood's preoccupation with carefree, "innocent" college campus male sexual hijinks that recognizes women as a demanding yet necessary catalyst for male pleasure (*Animal House* would reconfigure the genre seven years later) and a much darker vision of the committed relationships that ensue after heterosexuals who have graduated from college quite uncomfortably move on to pursue a version of "adult life" that threatens to mimic the "square" values that their parents' relationships epitomized. By the time of Hollywood's early 1970s marriage cycle, the problem of what comes next for the generation of the sexual revolution is both complicated and wholly enriched by newly articulated options available to American women.

Following the directives of the civil rights movement and the sexual revolution, which politicized the practice of sex by moving it from the bedroom to the social arena, the women's liberation movement announced itself to popular American consciousness at the beginning of the 1970s as a phenomenon of social and political awakening. "Sexual freedom has never been the primary concern of women's movements . . . nor are the feminists of the Pill generation particularly partisans of the sexual revolution," *Time* magazine announced in 1969 ("the New Feminists"). If the sexual revolution's promises of free love and release from the constraints of monogamy ultimately served male sexual libidos while securing women more inflexibly in the position of objects of desire, by the early 1970s second-wave feminists such as Kate Millett and Germaine Greer were guiding women in other directions, articulating new choices available within and beyond the contractual married relationship, and offering them a "way out." While the leaders of the movement collectively invested in the project of debunking archaic social assumptions and myths that enslaved women, their strategies varied widely, with Millett advocating widespread social action and Greer focusing on more immediate steps that each woman could take to better her life situation. As she suggests in her phenomenally successfully 1970 book *The Female Eunuch*, the woman "could begin not by changing the world, but by re-assessing herself" (16).

Coterminous with the women's liberation movement, and as a carryover of the slowly waning effects of the sexual revolution, the American public of the early 1970s was bombarded by reports of the long- and short-term effects of marital communication breakdown and rapidly rising divorce rates, which would total a record of approximately 840,000, or 9 percent, by 1972, more than twice as many as in the mid-1950s ("Who Stays Married Longer").[1] Alongside the attempts of feminist leaders to frame these phenomena as logical outcomes of the public's growing awareness of outworn myths and institutions, the era produced specialized and popular literature from psychologists committed to regrounding marriage problems inside the home. Intent on producing healthier marriages rather than radical alternatives to the marriage contract, these psychologists maintained that marriage was indeed salvageable at the institutional level, and they would attempt to prove this by reintegrating fractured relationships between individual couples. Some, such as Herbert Otto, would contend that "any marriage can be envisioned as a framework for actualizing human personal potential" (25). Others, such as Nena and George O'Neill in their 1972 best seller *Open Marriage: A New Life Style for Couples*, maintained that true interpersonal commitment was accessible only through marriage:

> Only through knowing another in significant and authentic dimensions can we love, explore the potential of ourselves and others, and fight off the alienation of our time. And marriage, in some form or another, still provides the only framework in which people can find the stability in which to experience the full intimacy of a one-to-one relationship. (26)

With emerging and increasingly popular social and psychological discourses emphasizing the individual's—especially the female's—entitlement to an identity that marriage only serves to complicate, the prevalence of loneliness among spouses became a phenomenon worthy of analysis. In a popular, influential 1969 study of marital conflict entitled *The Intimate Enemy: How to Fight Fair in Love and Marriage*, psychologist George Bach and *Ladies Home Journal* executive editor Peter Wyden describe a class of marital loners as pathological cowards who are:

> all grappling with the same dilemma. They are trying to exist psychologically alone and bear the stress of isolation rather than live as authentic twosomes and bear the stress of intimacy. Most loners are nominally attached to someone. . . . But they cannot abide being emotionally dependent. They don't get truly involved. They detest tension and personal hostilities. The true loner would rather split than fight. (32)

Such individual and interpersonal alienation become common elements of couples' domestic situations in the films of the marriage cycle. In Mel Stuart's film *I Love My Wife*, medical doctor Richard Burrows (Elliott Gould) relieves the stress of a troubled marriage through a series of extramarital affairs, and only with these other women is he able to articulate his alienation from his wife Jody (Brenda Vaccaro). After deciding to leave Jody, however, he feels even more lost and isolated in his newfound freedom, but by the time he realizes this and attempts to reclaim what he has lost, Jody has decided to move on to her own stress-relieving relationships.

Lawrence Turman's *The Marriage of a Young Stockbroker* more overtly circumscribes the problem of loneliness in marriage as a potentially pathological condition that arises out of unacceptable social circumstances. The film begins with a long, slow, high-angle, forward-tracking shot of a brokerage office, during which the figure of the eponymous antihero William Alren (Richard Benjamin) gradually becomes discernible amid the visual clutter of tickertapes and a distracting cacophony of competing voices. His feet are up on his desk as he doodles on a notepad, abruptly returning to the world of work only when his boss catches his eye, at which time he pretends to phone customers on his client list, placing imaginary stock orders on their behalf. Admiring the job performance of Mr. Franklin, the diligent and successful broker in a neighboring cubicle, Franklin tells him, "One of these days you'll be telling them what you want them to hear without even knowing that you're doing it. Then you'll be home free." When Franklin dies of a heart attack at the office later the same afternoon, William takes this as evidence of the ultimate futility of his own professional aspirations.

As much as he recognizes his own alienation, however, throughout most of the film he remains entirely incapable of expressing it. Despite his determination to speak openly with his wife Lisa (Joanna Shimkus), he communicates his dissatisfaction only introspectively through voiceover narration. The manifestation of William's inability to share takes the form of an obsessive voyeurism. William's visual probing remains harmless as long as he confines his activities to the office or the local porno theater; when on a vacation Lisa catches him spying on a group of bikini-clad women at the beach one night, she decides that she has had enough and tells him that she's leaving him. While the film certainly emphasizes the pathetic nature of William's failed attempts to express his feelings to his wife, *The Marriage of a Young Stockbroker* aspires to be equally concerned with investigating the reasons for Lisa's own silence, even as it attributes this silence to a social and cultural power imbalance that has denied her a voice as a woman to speak out about what's wrong. In the terminology of Bach and Wyden, instead of risking conflict or momentary discord, this husband and wife have settled for seething silently in a "fight-phobic household" where the penalty is "emotional divorce" (6). Such behavior comprises a form of "gunnysacking" in which man and woman secretly accumulate grievances that eventually erupt in a vengeful Vesuvius ("Fight Together, Stay Together," 64).

Even as the film explores the contemporary discourses of couples' counseling and women's liberation, however, it questions the efficacy of these emerging discourses to disrupt age-old conventions that have guaranteed the primary of heterosexual male power. Lisa's expression of dissatisfaction comes as close as any Hollywood film of the era to articulating the plight of the contemporary married woman:

> I have no power with you. It's that simple. . . . If you could find some way of giving me power, I'd stay with you, but you can't. . . . Over myself. I want the feeling that I can make things happen. I can't take it anymore. You sit over in your office all day; I sit at home. As long as you're over there, I can kid myself. I can sit there staring out the window kidding myself into thinking that sometime, things will change. Then you come home, all hostile and sullen and making idiotic small talk and I say to myself, "It's because he's tired, it's because he's worked hard all day, making money so that one day, our lives will change. . . ." But it won't Bill. It can't.

If Lisa's capacity for self-expression identifies her as a healthy woman attempting to establish a sense of identity and difference from her husband, the narrative undermines the health of this "new" Lisa by emphasizing that these thoughts are not her own: when Lisa finally does speak out, she only does so because her ultrafeminist sister Nan (Elizabeth Ashley) has successfully exerted her own form of control over Lisa's thoughts. Indeed, Nan is characterized as what Jonathan in *Carnal Knowledge* might describe as a ballbuster, a stereotyped composite of contemporary male heterosexual anxieties over what women might be capable of doing if gender differences were erased. To convince her sister that William's voyeurism is both pathological and incurable, Nan does her best to force William to concede that he would love to "look at her naked" if he were given the chance. When he refuses to take the bait, she arranges for the strap of her bikini top to come loose and expose part of her breast in front of Lisa and William, who *does* look this time around, thereby ultimately proving Nan's point. "It's the old story: male oppression of the female," Nan explains, the irony clearly marked by the fact that she has trained her own husband Chester (Adam West) to relinquish his own voice for fear of retribution from her. As it plays out, then, Nan's ability to dictate Joanna's needs is on a par with William's own manipulation of his wife's desires evidenced, for example, by his decision to tear up the application letters that Joanna has written to New York modeling agencies on the basis of his assurance that she really does not want to be a model. Indeed, as a narrative that maintains an alliance with the central male protagonist's perspective and that accordingly asks its audience to identify with that point of view, *The Marriage of a Young*

Stockbroker manages to redefine a woman's gender identity problem as part of the larger network of a problems with which the heterosexual married male is forced to contend in a post–sexual revolution, feminist era that threatens *his* identity and reinforces *his* sense of alienation.

Staying Straight

If, according to Bach and Wyden, fighting is a constructive activity for marriage partners who are not afraid of taking risks, the intimacy-averse couples in the marriage cycle films end up unleashing their explosions of anger erratically, in nonconstructive character attacks that reduce their disagreements to personal problems in which blame must be assigned. In *The Marriage of a Young Stockbroker* and elsewhere, the arguments concern assumptions about gender roles, especially, as in Joanna's case, the confinement that the woman feels as a result of the inflexibility of these roles in their relationship, and male anxiety about the integrity of the roles of man and husband in light of the woman's assertions of individuality. One attack strategy that many of these wives favor is the tried-and-true accusation that their husbands are not "real" men at all. In the larger context of the sexual revolution, with its expectations of sustained male prowess, labeling a man a "fag" in the marriage cycle serves as a most effective shorthand for connoting his ineffectiveness as a heterosexual partner.

Although all of the films of Hollywood's marriage cycle were released after the Stonewall riots of June 1969 and in the context of other sustained and burgeoning contemporary equal rights movements, the "presence" of homosexuality had met with neither widespread acceptance nor cultural tolerance by the early 1970s. The suggestions of professional psychological communities rarely if ever sanctioned homosexual practice as an acceptable "alternative" to the monogamous heterosexual marriage contract; instead, homosexuality maintained the status of a now more visible psychological and social problem. In a 1970 cover article for *Harper's*, Joseph Epstein contends at length with ways that heterosexuals like himself have had to negotiate the increasing presence of homosexuality in contemporary culture:

> Now that the notion that heterosexuality is primarily a purpose of procreation no longer has any real direct force in most people's lives, heterosex, being officially recognized as an agency of pleasure, has itself taken some very fancy turns. (All those marriage manuals describing all those new positions, tricks, little surprises!) Certainly, nowadays it is not so easy to say, heterosexually speaking, what is

> natural and what is not. . . . This being the case, one can't say with the same old confidence that homosexuality is unnatural, however deeply one might feel that it is. One cannot even any longer say that it is uncustomary. . . . (50)

Instead of embracing or resigning himself to this homosexual cultural presence, Epstein constructs an ideological argument that continues to relegate same sex relationships to the realm of the "other," establishing a distinction that maintains a pathological nature of homosexuality that was still officially aligned with the American Psychiatric Association's official position on this issue. "With the possible exception of prostitutes and heterosexuals driven by abnormal appetites," Epstein argues, "the general run of heterosexuals are not defined by their sexuality at all . . . [while] homosexuality, on the other hand, is a full-time matter, a human status—and that is the tyranny of it" (50). At the same time that the developments of the sexual revolution were problematizing the maintenance of gender difference in heterosexual relations, then, heterosexual culture began to mark difference in terms of the increasingly visible "phenomenon" of homosexuality. And if, as evidenced by *The Marriage of a Young Stockbroker*, the Hollywood film industry was slow to acknowledge the women's rights movement as anything but another threat to the heterosexual male psyche, Hollywood was even more reticent to conceive of homosexuality in any terms beyond the strictly stereotypical.

While the films of the marriage cycle include no avowed male homosexual characters, homosexuality is primarily relegated to a function, an indication of that against which the heterosexual male norm must define itself to ensure its stability and integrity. In the process, male homosexuality also begins to reveal unresolved anxieties in male heterosexual performance at a historical moment that demanded free sexual expression while busily marking off the acceptable limits of this freedom. Given a sufficient dose of sexual ingenuity, the single, heterosexual male could manipulate homosexuality to his advantage in short-term relationships with women. In *Three in the Attic*, for example, Paxton Quigley manages to "score" with cosmically enlightened co-ed Jan by concocting a traumatic experience with a villainous high-school swimming coach who "made" him "queer." The confession spurs Jan to attempt to cure him by demonstrating what a real woman can make him feel, and Paxton's deception is successful enough for him to confide to the audience in voiceover narrative that he envies "faggots" for their ability to score: "Thank God for faggots. I sometimes think that faggots make it with more chicks than guys do."

Once the marriage contract is in place, however, a wife's suggestion of her husband's homosexuality becomes very serious business, whether it is made in jest or in the heat of argument. In *The Marriage of a Young Stockbroker*, for example, a form of what Epstein might describe as "abnormal sexual appetite" becomes the basis of a potential sexual pathology which—momentarily, at least—renders William's heterosexuality suspect. While his voyeurism remains a purely heterosexual obsession, his wife Lisa identifies this problem as the one that has had the most profoundly negative effect on their marriage. From Lisa's perspective—especially as it is filtered through the enlightened consciousness of his sister-in-law Nan—amid all of other problems with their relationship, William's scopophilia becomes the most convenient site of marital pathology. Accordingly, after the couple has separated and Lisa is more convinced than ever that he will never stop looking at other women, she exclaims, "You're a fairy. . . . I'm married to a fairy!" William never even bothers to contest the validity of what he perceives as a wholly absurd assessment on her part: if in his eyes she is not strong enough to know what she wants, she is hardly in a position to assess his identity or his desires. Interestingly, however, the narrative trajectory ultimately erases any possibility of William's latent homosexuality by entirely removing William's obsessive behavior from the realm of the pathological. At the end of the film, after husband and wife have safely reconciled their problems, a beautiful woman crosses their path and catches William's wandering eye. This time around, however, William and Lisa subsequently exchange knowing looks of acknowledgement followed by easy laughter. In the end, a man's recognition of any form of feminine beauty is not only normal, but also expected as a harmless confirmation of male heterosexuality.

Elsewhere in the marriage cycle, however, a woman's accusations of a man's homosexuality cut more deeply to suggest a fundamental problem in discerning what being heterosexual in the early 1970s means. Curiously, the propensity for unmarried males to have multiple sexual partners—a phenomenon sanctioned as a form of healthy and playful experimentation in the college campus films—takes on a more sinister and potentially pathological feel in marriage narratives that attempt to account for women's needs and feelings. In Frank and Eleanor Perry's *Diary of a Mad Housewife*, the unhappily married Tina Balser (Carrie Snodgress) engages in an extended extramarital affair with the solipsistic novelist George Prager (Frank Langella), who is every bit as demanding as her ambitious lawyer husband Jonathan (Richard Benjamin). Although they set up and carry out their contemporary casual arrangement with no expectations from either side, George becomes scornful and jealous when Tina prioritizes the needs of her family over his needs, and Tina becomes enraged when she is confronted by the fact that George has other women in his life. When she refuses to accept George's edict that they should cool their relationship for awhile, she accuses him of being a "rotten and sadistic son of a bitch," prompting him to retort that she's the "perfect willing victim." After George throws her down and pins her shoulders to his couch, Tina's final attempt to subvert control in this relationship takes a form of sharp accusation: "You're sick, sick. You have to put on this big, virile act, because you're really a fag." The accusation definitely strikes a nerve (he literally throws her out the door), and the scene ends with a reaction shot of a stunned George alone in his apartment. Whether Tina's assessment of him is ultimately accurate, however, the narrative clearly contests the presumed "innocence" of aggressive and insensitive hypermasculinity, at the same time, perhaps not so radically, identifying an unwillingness to commit oneself to a relationship as a deeply pathological phenomenon. As an attempt to rectify a power imbalance, Tina's speculation about George's homosexuality introduces another dimension of the problem of difference in heterosexual relationships. She wants more communication and reciprocity from her lover, an amelioration of the enforced difference between gender roles that paralyzes her in her relationship with a husband who barks commands, insults her in private and in front of their children, and acts out whenever his needs are not immediately met. Her inability to connect with George on equal footing is precisely what enables her to perceive how different he is from her and how oblivious he is to what she wants. Ultimately, this recognition of difference leads her to label him as something other than the type of man capable of attending to her sexual needs. If in one sense the accusation of homosexuality comprises a convenient practice of scapegoating, it also constitutes the sliding of an undesired difference of gender onto a misunderstood difference of sexuality.

Such curious connections between gender and sexuality in and beyond marriage play out even more elaborately in the marriage cycle's most light-hearted romantic comedy, *Lovers and Other Strangers*. Although the plot concerns the forthcoming marriage of the working-class Mike (Michael Brandon) to the upper-middle-class Susan (Bonnie Bedelia), the film focuses less on specific class differences than on gender connection problems that are deemed heterosexually universal: fear of commitment, the complications of adultery, the possibility of divorce, sexual performance anxiety, and most emphatically, gender difference. Much of the film's comedy stems from its intricate gender role reversals, as evidenced by the swinging playboy Jerry (Bob Dishy) who is intent on "scoring" with his blind date Brenda (Marian Hailey), a woman who at first appears to be too analytical and intellectual to "let go" but ends up driving Jerry to sexual exhaustion. Some of these reversals are merely playful, such as when, at the wedding ceremony, husband and wife switch genders in address (she says "Hi, Phyllis; he responds, "Hi, Nick"), but even this instance demonstrates how extensively the transition to marriage threatens to eliminate difference.

The most emphatic demonstration of gender confusion ensues between Johnny (Harry Guardino) and his wife Wilma (Anne Meara), whose twelve-year marriage has begun to show signs of strain. In their first scene together, he makes excuses for not wanting sex that night, telling her that he feels pressured by her nagging and her detailed reminders about how long it has been since their last time ("You owe me two, now"). Her scorekeeping compromises his virility and his interest in being intimate with her. "Out of all the women in the world, I had to go and marry an equal time orgasm fanatic," he complains. "You read a couple of *Ladies Home Journals*, and all you can think of is 'me too, me too.'" When, in their subsequent argument, he accuses his wife of being "butch" ("Butch? I'm more feminine than you'll ever be."), she retaliates, hitting him where it hurts: pointing to a picture of Harry in his U.S. Marine Corps uniform, exclaiming, "Those tough marine drill sergeants are the biggest fags in the world! . . . They're latent fags. But they're not real men. A real man is warm and understanding and tender and gentle and loving and sensitive." When he asks her what a woman is, she struggles with her response, "A woman is strong, responsible, and brave—I don't know what a woman is. I don't see any difference between us anymore."

Wilma's unmet expectations of what a man could ideally be for her are not so far from Tina's in *Diary of a Mad Housewife*, except that here, ensuing between the husband and wife themselves, the argument is precipitated by a man's problems with fulfilling a *woman's* desires; more curious in this case, however, are the contradictory configurations of gender and sexual identity that this couple constructs. Johnny's perspective on Wilma's behavior mirrors William's take on Nan in *The Marriage of a Young Stockbroker*, although *Lovers and Other Strangers* more explicitly articulates the parallel between a sexually assertive woman and a "butch" lesbian. Wilma, however, perceives Johnny as both soft and hard, brusque and excessively macho on the basis of his military status, but also ultimately duplicitous and false because of what she perceives as the performative aspect of this machismo, one that ultimately makes Johnny less of a "man." Given Wilma's concept of the ideal heterosexual man as someone whose strength stems from his tenderness and sensitivity, would it follow that a man with an opposite set of attributes would be a "fag"? Not exactly because Wilma's defines "fags" not as people who lack gentleness or sensitivity; instead, "fags" are simply not "real" men. If one extends this process of definition by exclusion or negation to what Wilma describes as a "woman"—someone strong and brave—we derive another version of "not man" that is also not the same as a "not fag." The results, accordingly, posit a conflicted notion of homosexuality that, because it is defined by negation, also renders the category of heterosexuality incoherent.

What *Lovers and Other Strangers* ultimately hypothesizes—albeit largely unknowingly—is the absurdity of pegging individuals into conventional and acceptable patterns of behavior on the sole basis of their gender or, by extension, sexuality. The attempt to preserve the integrity of such conventionally defined categories becomes the basis of several interpersonal conflicts in films of the marriage cycle, and as Wilma and Johnny's conflict illustrates, to insist that these categorical descriptions be reiterated and rehearsed (as Johnny does) is to invite them to be dissected (as Wilma attempts to do) in a way that ultimately reveals their incoherence. Wilma's conjecture that "I don't see any difference between us anymore" is hardly intended as a satisfactory condition, and no wonder, then, that in a film whose ultimate goal is to preserve the possibility that conventional marriages can still work, Wilma and Johnny's conflict later resolves itself as a reconciliation in which Wilma lets Johnny be the dominant partner on the sole condition that she make him aware that she is *permitting* him to do so.

In the marriage cycle of films, matters of "difference"—in both heterosexual and homosexual relations—often become problems of an "excess" that is measured in relation to the "norm" of monogamous heterosexuality. As much as *Lovers and Other Strangers* attempts to give a voice and an identity to unsatisfied, married women, it also infers that both wanting something more (an extramarital relationship) and wanting more of something (happiness or sex) equally invite trouble. When Richie (Joseph Hindy), the groom's brother, tells his parents that he and his wife are about to be divorced because they are no longer happy, his mother Bea (Beatrice Arthur) and father Frank Vecchio (Richard Castellano) take this as a sign of his weakness, an indication that he has been "spoiled"; "happiness" is neither masculine nor heterosexual, but duty, obligation, and tradition are, and as much as the film strives to present more contemporary alternatives to this conventional perception of marriage, it retains a bittersweet nostalgia for a time when such questions of happiness held less primacy. George Schaefer's melodrama *Doctors' Wives* (adapted from the bestselling Frank Slaughter novel) more insistently renders all forms of excess as inherently pathological, through the eponymous group of women who cover a wide spectrum of the neurotic symptomatology of everyday heterosexual life among the upper-middle class, from the sex crazed, to the sex starved, to the alcoholic, to the pain killer addict. Although the root of all of their ills appears to be their inattentive, profession-centered husbands, the narrative generates no sympathy for anyone in this privileged class, preferring instead to demonstrate that because they already have too much, they must end up with nothing.

The film's opening scene depicts a typical evening out for this group as clearly marked by gender division: at a social club, the male professionals and their wives sit in adjoining but separate spaces playing poker; the doctors "talk shop" while the women, led by the free spirited and universally despised Lorrie Dellman (Dyan Cannon), talk about sex. Lorrie identifies the afflictive condition of these "uptight" women as "sexual malnutrition" ("you know what I say: 'an orgasm a day keeps the headshrink away'"), exposing through her probing questions the sexual alienation that each of the women feels in her marriage. To rectify these problems, the self-proclaimed "horny" Lorrie follows her initial offer to "step out into the parking lot for awhile" with any of the women with the proposition to "sleep with each of your husbands and tell you what each of you is doing wrong" as a service to her social community, adding that she's "already covered 50 percent of the territory." Aside from making for a rather brief appearance for the star-billed Dyan Cannon, the fact that by the next morning Lorrie's husband has murdered his wife after discovering her in bed with a colleague is not so surprising: Lorrie represents an excessive sexuality that threatens the foundations on which all of these couples have built their marriage, uptight, frustrated, and incommunicative though these women may be. If the act of committing adultery were not sufficient to place Lorrie in jeopardy, the idea of having casual sex with a female friend is certainly much less tolerable, and talking so openly about either in the spirit of sexual "liberation" is perhaps the most severe institutional violation of all. If one of the men had not killed her, one of the women might have done so—perhaps Amy Brennan (Janice Rule) or Della Randolph (Rachel Roberts), both of whom express their disdain for her crudeness.

Lorrie, however, is by far the most content and fulfilled of this lot, and as the plot unfolds, her estimation of the other couples' marital problems is revealed to be largely accurate: the women, according to the logic of the narrative, are not getting enough sex and all of their problems are rooted to this lack. The most curious of these sexual "blockages" manifests itself in the character of Della, who alternates between sarcasm, bitterness, and anger for most of the film until husband Dave

(Gene Hackman) forces her into a most curious confession: after too many drinks one night, Della submitted to Lorrie's advances and the women had sex. What has been so traumatic for Della is not only that the incident occurred, but also that she actually enjoyed it! The most remarkable aspect of this confession, however, is that immediately on unburdening herself to her husband, Della is not only absolved but also entirely cured of both her neurosis and her homosexual predisposition, so that she can regain productive married life with her husband.

Marriage, Excess, and Therapy

If for Della confession manifests itself as a purgative and cathartic experience that immediately relieves her of excess desire and redirects her needs to more culturally acceptable heterosexual endeavors, most of the troubled men, women, and couples of the marriage cycle films must resort to a more prolonged investment of resources to effect cures to their ills. As is the case with Della, however, these investments share the presumption that the proper method of rectifying marriage problems is to repair them, to engage in a therapeutic process whose ultimate result is a renewed belief in the efficacy and integrity of heterosexual marriage: perhaps the couples should try harder and learn from their mistakes; perhaps they should invest more energy in finding the right partner; or perhaps they just should not complain quite so much. As much as *Diary of a Mad Housewife* attempts to sustain a woman's perspective on unhealthy marital and extramarital relations, the events of the narrative providing Tina with more than enough reason to back out of a contract with a demanding and unappreciative husband, the final scene reveals her to have narrated her entire story in a group therapy setting, struggling now to decide whether she should have told her husband about her affair after he divulged to her the details of his own.

If *Diary of a Mad Housewife* manages to preserve some ambiguity about the therapeutic process by implicating intolerable social and institutional conditions as catalysts for Tina's "madness," other therapeutic situations among films of the marriage cycle more insistently maintain that the problems to be addressed are personal rather than social or political.[2] Despite the prevalence of contemporary discourse devoted to matters of heterosexual marriage therapies, most of these films retain a skeptical position regarding the efficacy of having outside "experts" intervene in personal matters, especially because the goal of these therapists is most often to erase the gender differences on which their marriages are firmly founded. In *The Marriage of a Young Stockbroker*, the backyard patio group therapy session that Nan insists on arranging allegedly to help her sister and brother-in-law reconnect plays out as an extended joke. The therapist—who has already demonstrated her success by having "fixed" Nan and her husband's marriage—turns out to be so lame, inept, ineffectual, and self-serving that her presence ends up emphasizing even further that the couple's only hope—and indeed, their responsibility—is to work through these problems together.

The therapeutic entanglements of the black comedy *Bob & Carol & Ted & Alice* yield insight into contemporary perceptions on the management of gender difference in Hollywood's marriage cycle films. The film begins as Bob (Robert Culp) and Carol (Natalie Wood) Sanders arrive at The Institute, a remote southern California facility for a weekend marriage encounter marathon. In group sessions the participants reveal their sexual problems (inability to refuse sex with anyone, impotence, unsatisfactory orgasms) using techniques such as touch and aggression therapy to bond in small groups and ultimately with their partners. The encounter is a model for bettering communication between husband and wife, as contemporary marriage and sexual therapists were recommending for their clients. Before long, Bob admits to Carol, "I hide my feelings and I accuse you of hiding yours," leading to Carol's insight, "I do hide my feelings. I'm afraid of you." After the weekend, the couple returns to their home with a renewed confidence in their communicative abilities, convinced that they have eliminated the unhealthy differences. Their more conventional and largely unenlightened friends Ted (Elliott Gould) and Alice (Dyan Cannon) Henderson seem puzzled by Bob and Carol's transformation, especially after Carol, to confirm her closeness to her friends, reveals to them that Bob recently had an affair on a business trip. Shortly afterward, when Carol informs Bob that she has invited her tennis instructor Horst (Horst Ebersburg) for home bedroom sex, his initial reaction of rage and hurt ("What are you doing to me? I'll kill the sonofabitch.") is soon supplanted by his "insight" that he has no reason to be upset; in fact, he is delighted that Carol cared enough to trust him with her admission. By the time that the foursome end up in a Las Vegas Riviera Hotel suite getting dressed to see Tony Bennett, Ted has joined the group of self-admitted, carefree adulterers; in response, partly in retaliation, an emotionally distraught Alice proposes that the four have an orgy. Although the others initially see her invitation as a self-punishing act, Bob is soon convinced that the orgy would help the foursome to connect on a new sexual level. As it plays out, however, after some slow motion shots of Bob romancing the two women in bed (while Ted obsessively brushes his teeth in the bathroom), the four-way orgy devolves into an uncomfortable silence and awkwardness that is interrupted only when the friends start putting their clothes back on. Accompanied by the song "What the World Needs Now Is Love," Bob and Carol and Ted and Alice march out of the casino with smiles of wisdom on their faces, presumably realizing (without verbal acknowledgment) that they have gone much too far with this unleashed "free love" phenomenon. The friends' experiment certainly falls short of what Robert Rimmer in *The Harrad Experiment* (1967) had described as the ideal of the sexually liberated group relationship that defies the conventional and "square" emotions of jealousy and secrecy.

Finally, the college campus and problem marriage films of the late 1960s and early 1970s exemplify Hollywood's strategy of "having it both ways" in their dealings with sociopolitical movements that attempt to disrupt the foundation of traditional institutions such as heterosexual marriage. The films employ a contemporary and popularized discourse of liberation at the same time that they warn their protagonists and their audiences that while sexual freedom is permissible and even necessary in a period of experimentation, it is so primarily only for heterosexual men, and even here being able to recognize when enough is enough is important. This same precautionary attitude governs the industry's construction of gender and sexual difference in this more "liberated" time, emphasizing that social or institutional deviance in any form must be identified so that it may be recognized as not only undesirable but also excessive and unnecessary. And in the spirit of a nostalgia for some seemingly less complicated time for relationships, if "heterosexuality" emerges only through such means in this historical period as a category of identity and behavior, then the category remains wholly unstable, preoccupied as it is with managing the potentially invasive effects of incipient discourses of women's liberation and of homosexuality, both of which threaten to redefine and rewrite the terms of the marriage contract.

Notes

1. In the late 1960s and early 1970s, the problem of divorce attained such a prominent position on the national agenda that it was often noted in popular weeklies by well-known public figures as confessional, self-reflective commentaries on the breakdown of their own marriages. A particularly insightful and disturbing instance of this phenomenon occurs in "A Problem of Making Connections" in the December 5, 1969, issue of *Life*, where Joan Didion frames her alienation from her husband in terms of a wider, metaphorical alienation from contemporary sociopolitical conditions.

2. Ernest Lehman's adaptation of Philip's Roth controversial novel *Portnoy's Complaint* (1972) takes this matter of personalizing problems to its extreme. Relationship-averse Alexander Portnoy (Richard Benjamin) spends five

afternoons per week on the couch of his entirely silent psychiatrist Dr. Spielvogel (D. P. Barnes), engaging in an elaborate confession of a series of sexual escapades that have left him with the neurotic affliction of deriving sexual pleasure only from masturbation.

8

BHASKAR SARKAR

Hetero-nation

Toward a "New and Improved" Global Public Image

THE CONTEMPORARY GLOBAL PUBLIC sphere presents us with a remarkable conundrum: as novel transnational configurations call into question the primacy (even legitimacy) of the nation form, new and resurgent nationalisms keep surfacing all over the world. In the South Asian context, we have witnessed the rapid "opening up" of the Indian economy. Steps toward economic liberalization, adopted since 1991, included the removal of four decades–old licensing policies and financial regulations, the dismantling of barriers to foreign investment and trade, and the widespread privatization of important sectors such as energy and heavy industries. There has also been a restructuring of India's national media (the official recognition of cinema as a legitimate industry, the advent of cable and satellite television, a massive overhaul of the telecommunications networks, and tremendous growth in print media, radio, and marketing). Culturally, large segments of the Indian citizenry have been exposed to and influenced by globally emergent lifestyles and worldviews; yet, at the same time, the disorienting winds of change have precipitated a strong conservatism, congealing most notably around a resurgent fundamentalist Hindu nationalism. This chapter begins with this confounding duality, which calls for imaginative modes of apprehending the vertiginous encounters between the global and the local, a necessity that has generated glib neologisms such as the *glocal*.

How does popular Indian cinema—particularly the Mumbai-based Hindi film industry and its ancillary sectors,[1] now widely referred to as "Bollywood"—negotiate this ambiguity at the heart of contemporary national agendas? In particular, what cinematic fabulations become necessary with the rapid jettisoning of the cornerstones of postcolonial official policies, and the sea changes in sociocultural structures? How does the Indian nation-state regenerate itself through popular cinema? Consider the following example from the 1999 film *Dulhan Hum Le Jayenge*. Whenever Swapna, the female protagonist, faces an important moral choice (Should she drink beer in a public bar? Should she marry someone against her family's wishes?), Raja, her boyfriend, asks her questions striking for their recursive banality: "Are you French? Are you Russian? Are you German? Are you Italian?" Every time, the queries reduce Swapna to an infantile and simpering girl who replies she is an Indian who, therefore, knows exactly what to do: evidently a real Indian woman always stays true to a national ethos, neither drinking in public nor acting against her elders' wishes. The strategy adopted here centers on a specific trope of negotiation common to Indian epistemic and aesthetic traditions: I am referring to the *sawal/jawab* (that is, question/answer) structure of Indian rhetorical systems, a structure with which all connoisseurs of Indian classical music will be particularly familiar. Indeed, the improvisational mode of Indian classical music builds around imaginative detours from anchoring melodic and rhythmic patterns, and establishes a creative dialogue between various musicians to settle all tensions in a final harmonious resolution—a point of stasis referred to as *sama* (eqivalence, unity). If the performance stages stimulating musical development, the end point (a tonic-rhythmic *home*) is already known: the pleasure derives from knowing this predetermined goal, in diverging from it, and eventually in reaching it. The obsessively iterative questions about national identity, which maneuver Swapna toward a fixed and self-evident "realization" about the correct mode of behavior, form precisely such a discursive structure.

The recurring point of narrative stasis in the film is the anchoring ideological institution of the family. Stepping out of this particular text, we encounter numerous Hindi films in the 1990s that engage questions of sociocultural transformation within the genre-scape of the romantic melodrama, returning us time and again to the traditional family fold—now bearing the unmistakable trappings of affluence and confidence that have become emblematic of a post-liberalization Indian upper-middle class. *Hum Apke Hain Kaun* (a.k.a. *HAHK*, 1994) and *Dilwale Dulhaniya Le Jayenge* (a.k.a. *DDLJ*, 1995), which remain the most paradigmatic of this new breed of family films, are celebrated as wholesome entertainment, as well as for upholding immutable family values. Commentators have observed that these "clean" films focusing on family life and kinship loyalties coincided with several other trends. During the decade, a drive began to "clean up" the industry through its corporatization and professionalization. Simultaneously, the industry recognized the development of extensive diasporic audiences with a specific need for cultural and identitarian moorings (not to mention recognizing non-resident Indians as potential investors). Meanwhile, a Hindu chauvinist nationalism emerged at the center of India's political mainstream (Mehta; Uberoi, 138–216). In Monika Mehta's astute summation, through these strategies, the nation-state "reproduce[s] itself in the context of globalization" (136).

Intriguingly, while such efforts to reproduce national identity forge family-oriented tales upholding heteronormativity, they perform deep anxieties about what constitutes an essential Indian-ness in the face of a rapidly mutating world. Indeed, their insistence on an immutably Indian way of being intimates something like a "national panic." A closer look at these overwrought films reveals strategies of doublespeak and surreptitious accommodation complicating the process of ideological reproduction. Drawing broadly on the 1990s' cinematic field marked by morally righteous tales promoting heteronormative family values and gender roles and focusing primarily on the aesthetically unremarkable but discursively fascinating film *Dulhan Hum Le Jayenge*, this chapter demonstrates that: (1) the eventual narrative resolutions, which seem to shore up traditional heterosexual family structures, paradoxically help to consolidate an emergent middle-class consensus about the need to globalize; (2) the initial vacillation and the process of cultural arbitration precisely render the disorienting changes acceptable; (3) the conservative resolutions can neither fully shut down a heterogeneous space that the narratives now routinely present nor eradicate its radical promises; and (4) if the reproduction of the hetero-nation is crucially dependent on the marginalization of unorthodox modes of being as "deviant,"[2] then the same deviances are now being marshaled to signal a new openness (that is to say, the entanglements of the hetero-nation and its "dangerous supplements" become the sites for negotiations between continuity and change). At issue are a deliberate, if cautious, reinscription of the national in relation to the global and a repositioning of the heteronormative within a potentially diverse range of identities.

National Identity in a Global Frame

Lavish weddings—complete with huge congregations of kith and kin, party and games (typically, ritualistic exchanges that bring the bride's and the groom's families closer through playful competition, and the game of *antakshari* in which participants exhibit their knowledge of popular film songs), music and dancing, elaborate rituals and feasts—emerged as a *de rigeur* component of the 1990s family films. *HAHK*, a 206-minute opus, appears to be one endless if entertaining process of anticipation, deliberation, engagement, planning, and staging two weddings over several years; they bookend an intervening period of family transactions and ceremonies, vacations, and visits, through the course of which the plot's core romance blossoms. The young lovers now negotiate the mores of courtship and nuptials within the socially sanctioned extended family, all along attending to their familial loyalties and responsibilities. Widely hailed for its eschewal of violence and vulgarity, *HAHK* broke all previous box office records and ushered in a new era for Hindi films. *DDLJ*, which was released the following year (1995), fared even better by staging the complications of romance in a transnational setting. Raj and Simran, the young protagonists, are diaporic Indians traveling across Europe and India: they have to work out the nature of their courtship in relation to familial expectations while being away from home, and they eventually overcome parental opposition to their union by embracing conventional values. *Pardes* (1997) offers interesting variations in a tale about the protracted process of arranging a marriage between an "urbane" NRI (non-resident Indian) guy from the United States and a "traditional" young woman from a village in North India. The unwilling but obedient groom comes to India at his father's insistence; when he falls for his prospective bride, she travels to the United States to meet his extended family and to get a sense of his life. But the young man's best friend turns out to be the "authentic" Indian, capable of respecting and preserving Indian social institutions and customs, thereby emerging as the rightful inheritor of patrimonial privileges; needless to say, he also wins over the bride.

In contrast to the defiant macho figures of the 1970s, 1980s, and early 1990s epitomized by the proletarian "angry young man" persona of Amitabh Bachchan (for example, in *Deewar* [1975]) and the even more violent "one man army" of Sunny Deol (for example, in *Narasimha* [1991]), the family-oriented heroes of the post-liberalization era are kinder, gentler characters. They usually start out being fun-loving, happy-go-lucky innocents from affluent families, enjoying great spatial and social mobility, appearing in tune with—and at ease in—a cosmopolitan habitus. As time goes on, they learn to cherish their familial and social duties, evolving into responsible national subjects. The heroines are also mobile subjects capable of expressing and pursuing their hopes and desires; but their agency outside the domestic fold is largely ornamental and performative, relegated to the realms of consumption and spectacle (hanging out in trendy cafes and discotheques, shopping in metropolitan boutiques). Even when they are college students, their lives seem like an endless party. Parallel to the evolution of the male protagonists, these young women come to appreciate the value of personal sacrifice and step into the regulated and highly symbolized roles (wife, mother, and custodian of continuity) a heteropatriarchal society assigns to them. In sum, the family-films of the 1990s provide the mise-en-scène for intense cultural transactions in the face of changes wrought by globalization: they position the legitimacy and sanctity of heteronormative structures as cornerstones that will (and must) uphold the nation-state (Mankekar).

Ultimately, the young transnational Indian subjects must get in touch with their inner national self. The eventual triumph of an essential (that is, traditionally heterosexual) Indian way of life cushions the onslaught of global transformations, providing desperately needed cultural anchoring in uncharted waters. Yet, this argument about identitarian transactions indexes an economy of competing demands on contemporary national subjects, involving intricate trade-offs. The balance in the 1990s blockbuster Hindi films usually favors entrenched norms, but not before making a substantial case for adjustment and accommodation. With the "opening up" of Indian economy and society to global trends, a certain measure of recalibration becomes inescapable and imperative. Therefore the films register individualist aspirations and recognize a semblance of autonomous subjectivity before absorbing these impulses into a matrix of "the collective good." Thus these popular mediations of a transitional era help manage social anxieties, allaying fears of the unknown and rendering the impending changes attractive. After all, on the evidence of these cinematic fabulations, Indian middle-class life is a plush and privileged domain—and is only getting better. In other words, the films help secure a broad consensus among the ruling elites on the need to embrace globalization as a strategy for national growth.

Not surprisingly, even as the Indian state adopted the mantra of liberalization, a range of measures was necessary to bring the interests of the Bollywood culture industry into synergy with its own programs. After decades of suspicion, indifference, and official policy centering on censorship and regulation, the state recognized popular cinema as a significant partner in a national hegemony. As the state capitulated to the forces of global capital, it sought to deflect attention from the resultant loss of economic and cultural sovereignty through a neurotic insistence on the preservation of an imputed national ethos (whether in the form of *hindutva*, an essential Hindu identity, or its more secular versions). While flexing its nuclear and information technology muscles, the Indian state came to depend on popular cinema to shore up support at home and to act as its cultural ambassador abroad. The genius of the new Hindi cinema is evident in its creative response to these expectations: presenting a picture of plentitude on the metonymic home-nation front, engaging global (especially Western) stereotypes about arranged marriages and turning traditional weddings into dazzling national spectacles for a transnational market. But this trope, which Mira Nair acknowledged and capitalized on in her globally fêted film *Monsoon Wedding* (2001), cannot be reduced simply to a process of orthodox reification. Rather, this new cinematic "wedding complex," which extends the idea of arranged marriages to "romance sanctioned by the family leading to matrimony," performs a dual ideological function: enabling change tempered by conformism and continuity, and reframing the national in relation to the global. When the elders propose the *rishta* or matrimonial alliance, the prospective couple is allowed a space of courtship, which the norms of social interaction between the sexes incribes. While proxy guardians often oversee this period of getting to know each other, they prove to be comically inept chaperones, presenting at least the possibility of transgression. If, on the other hand, the two meet and fall in love on their own and have to contend with initial opposition from their families, the youth eventually win the elders over with their responsible conduct and respect for authority. Both scenarios thus present a new horizon of freedom in matters of the heart, invoking a bourgeois-liberal rhetoric of individualist choice and a universalized paradigm of romance and conjugality; they also qualify this freedom in terms of an unassailable vernacular deference to the family and the community.

Consumption becomes a principal conduit for the mutual rearticulation of the national and the global in the films of the liberalization era. Two tropes of consumption, shopping and tourism, take on particular significance because of their ability to conjoin disparate spaces and signal new modes of being. As the heroine of *Dil To Pagal Hai* (1997) waits to find "true love," she nevertheless gives in to the seductive promises of Valentine's Day and goes shopping to buy herself a gift. This act of self-indulgence is important in two respects: it marks the arrival of a global-popular ritual on the Indian scene (soon to become the site of a pitched cultural war—with conservative groups unleashing their ire against public displays of romantic affection and the commodification of *amor*); it also stresses a romance with self-absorbed individualism and its actualization through consumption. The films of the 1990s are replete with explicit shopping activities: shopping for contemporary fashion in Europe or the United States, shopping for wedding trousseaux, shopping for identities—frequently marked in terms of semiotically loaded consumption goods such as alcohol or mini skirts. At other times, consumption activities remain embedded in the details of characterization, set design, and performance—for example, in youngsters adopting the gestures and paraphernalia of globalized youth cultures (posters, T-shirts with identifiable logos and quips, music, and in a memorable scene from *Pardes*, an iconic guitar invoking not only a youthful passion for rebellion and change, but also commercial incorporation of the kind epitomized by the globally popular Hard Rock Café franchise). The dual invocations of the arcade and the arcadia serve to capture the interpenetrations of the national and the global.[3] With tourism, another leisure activity in vogue in 1990s Hindi films, cinematic spectacles of exotic foreign locations are harnessed to conjure up deterritorialized subjectivities. Characters "find" or reinvent themselves as they move through the *terra infirma* of transnational space: the young protagonists of *DDLJ* and *Pardes* romp through Switzerland and Austria, Las Vegas and California; the NRI patriarchs "return home" to pose at Indian tourist hotspots. For instance, in *Pardes*, North American industrialist Kishorilal travels from Rishikesh to Agra, his nostalgic patriotism expressed largely through a tourist gaze: the verdant northern plains, bucolic farmsteads, shots of the Ganges, holy men on a boat chanting "Shoham," and the legendary locales of the Taj Mahal and Fatehpur Sikri rendered in the style of picture postcards.

My point is that the 1990s family-oriented films self-consciously thematize the global-local dialectic. Indeed, this dialectic is typically harnessed as the central dilemma driving the narrative, and thus turned into a marketable commodity. The strategy works at the box office because it resonates with audiences' experiences and expectations. The negotiation in these films is not so much between tradition and modernity (a polarity that preoccupied Hindi popular cinema of the 1950s and 1960s) as between *parallel modernities*. At stake is the articulation and consolidation of local versions of the modern that subsume a refigured traditional. The persistence of archaic social institutions does not imply a failure to modernize or to become cosmopolitan; rather, accommodating both the time-honored *and* the contemporaneous points to a *local* modernity, a *vernacular* cosmopolitanism. It is useful to remember here that tradition, as the necessary and defining other of modernity, was always a modern category. Only from a modern perspective can "tradition" be construed as such. In our current conjuncture, a homologous reframing is under way: a resurgent core national identity is now posited as the necessary foil to transnational affinities. In other words, contemporary nationalism has to both assert and negate itself in relation to a transnational imagination, each category functioning as the other's condition of possibility. This equivocal logic allows for the gradual recalibration of the national in the context of globalization.

Let us return to the moments in *Dulhan Hum Le Jayenge* that stage a crisis of identity in terms of the rhetorical questions, "Are you French? Are you Italian? Are you British? Are you German?" The implication of this iterative structure (note the precise series of nationalities invoked shifts ever so slightly) is loud and clear: as long as Indian youth agree to return to the family fold, they can venture into uncharted terrain; as long as they remember *who they really are*, they are allowed some behavioral latitude. The volley of redundant questions, always propelling one toward a self-evident truth, continues a long cinematic tradition of reassertions of an immutable national identity: from *Shri 420* (1955), in which the Chaplinesque tramp played by Raj Kapoor sings, "My shoes are Japanese, my trousers are English, and my hat is from Russia, yet my heart remains Indian"; through *Purab Aur Paschim* (1970), in which Manoj Kumar's hyper-patriotic character asserts his Indian-ness in the face of diasporic deracination (most notably in a London restaurant sequence); to the more recent *Phir Bhi Dil Hai Hindustani* (2000), whose title and eponymous song, a quote of the *Shri 420* number, proclaims, "And yet my heart remains Indian."

Dulhan Hum Le Jayenge may strike many as an odd choice on which to hinge one's arguments. After all, it is a lesser known work by David Dhawan, successful auteur of heavy-handed, low-brow comedies; its box-office performance is considered "average"; its title ("We shall take the bride home") brazenly echoes the blockbuster from four years ago, *DDLJ* ("The brave-hearted shall take the bride home"); its plot, an amalgam of formulaic elements from other films, often veers toward the incoherent, settling for highly contrived resolutions. Yet, it brilliantly engages the shifts and negotiations this chapter has been charting. Take, for instance, the film's use of the wedding trope. It begins with a discussion about Raja's marriage, necessary for the continuation of the family line: the housekeeper tells his parents of an excellent bridal prospect—Swapna, a beautiful and smart young woman raised by her three uncles. Raja pursues Swapna across Europe at his parents' behest; of course, he is allowed a peek at her photograph to establish his own willingness. The ensuing romance is then interwoven with misunderstandings between the two families and Raja's good-natured, if devious, attempts to win over Swapna's intransigent uncles. The film ends with the customary group photo at Raja and Swapna's wedding. As if this diegetic arc were not enough, the film reflexively alludes to the generic significance of the wedding in contemporary Indian cinema: hearing band music at a wedding, the uncles forget their immediate mission and begin dancing on cue—not unlike audiences who might be drawn to wedding films largely because of the sheer spectacle of celebration and a merry, old time. But there is more to the film that complicates its overall heteropatriarchal conservatism (a conservatism that incredulously requires Swapna's grandfather to come out of narrative oblivion and set things right—the grand patriarch figure still has ultimate authority, social and narrative). As the rest of the chapter shows, compared to the more well-known and written-about family values films such as *HAHK*, *DDLJ*, and *Pardes*, this one may be more crass, but it is also more radical. Feminist readings of the genre have assembled a certain canon over the last decade—a canon that provides evidence about the new cinematic conservatism (and strengthens critiques linking cultural mediations to a resurgent sectarian nationalism), but also excludes the more disruptive moments in popular cinema. A class dimension is at work in such exclusions, in critics' unwillingness to engage with the inane and vulgar. But in its crass, over-the-top elements, thematic and formal, *Dulhan Hum Le Jayenge* produces a queering, as it were, of the heteronormative national pitch.

Family Loyalties, Individualist Aspirations

Such a queer impulse is evident in the film's focus on a most unusual family. Swapna's family life is anything but heteronormative: after her parents die in an accident, her three uncles raise her. Fearing that their own conjugal aspirations might get in the way, the uncles remain bachelors, dedicating themselves to bringing up the baby. With three father figures, the family is so excessively and redundantly "patriarchal" that the structure devolves into its own surreal parody. The basic idea is from the French film *3 Hommes et un Couffin* (1985) and its Hollywood remake *Three Men and a Baby* (1987), except Bollywood reimagines the trio in terms of local stereotypes. The eldest uncle, Bhola Nath, is a *palwan* or bodybuilder: he extols the virtues of a high-protein, carnivorous diet, imposes a strict workout regimen on Swapna, and chases away every Romeo who dares to ogle at her. The youngest uncle, Prabhu Nath, is a *pujari*, a devout Hindu spending his days in meditation and worship, eating a strictly vegetarian diet, and expounding on the importance of spirituality. The two brothers appear to stand in for the two pillars of a militant Hindu nationalism associated with organizations such as the Viswa Hindu Parishad (VHP) and the Rashtriya Swayamsevak Sangha (RSS): the film acknowledges the centrality of these tendencies in 1990s

Indian society and simultaneously lampoons them. The middle brother, Vicky (most likely an Anglicized diminutive for Vikram) Nath, is literally the odd man out: flamboyantly effeminate, he is a fashion designer by profession, eats only "continental food—no oil, no masala, no calories," and prefers a cosmopolitan lifestyle. The film introduces the characters in telling ways: Bhola lifting weights, Prabhu singing a devotional *bhajan*, and Vicky making a grand appearance on the ornate staircase, prancing to the Ricky Martin dance ditty, "Livin' la Vida Loca."

As the object of her uncles' obsessive affections and their competing demands, Swapna feels stifled. She complains to Mary, the sympathetic housekeeper, that she cannot do anything of her own *marzi* or volition: all her desires have to be secondary to her doting uncles' wishes. Even with something as basic and essential as meals, she is scared of offending the divergent tastes of the carnivore, the vegetarian, and the health conscious. When the uncles gather in her room to coax her into eating, the situation quickly devolves into a quarrel among the three. Unable to get a word in, Swapna finally screams in desperation: evoking the trick films of the early twentieth century, a simple edit makes the bickering brothers disappear in thin air. The implication of this scene is quite unambiguous: if Swapna is to come into her own as an autonomous subject, she must make the overprotective uncles "disappear" from her life for a while—that is, she must run away from them and live her own life on her own terms. In this struggle between patriarchal expectations on a young woman and her embodied existence, Swapna finds an ally in her Uncle Vicky, clearly coded as gay and presumably more in tune with her desires than the other two uncles (more on this later). Unbeknownst to Bhola and Prabhu, Vicky arranges for her to join a group tour of Europe. Swapna has a chance to break out of the family cocoon and to live life without having to accede to her uncles (or to her future husband).

Of course, the terms in which the film presents Swapna's temporary "liberation" remain circumscribed within patriarchal structures and conventional cultural polarizations. Thus she goes to Europe in traditional *salwar kameez*, and changes into trendy mini skirts and slinky dresses; as one character retorts, she leaves as Seeta (the mythic ideal of Hindu-Indian womanhood), and returns as Suzie. The reference to Seeta is significant in the light of contemporary conservative campaigns often, although not exclusively, spearheaded by *hindutva* brigades against young women wearing Western clothing (skirts, jeans, T-shirts) on college campuses and in small towns. The idea here is that a woman's dress code signifies her purity or her corruption (see "Obscenity? It's in Your Jeans"). No wonder, then, that Swapna soon gets into trouble with drunken revelers in a bar. Raja blames her for drinking beer and cavorting with strangers, ignoring her honest if bewildered plea that she was "only dancing." Apparently in this film's moral universe, women as wily seductresses are ultimately responsible for men's carnal transgressions. Therefore Raja gets to slap Swapna, his punitive outburst legitimized by the narrative's regulatory paternalism vis-à-vis women. This chapter will later argue that the film reveals a far more complicated attitude toward gender relations and the tension between individualism and conformism; for now, let us note the slight reprieve for the young woman before she is returned to her pedagogical role. Swapna manages to turn the iterative question/answer structure back on Raja to make her point that a real Indian man would beat up her assailants to protect her honor. When Raja complies gruffly, she turns into a quivering girl, signaling her capitulation to the hero's macho charms. Still smarting from Raja's accusation, she follows a long line of hyper-romantic and whimpering Hindi film heroines to lie down on nearby train tracks. This compound gesture of hurt indignation/abject submission seals her fate. From now on, she will be Raja's loving and all-forgiving consort. The scene ends with Raja literally carrying her in his arms back to the hotel: as the film's title suggests, we (that is, male national subjects) shall sweep the bride off her feet and carry her away.

Interestingly, it is Swapna who experiences trouble in being integrated within a heteropatriarchal regime, as she negotiates the tussle between her desires and what is expected of her. In contrast, Raja is the effortless social subject—his life is a seamless fit with the normative

Figure 9. Swapna (Kajol) and her uncle Vicky Nath (Anupam Kher) in *Dilwale Dulhaniya Le Jayenge* (1995).

order, and he has no problem being the perfectly obedient son at all times. Indeed, when the uncles spurn the wedding proposal from Raja's parents a second time, Swapna gets fed up with their unreasonable and obdurate attitude and is ready to leave; but Raja, evoking the film's litmus test of Indian-ness, maintains that because they are neither Russian nor German, they cannot marry without their loving guardians' consent. Raja's parents do not have to struggle like Swapna's uncles in dealing with their ward, although their ease may be construed as evidence for the social efficacy (thus, desirability) of the heteronormative family. Raja's family comes across as a model of heteropatriarchal stability (although with an update—Raja and his father act like buddies) when compared to the heroine's decidedly queer family with three daddy figures. This contrast puts a further twist on the continuing "feminization" (and subservience—in the end, the three uncles have to kneel in front of and plead with Raja's parents) of the bride's side in typical Indian wedding scenarios. After all, the groom's family *is* the scene of heteronormativity, the "home" where the bride will live from now on, carry out her wifely duties, and breed. Swapna's grandfather, who finally makes their union possible, enjoys his authority because he is the eldest of the two families. He is an iconic figure straight out of old oil paintings of forbears towering over present generations: his gravelly voice, his firm bearing, and his moustache speak volumes about his patrician authority, masking the abruptness and improbability of his appearance as the living vestige of an archaic social order.

In spite of these blatant and strained narrative maneuvers aimed at securing ideological reproduction, the film ultimately communicates marked ambivalence about its own ostensible project. From the moment when Mary, the loving housekeeper, advises Swapna to run away (advice that costs Mary her job), we realize that the narrative is in deep empathy with the young woman's dilemmas. The fact that Mary is Christian, and thus part of a religious minority, brings a marginalized critical gaze to bear on mainstream Indian society, revealing its entrenched Hindu unconscious: we are forced to remember that in the Indian context, women such as Swapna have to live up to the ideals of Hindu womanhood and subject themselves to quasi-religious containment. Mary, a surrogate mother figure, understands a maturing Swapna's emotional and physical needs, and it is she who initiates the matrimonial arrangement. The film is by no means feminist; however, a proto-feminist case can be made for its empathetic and affective truck with real women's hopes and aspirations in the face of the tyrannically prescriptive and proscriptive norms. It allows Swapna her moment of autonomy, all too short-lived, in the European sun. The foreign locale (locations in Switzerland and

Mauritius doing duty as generic Europe) is significant, as it takes the protagonists beyond the territorial bounds national borders impose, and beyond the possibilities familiar social institutions circumscribe. There is a long literary and cinematic history of European subjects "finding themselves" on a trip to India: E. M. Forster's *A Passage to India* (with its real and imagined sexual transgressions) may be the paradigmatic text in this respect. Now, more than ever before, globalized Indians turn the traffic of self-realization around, traveling to Europe to find themselves. On the evidence of the 1990s conformist films, they actually discover their innate national identity while traveling through Europe (and in some cases, in the United States or Australia). However, such self-realization cannot fully contain, nor quite erase, the preceding and substantial confusions. Just as a Christian gaze shakes up—queers—the immanent naturalness of Hindu-Indian behavioral strictures, so does the territorial displacement present new opportunities, extending—queering—the realm of potentialities for Indian identities and lifeworlds; thus certain queer portals open in the midst of the cinematic hetero-nation. The following presents a queer reading of *Dulhan Hum Le Jayenge* in terms of its themes, characterizations, iconographies, and formal predilections.

Queer Windows

The two family habitats are a mish-mash of design elements, with ornamental flourishes in garish colors and ostentatious materials. Even as the decor spells "affluence," it brings to mind architecture critic Gautam Bhatia's acerbic appellations "Punjabi pop" and "*baniya* [mercantile] baroque" with their connotations of excess and brassiness. It also reminds one of camp aesthetics, although that term designates a consciously ironic intentionality that may not be operative in the set designs here. (And this lack of irony seems to be a part of Bhatia's point.) A camp tonality is more in evidence in the deliberate camera movements, in the flashy costumes, the larger-than-life performances, and in the embellished sound cues that elicit mirth with all the subtlety of the laugh track that punctuates television sitcoms. These overblown formal elements are all essential components of filmmaker David Dhawan's stylistic repertoire; in this film, they parody and thus trouble the very upper-class privileges and heteropatriarchal sanguinities that they seemingly represent. Thus, as Swapna dances with two men in a Swiss bar as Raja looks on irately, the camera repeatedly dollies in on him in a suggestive swoop to the accompaniment of a metallic swoosh. Watching the film twice with very different audiences in Kolkata and in Jackson Heights, New York, I noticed both times that viewers gleefully anticipate the macho hero's impending outburst. What is not obvious is whether they expect him to direct his ire toward the two lotharios or toward Swapna. Many viewers might find it entirely credible that our hero gets infuriated with his love interest for her "wayward" behavior; thus they might accept his public slapping of Swapna as entirely justified. Indeed, the inane formalist flourishes could be bolstering an archaic masculinity that thrives on subjugating women as objects of protection and control. And yet the unabashedly corny camera and the soundtrack could, just as well, insinuate something else for viewers: that Raja's anger is misdirected and ridiculous and that his masculinist mindset is utterly outmoded. That Raja physically reprimands the heroine and beats up her molesters is a measure of the film's ideological doublespeak. It wants to disparage patriarchal norms even as it supports them.

The performances are all canted to a high pitch: Bhola's exaggerated machismo, Prabhu's projected other-worldliness, Vicky's swishy affectations, Swapna's naivety, Raja's beefcake postures, the tour manager's relentless hamming—all register both affection and incredulity about the characters and their lifeworlds. The comedian Johnny Lever dons many garbs: first as manager of the European tour group, then as a waiter in a restaurant, then as a fake wrestler, and finally as Raja's trusted sidekick. If he is the most explicit drag performer (especially in the superhero-style tights and cape he wears as the wrestler Chirkunda), the film features a bevy of impersonators. The fiendish "diamond smugglers" who shadow Swapna are actually Raja's cousin, and the man he fights on the road to "protect" (and impress) Swapna turns out to be his close friend.

The most prominent camp performance here is that of actor Anupam Kher[4] in the role of Vicky Nath. Kher has taken on roles of ambiguous sexualities on multiple occasions. One of his most memorable screen turns is as Pinkoo, the swishy villain of *Mast Kalandar* (1989) who openly comes onto other men and winks at the audience from behind the bars of his prison cell, letting them in on his amorous/carnal designs on his cellmate. In this, Kher joins other revered "character actors" (an epithet reserved for versatile actors who, in spite of their supporting roles, often walk away with the films) tackling popular queer roles throughout the 1990s: thespians such as Paresh Rawal (seen as the spiritual uncle in *Dulhan Hum Le Jayenge*) in the role of the *hijra* or hermaphrodite Tikoo who serves as surrogate mother to the female protagonist of *Tamanna* (1996), and Sadashiv Amrapurkar who brings to life the villainous *hijra* pimp Maharani in *Sadak* (1991). In his landmark essay on "the profuse and richly ambiguous indigenous male-male sexual iconographies" in popular Hindi films of the 1990s, Thomas Waugh notes the cinematic ubiquity of the "highly visible intersex persona" of the *hijra* icon essentialized alike by Northern (or Western) anthropologists and gay rights advocates (282). In particular, he observes that the *hijra* figures are promoted from the status of the "epicene sidekicks" *and* "low comic diversion[s]" to the "complementary narrative functions of supermenace or supermother," instantiated by Maharani and Tikoo, respectively (286).[5] He also argues that Kher's characterization of the male-identified Pinkoo is more of an exception for 1990s commercial Hindi films. More than the third gender,[6] Pinkoo embodies emergent explicit "queer cravings in terms . . . of middle-class metropolitan movements and identities" or MMMIs (284).

Pinkoo predates *Dulhan Hum Le Jayenge*'s Vicky Nath by a decade with one significant difference. Although Pinkoo's flashy villain is allowed the expression of his homosexual desires, the more respectable Vicky Nath has to sublimate his yearnings into an avuncular aspiration to see his beloved niece get her beau (except for one passing moment in a restaurant scene when Vicky seems smitten with the flamboyant Chirkunda). Like his two brothers, Vicky eschews any possibility of conjugal happiness, conventional or otherwise, to devote himself to raising his orphaned niece. In sharp contrast to his brothers, however, Vicky understands and empathizes with Swapna's plight. In a displaced articulation of his own (as yet impossible) desires, he wants her to live her life—if only briefly—on her own terms and to find fulfillment in heterosexual romance. He not only sees himself as Swapna's father *and* mother, but also seems most capable of fulfilling both roles. Note that Raja's father, Seth Oberoi, openly expresses *his* desire for a beautiful daughter-in-law, Heteropatriarchal family ties permit, even encourage, such social pleasantries about intergenerational, quasi-incestuous dynamics. In contrast, Vicky only hopes that his niece will marry a swanky and up-to-date young man without personalizing this hope in terms of his own needs. Normative kinship structures do not allow a more direct bond between men brought together through the institution of marriage.

If Vicky's desires remain inscribed within a regime of heteronormativity, in what sense does he personify the "queer cravings" of "middle-class metropolitan movements and identities?" The fact that he is an internationally successful fashion designer is not an inconsequential narrative bleep, nor simply a stereotypical professional choice for an imputedly queer character. Worldly and cosmopolitan, he is projected as being savvy to the ways of contemporary life. No doubt, such a notion of contemporaneity remains problematically glib. To be contemporary, for example, typically implies to be individualistic with a narrow insistence on one's "freedom of choice." Again, freedom now is realized largely within the realm of consumption (how many kinds of cereals or detergents do we get to choose from?)—a realm to which fashion belongs. In a rapidly globalizing India, the middle class has overcome the stoic austerity of an earlier, more insular project of nationalist development with its obsessive stress on self-reliance. Transnational lifestyles, grooming standards, and modes of self-presentation infiltrate and "queer" prior nationalist standards. Most striking are the transformations in male attitudes and deportment—Waugh's MMMIs—not all of which are skin-deep. Note the shift away from rigid gender roles with a rise in the number of educated female professionals and in the willingness of younger urban men to share the responsibilities of domestic work and child care. Note also the primed self-consciousness among men about their looks and their fascination with global grooming norms, indexed by proliferating men's lifestyle magazines, exclusive health clubs and beauty salons, and new products such as Fair and Handsome cream.[7] Male supermodels-turned-actors such as Arjun Rampal and John Abraham are the new national role models, inspiring young men to become fashion conscious and earnestly vain; Bollywood superstars such as Shah Rukh Khan and Saif Ali Khan play with and around queer yearnings both on-screen (most famously in the hit film *Kaal Ho Na Ho* [2003]) and off-screen (Indian gossip columns have been rife with rumors about Shah Rukh's alleged bisexuality; Saif has expressed his deep appreciation of his gay fans). If consumption and the body are the foci of a new cultural-political imagination, then the transfigured, queered male identity has emerged as the condensed node of a host of less inhibited, norm-bending desires (covering a range far beyond homosexual yearnings).

The term "metrosexual," coined by the British journalist Mark Simpson in the mid-1990s, is the much-hyped global signifier for the new male. The Indian popular media has enthusiastically embraced the term not simply because it makes for "good copy," but also because of its strong resonance with social trends. In October 2005, Mumbai hosted the first Met-Fest, "a 10-day exploration-cum-celebration of this new urban phenomenon" (Rao). Mangesh Kulkarni quotes Simpson to point out the latter's astute linking of this "male makeover" phenomenon to forces of global political economy:

> For quite some time now, old-fashioned (re)productive, repressed, unmoisturised heterosexuality has been given the pink slip by consumer capitalism. The stoic, self-denying, modest straight male didn't shop enough (his role was to earn money for his wife to spend), and so he had to be replaced by a new kind of man, one less certain of his identity and much more interested in his image—that's to say, one who was much more interested in being looked

> at. . . . A man, in other words, who is an advertiser's walking wet dream. (quoted in Kulkarni)

Kulkarni argues the transformations in gender roles and sexuality cannot be understood in isolation from the New Economy with its stress on "the knowledge-driven service sector" and the "non-traditional, varied patterns of consumption" (Kulkarni).

A far more disjunctive domain comes to view when one surveys transformations in social outlooks and mores regarding gender and sexuality. The national child sex ratio (number of girls per thousand boys from birth to age 6) has dropped since the 1990s, dipping below 800 in many districts of the wealthiest states of Punjab and Haryana ("No Girls. Please, We're Indian"): higher income levels, expected to improve reproductive health, may actually encourage pre-natal infanticide by allowing access to ultrasound imaging technologies. A Bangalore study on youth sexualities finds continuing differences and inequities across gender lines. Young women are more prone to talk about their reproductive responsibilities, generally skirting the issue of sexual pleasures. Young men, on the other hand, freely discuss their sexual proclivities. They read "sex books" with graphic illustrations and language that frame male organs as "weapons" and female genitals as "passive receptacles"; they even recount "[s]tripping, masturbating and passing crude comments" as part of their enjoyment.[8] Alongside these deeply entrenched beliefs and practices, the past two decades have witnessed gains in the legal rights of women, the establishment of pro-feminist men's groups, and the institutionalization of gay rights—including the appearance of the newsletter *Bombay Dost* in 1991 (the very year the Union Budget officially triggered economic liberalization), establishment of the Humsafar Trust in 1994, and perseverant attempts to repeal anti-sodomy laws dating back to colonial India. The HIV/AIDS crisis and strong anti-prostitution blocs (covering the entire range of the political spectrum) have forced the national establishment to engage and address heretofore marginalized, even taboo, forms of sexualities. One might mention the AIDS awareness campaign in Bengal, featuring the adorable ragdoll Buladi (a familiar, caring elder sister figure), and hard-hitting photography exhibits and documentaries on sex workers (including Shohini Ghosh's film, *Tales of the Night Fairies* [2002]). The visibility of queer subjects in mass media has recently reached a new apotheosis with a spate of films centering on queer characters (including *Sancharram* [2004] and *My Brother Nikhil* [2005]), and the runaway success of the television talk show *Koffee with Karan*, which the openly gay filmmaker Karan Johar hosts on the Star Network channels.

The contemporary queer subject embodies, in more ways than one, the nation's highly disjunctive and plastic participation in the movements toward globalization. The recent shift from the *hijra* to the MMMI persona in commercial films constitutes a semiotic passage from the realm of the subaltern to that of the global-popular. The transitional figure of Vicky Nath signals this class dynamic: transitional because he retains the reified mannerisms of the earlier stereotypes of marginal sexualities, yet he projects a new social mobility, a worldly confidence. Still, one significant commonality remains between such transitional icons and the playfully queer cosmopolitans the most popular stars project. Within the domain of popular cinema, they all articulate and flirt with the forbidden, but ultimately return us to the safety of conformism (Vicky Nath cannot articulate his sexual desires, and the younger heroes tap dance around a queer sensibility but eventually confirm their heterosexuality).

The contradictions faced by a globalizing national social space produce these cinematic interdictions—screen mediations whose enunciations simultaneously defer to the limits of the permissible and transgress those very boundaries. Such ambivalent maneuvers require a supple analytical lens unencumbered by the value-laden, obscuringly polarizing categories of "progressive" and "regressive." Borrowing from the terminologies associated with computer operating systems, contemporary Hindi popular cinema's frequent but highly circumscribed invocations of queer subjectivities[9] function as windows on our computer screens. We open multiple windows to work out subsidiary problems, and then we subsume the results into the main task. These "queer windows" of cinematic doublespeak allow us to romance the unconventional, even the subversive, before we settle back into the heteronormative fold; and the (necessarily temporary and controlled) invocations of these transgressive impulses harness a certain "progressive" chic, securing for the nation a "new, improved" cosmopolitan public image. Interestingly, traces of these partial transgressions linger in our imaginations and our material lifeworlds: these traces coax us, ever so slightly, into a novel and open sensual field. As Mahesh Kulkarni notes, this is "the vast grey zone between the media-bolstered façade of metrosexuality and the deep-rooted structures of heteropatriarchy. This is the space to watch for those seeking to understand and shape gender dynamics in the country" (Kulkarni).

This chapter demonstrates that the heteropatriarchal family, which has been a metonymic bulwark of the modern nation, has become one such "grey zone" in its encounter with contemporary conundrums. Drawing on my analysis of an unabashedly mainstream Hindi film, I have explored the following questions: What happens to the ideologically linked and painstakingly delineated and reified categories (for example, male privilege, patrilineal inheritance, normative sexuality, social reproduction) that shore up and naturalize the entire complex of social relations comprising the hetero-nation? If the current conjuncture unhinges many of these terms from their imputed verities, what fuzzy zones of individual and collective being become available to us? At stake is the apprehension and realization of these new possibilities for a (trans)national publicity, where the radically heterogeneous potential always, already inherent in the hetero-nation is made explicit, concrete, and, perhaps, even more normal.

Notes

I would like to thank Swati Chattopadhyay, Bishnupriya Ghosh, Sean Griffin, Amelie Hastie, and Angelo Restivo for their comments and suggestions.

1. These include cinema-related radio and television programming, magazines, posters, coffee-table books, music and music videos, as well as "new media" products such as videogames, Web sites, downloadable screensavers, and cell phone jingles.

2. To take one salient example, the marginalization of homosexuality within modern national imaginations have a long and pervasive history: for instance, Paragraph 175 of the German Penal Code outlawed homosexuality at the inception of the modern German nation-state in 1871. In India, the British Raj instituted antisodomy laws in Section 377 of its Criminal Code in 1861; after independence (1947), the post-colonial nation-state inherited these laws.

3. For an interesting discussion of utopianism and commercialism in recent Hindi films, see *Inden*.

4. Global audiences will remember him as Jesminder's strict but sympathetic father in Gurinder Chadda's film *Bend It Like Beckham* (2002).

5. One might add that practically all the major male stars of the period donned drag in at least one film, including Akshay Kumar in *Khiladi* (1992), Sanjay Dutt in *Khalnayak* (1993), Amir Khan in *Baazi* (1995), and Shah Rukh Khan in *Duplicate* (1998). However, their drag performance is either an instrumentalist ploy in the story (often to hoodwink the villains, or to get the girl, or both), or a comic diversion that spectacularizes the star's capacity for hamming: never is the queering indicative of the characters' sexual confusion. On the other hand, a handful of "offbeat" or "alternative" films such as *Daayraa* (1996) and *Darmiyan* (1997) focus on intersex or transgender subjectivities.

6. As Waugh suggests, industry insiders and mainstream audiences do not really bother to distinguish between the categories of sex and gender: the stereotypical *hijra* is a composite icon of sexual indeterminacy, gender trouble, and forbidden yearnings—all in all, a radically marginalized subaltern figure that is still a potent threat to social normativity.

7. Realizing that nearly one-third of the customers of their best-selling Fair and Lovely complexion-lightening cream were men, the cosmetics manufacturer Emami decided to bring out its "exclusively for men" version.

8. Vasan reports findings of the study, which the Foundation for Research in Health Systems conducted with funding from the Department of Health Education, NIMHANS, Bangalore.

9. This strategy involving part-time queer subjectivities—a kind of queer impersonation or "queer drag"—is also characteristic of other cinemas (for example, Hong Kong, Mexican) originating from social contexts in flux.

9

DIANE NEGRA

Time Crisis and the New Postfeminist Heterosexual Economy

One of the signature attributes of postfeminist culture is its ability to define various female life stages within the parameters of "time panic." Postfeminism has accelerated the consumerist maturity of girls, carving out new demographic categories such as that of the "tween"; it has forcefully renewed conservative social ideologies centering on the necessity of marriage for young women[1] and the glorification of pregnancy; and it has heightened the visibility of midlife women often cast as desperate to retain or recover their value as postfeminist subjects. Crisis and fulfillment in virtually all these life stages center on the discovery of personal destiny, the securing of a heterosexual romantic partner and motherhood and the negotiation of the problem of paid work (seldom its rewards). Thus, the life stages and archetypes of femininity postfeminist popular culture so vividly draws, consistently and insistently display and perform femininity as heterosexual, white, affluent, and family-focused, and those women who cannot be recuperated into one of these life stage paradigms generally lose representability within a landscape dominated by these categories.

Yvonne Tasker and I have noted elsewhere that "postfeminism evidences a distinct preoccupation with the temporal—women's lives are regularly conceived of as time starved, women themselves are overworked, rushed, harassed, subject to their 'biological clocks,' etc. to such a degree that female adulthood is defined as a state of chronic temporal crisis" (10). Women are often depicted as particularly beset by temporal problems that may frequently be resolved through minimization of their ambition and reversion to a more essential femininity. That reversion is often expressed through corporeal concepts and procedures—the "biological clock"; intense adherence to regimes of diet, exercise, personal grooming; and the decision to have plastic surgery or Botox injections are all manifestations of and responses to a postfeminist cultural climate. (Indeed, the intensification of a personal aesthetic regime that now normatively entails the services of day spas, nail salons, cosmetic dentistry, and tanning salons is one of the signal characteristics of the postfeminist economy.) A youthful appearance achieved through consumerist "empowerment" is positively encoded even as it is disingenuously celebrated in some quarters as a genetic birthright or the natural outcome of a well-lived life. New exhortations for one to demonstrate that one is "aging well" employ such rhetoric as cover for the class and wealth bifurcation that enables an affluent minority to tap into a growing marketplace of products and services to forestall and camouflage the effects of the aging process. These formulations of age-beset femininity also fortify male heterosexual desire as the cynosure for women's concepts of self and their consuming behavior.

While women's lives are represented as profoundly governed by the passage of time, postfeminism also extends the promise of new freedoms to transcend or cheat time (which will be discussed shortly). However, these putative temporal freedoms are countermatched by an intense calendarization of women's lives with a return to demographic-defining rituals including sweet sixteen parties, bridal showers, weddings, and baby showers, which are positioned as markers of female identity legitimation in addition to life milestones. Women's lives are thus simultaneously not only increasingly governed by notions of temporal propriety and conformity but also assessed in relation to women's perceived abilities to defy time pressures and impacts, and the ensuing paradox is one that a variety of forms of female-oriented popular culture seek to manage.

Such rituals, not coincidentally, all celebrate the achievement of heterosexual maturity, marriage, or motherhood and thus one of the consequences of the heightened ritualization of milestones in the normative female lifecycle is that the lives of women without these experiences are temporally unmapped. This chapter suggests that the rampant temporal uncertainties so strongly associated with postfeminist femininities operate (among other things) as a cover for a heightened anxiety about the terror of losing heterosexual viability and worth. "Time panic" thus marks a deeper kind of heterosexual panic that urgently requires the performance of female sexuality and maternity to anchor "family values" paradigms now under threat of being set adrift. It emerges as a manifestation of, in Judith Halberstam's (2007) words, "the ongoing manic project of the re-naturalization of heterosexuality and the stabilization of relations between men and women." Seen in this light, the distinct overvaluing of female heterosexuality and maternity read as oblique recognitions of the ways in which alternate concepts of sexual identity and family have crept (however slowly) into the American ideological mainstream.

Ritualizing the Female Life Cycle

Given the blinkered nature of contemporary American life with its sense of unmanageable terrorist, environmental, and other threats and a conservative political climate, which advocates consumerism as a panacea for anxiety and an expression of good citizenship, we should perhaps not be surprised that large numbers of Americans have come to invest deeply in ostentatious ritualizations of family life and female sexuality. In the expansion of bridal and baby culture, and in the return of celebrations of female sexual maturity such as the sweet sixteen party, we can track a certain myopic sensibility, a celebration of the present moment. In an environment of rampant time anxiety, ritualization of the exemplary events of the female life cycle serves to pin down time. Such rituals also essentialize femininity as a biological experience, reinforce the connections between femininity and domesticity, rationalize event-related consumer spending on a grand scale, and connect to the nakedly hierarchical culture that postfeminism helps to produce.

The intensified U.S. bridal industry (a $32 billion a year "wedding-industrial complex" according to Chrys Ingraham, but more recent statistics suggest this figure should be upwardly revised to about $70 billion) and the heightened prominence of weddings within popular culture targeted to women—evident in television's lavish coverage of weddings on both niche cable (in such forms as the Learning Channel's *A Wedding Story*) and the networks (the greater frequency of weddings as television special events, particularly as season enders in primetime series and in programming such as "*Today* Throws a Wedding" on NBC's *The Today Show*—as well as in the emergence of the "wedding film" as a significant strand of the chick-flick genre have massively increased their cultural purchase over the last decade. While in 1999 Ingraham could legitimately observe, "clearly, weddings have become the most watched yet 'unnoticed' phenomenon in popular culture" (8); in the past five years scholarship in such fields as sociology, cultural, and media studies on bridal culture in the United States and the United Kingdom has grown exponentially (Freeman; Geller; Otnes and Pleck; Wallace).

In a hypermatrimonial, hypernatalist culture, motherhood is presented as the next normative plateau of temporal intensity and cultural celebration. In addition to such diffuse phenomena as the publicity campaigns for mother-focused sales strategies that include Target's Lullaby Club and the emergence of stork-designated convenient parking for mothers and pregnant women at supermarkets, a variety of other direct demographic symptoms of an intensified culture of family values abound. At least one state antipoverty program the Bush administration endorses conceptualizes marriage as a social and economic diagnostic for impoverished women, and in a so-called faith-based initiative, the federal government has extended generous support to abstinence-oriented high school sexual education programs (Boo). To qualify for federal funding such programs are obliged to teach that sexual activity outside marriage is most likely to be physically and psychologically harmful—their curricula often incorporate rituals that operate as "wedding warm-ups" such as abstinence ceremonies in which purity rings are worn (Ali and Scelfo). With marriage now presented in prescriptive terms for the young and the poor, the matrimonial mystique works to occlude a variety of social, economic, and ideological problems. Most evidently, as Halberstam notes, the consistent and insistent presentation of such state-oriented, capitalist-friendly imperatives emerges out of "a post-industrial landscape where the size of white families has plummeted, where the nuclear family has become something of an anachronism and where a majority of women live outside of conventional marriages" (Halberstam 2007).

Beating, Cheating, and Transcending Time: Disordered Temporalities in Recent Cinema and Culture

From self-help books on time management to cosmetic products and technologies that celebrate "age defiance" as personal empowerment to hyped-up rhetorical and ideological formulations such as the biological clock, women in a postfeminist culture are constantly exhorted to internalize and act on a sense of temporal urgency. Increasingly, the media generate alarmist coverage reinforcing "health panics" about women's susceptibility to time problems. Are midlife women behaving too youthfully? Are girls too mature? These worries are frequently crudely scientized in reports that the average age for the onset of menses has lowered or in accounts of a wave of "adult anorexia" that strikes women at a time when they fear their sexual desirability to their husbands may be fading (Bellafante; Newsome).[2]

The sense that women in particular cannot use time properly manifested itself in sensationalistic accounts in 2006 of a nation of sleep-deprived women worn-out by their work, exhausted by the burdens of child rearing in a culture of perfectionistic motherhood, or both. In a year when the *New York Times* reported on its front page that about 42 million sleeping pill prescriptions were filled over the preceding twelve months, the sleep crisis and its associated pharmacological dependency have revived 1950s-era images of pill-popping motherhood through their installment of archetypes such as the weary mother and the Ambien Driver (Saul, A1). (By mid-2006 a popularly gendered myth about Ambien-takers imagined male corporate workers falling asleep as they drove home from the office and female users waking in the middle of the night to binge on food, a particularly worrying side effect in a postfeminist culture of intense body maintenance).

Figure 10. Cover of *Newsweek* (April 24, 2006).

A cinematic response to the contemporary time crisis can be seen in the recent rather robust cycle of time-traveling romances.[3] While the time travel plot has a long history in Hollywood films pitched to female audiences (*Portrait of Jennie* [1948], *Somewhere in Time* [1980], and *Peggy Sue Got Married* [1986]), we have seldom seen a period in which this plot formula was so ubiquitous. The perceived commercial viability of this format is suggested by the involvement of several of the most high-profile chick flick stars (Meg Ryan, Sandra Bullock, and Jennifer Garner) in films of this kind such as *Kate & Leopold* (2001), *13 Going on 30* (2004), and *The Lake House* (2006). Even as other forms of postfeminist culture seek to fix time, this form extends the promise of correcting disordered temporalities or of transcending or cheating time.

In *Kate & Leopold*, the hard-edged New York advertising executive (Meg Ryan) meets an aristocrat who has traveled from the nineteenth century through a time portal into the present. Another in the long line of chick-flick representations of disappointed professional women, Kate leads a harried life that is suggested by our first glimpse of her hounding her former boyfriend for the return of her BlackBerry. Despite her executive status, Kate is trapped in an ethos of stultifying artificiality, spending her time manufacturing desire for synthetic products such as margarine through market testing and subject to the unctuous overtures of a boss who refers to himself unabashedly as a "people pleaser." Stuck in a superficial, alienated environment, Kate is by her own admission exhausted and disenchanted, and this disenchantment culminates near the end of the film in her increasingly numb response to the news of her long-sought promotion. The time-traveling hero arrives to school the heroine in a higher level of conduct steeped in the values of decency, kindness, and care the film represents as lost in the contemporary world, and Kate is reduced to weepy appreciation of Leopold's thoughtful and considerate gestures during what he perceives as their courtship. The film's concluding scene stages the only means of respite the film can envision for its heroine—a time-traveling return to 1876 where she rejoins Leopold, giving up her contemporary life to become a nineteenth-century duchess.

In one of the most recent incarnations of the time-traveling romance, *The Lake House*, *Speed* (1994) stars Sandra Bullock and Keanu Reaves are reteamed to play Chicago-based professionals (a doctor and architect, respectively) who find they can communicate through letters even though they are apparently living two years apart. While critics who deemed the more recent film "*Speed* in reverse" were probably sacrificing accuracy for glibness, the film does indeed abandon a conventional sense of a deadline in favor of a more complex struggle for time mastery on the part of its protagonists. Debates over whether the film was logically coherent tended to be showcased in its review coverage and on the Internet, but taken in a broader context such debates very likely miss the point. A movie such as *The Lake House* does not have to be logically coherent as much as it has to harmonize with the widespread perception that in everyday life time is somehow lacking, deficient, problematic, and blameworthy. Very much in keeping with the broader postfeminist rhetoric of female temporal crisis, *The Lake House* links the struggle for intimacy to a "time problem."

There's Still Time: The New Midlife Woman and the Mature Romance

Over the last decade a new matron culture has emerged driven by the expectation that mothers keep themselves fit and attractive in what another era would have deemed middle age. Perhaps unsurprisingly, the eroticization of pregnancy is increasingly extended into the eroticization of motherhood, a trend chronicled in a 2005 *USA Today* article, "Mommie Hottest," profiling women who maintain impeccable grooming and fashion, who workout, and who in general perceive themselves and are perceived by others as highly sexually desirable. Hijacking feminist rhetoric for postfeminist ends, the article maintains, "Mom has come a long way, baby. Of course, she's far beyond the ironed and buttoned-up June Cleaver archetype. But increasingly she's also moving past the soccer-mom look of the '80s and '90s. She pays attention to trends. . . . She indulges in a nip here, a tuck there. She stays fit, even buff" (Barker 2005).[4] By the early 2000s popular culture was regularly invoking the figure of the "yummy mummy," or (less politely) the MILF (mother I'd like to fuck) in television and in popular music. Youth films from *American Pie* (1999) to *8 Mile* (2002) have also showcased the desirable mother as a staple of the coming-of-age story.[5]

In recent years, an aggressively postfeminist representational culture has intensified the sexual visibility of midlife women. Grandmothers can now be attributed with "gray glamour," romantic comedy heroines are played by female stars in their late 30s and early 40s, and as noted earlier a variety of slang terms have emerged in popular speech to designate sexually desirable mothers, feeding a popular culture that encompasses everything from pop hits to Hollywood films. As plastic surgery and other cosmetic technologies adjust the sliding scale of age-based conceptions of femininity, the correspondence between the new sexualities and the depreciating capital of female maturity deserves fuller examination.

Stephen Katz and Barbara Marshall have ably shown how contemporary lifestyle culture is shifting the meanings of aging with "market and lifestyle industries creat[ing] an idealized culture of 'ageless' consumers and active populations" (Katz and Marshall, 3). Entangled rhetorics of individual empowerment and consumer agency increasingly camouflage the diminishing of state care for the aging and vulnerable in a fantasy of age transcendence that rests, in fact, on an intensified stigmatization of those who show the effects of an aging process. As Katz and Marshall argue, vocabularies of risk and loss increasingly supplant any notion of the benefits of maturity. I am interested here in how postfeminism cooperates with "the new aging" and its emphasis on marketing, consumerism, and personal responsibility for fending off the aging process.

Fantasy constructions of the sexually seasoned midlife woman in popular culture increasingly stand alongside putatively feminist celebrations of newly expanded conceptualizations of sexual attractiveness. A recent article listing a top ten of head-turning fortysomething female celebrities included stars such as Madonna, Geena Davis, Diane Lane, and Sandra Bullock and cited the editor of *More* magazine (a lifestyle publication directed to women older than forty) informing readers, "These stars are just a daily reminder that this is how 40 looks and this is what 50 looks like. It is certainly not the way your mother looked" (Holahan). Such celebrations have to be approached with caution, not only for the way they obfuscate the class and consumer power that facilitates "age transcendence" on selective economic terms, but also for the way they so often recast the pleasures and interests of adolescent boys as culturally universal, the defining barometer of mainstream taste and judgment. (One sign of this is the midlife woman's recent appearance in a rash of male sex comedies, shown later). In her research Suzanne Leonard finds, for instance, numerous contemporary films that "rely on the teenage gaze to posit the thirtysomething woman as an object of sexual desire, a move that privileges juvenile sexual proclivities and ways of understanding over articulations of female desire or agency" (3). Indeed, the expansion of teenage litmus tests for "hotness" into middle age is one manifestation of the way that "sexual freedom can be a smoke-screen for how far we *haven't* come" (Levy 2006b, 195).

In this sort of context we can begin to explain the phenomenal success of the ABC series *Desperate Housewives* (2004–). The series extends (and possibly culminates) a discourse of "housewife chic" that has been intermittently at work in both the U.S. and U.K. media for some years. This idealized category of femininity celebrates the affluent (usually white) stay-at-home mother for her retreatism, which is to say her opting out of paid work and largely out of the public sphere in favor of a reconnection with essential femininity that is deemed to be possible only in domestic settings. The celebration of the sexuality of the thirty- or fortysomething woman that has been so central to the series' promotion is consistent with the new availability postfeminism extends to women of various ages to be youthful and girly at midlife.

One of the most striking features of the chick flick in recent years has been its extension at both ends of the generational spectrum so that it now encompasses everything from fiftysomething romances (*Something's Gotta Give*) to "tween" and teen ones. Like their younger thirty- and fortysomething counterparts, women in the fifty- and sixtysomething age cohort are increasingly expected to maintain their sexual interest and sexual desirability further into life than in previous eras. In an analysis of the recent "girling" of the older woman, Sadie Wearing has examined the rejuvenation narratives of reality television makeover series and of films such as *Something's Gotta Give* arguing that such texts "offer a fantasy of escaping (or evading) time, but one that places clearly defined limits on that escape." Ultimately for Wearing, popular culture paradoxically presents the rejuvenation of older women as "simultaneously necessary and impossible" (373).

In a cycle of recent "mature romances," romance comes as a last-minute revelation to save the female protagonist from the fate of singlehood. The comeback stardom of Diane Lane in recent years has been particularly linked to the mature romance. In *Unfaithful* (2002), Lane's portrayal of restless midlife sexuality that undoes the family drew widely favorable critical notice, while subsequent performances in *Under the Tuscan Sun* (2003) and *Must Love Dogs* (2005) highlighted the actress' characterizations of sadly disillusioned women coping with the aftermath of divorce. In *Under the Tuscan Sun*, a "tourist romance" of the kind that Hollywood produced with some regularity in the 1990s and 2000s, the protagonist's acquisition of a Tuscan villa and expatriation to Italy is the catalyst for her to reimagine her life and transition from depression to vitality. In a key dialogue line centralized in the film's trailer Lane's Frances testifies, "Unthinkably good things can happen—even late in the game. It's such a surprise." In *Must Love Dogs*, Lane's Sarah Nolan is defined by her large Irish American family and their desperate need for her to find love again. (The provocation that single femininity constitutes within a family values mindset is suggested in the film's first scene, an "intervention" Sarah's family stages to try to get to her to date although she professes not to be looking for a partner). In a set of portrayals of restless housewives and emotionally questing divorcees, Lane's persona operates to take the measure of prospects and possibilities of midlife postfeminist femininity. Through plotlines featuring adultery and divorce, the films not only underscore the problems that arise from failing to conform to the time cycle, but they also frequently make guarantees about the possibility of romance predicated on midlife viability.

Celebrity Momism, Bravura Mothering, and Motherhood as Salvation

The postfeminist celebration of motherhood reaches heights unimaginable just a generation ago. In a range of films and television programs, in journalism, and in advertising motherhood redeems, it transforms, it enriches, it elevates. In recent years both the representational and social realms have fostered the display of hypermaternity among economically elite white women. As Ruth La Ferla has written, "To judge by the latest flurry of celebrity journalism and fashion advertising, for many women in the public eye becoming a mom is not just a momentous life passage but an opportunity to shine." While the hyperprocreative family film has been revived and recycled (*Cheaper by the Dozen* [2003, 2005], *Yours, Mine and Ours* [2005]) and television magazine programs such as *Dateline NBC* regularly air adulatory features on families with multiple single-birth offspring, a conspicuous upper-middle-class "baby boom" is underway in some of some of the more affluent socioeconomic pockets of the country (Siroto). In chick flicks that stage motherhood as empowerment such as *Mrs. Winterbourne* (1996), where a homeless young woman earns a class promotion through motherhood and finds not only a wealthy husband but also a kind and caring mother-in-law, the decision to give birth is lauded as courageous and life-changing in every sense.

In a related development, film and television dramedies have repeatedly employed a crudely conventional plotline in which improvised and unexpected motherhood is foisted on the unlikely or the unwilling for their betterment. In two particular examples, the ambition of a professional woman is abruptly checked by her sudden inheritance of children. In the 2004–2005 Aaron Spelling series *Summerland*, for instance, single fashion designer Ava Gregory is living a busy life in Southern California when she learns that her sister and brother-in-law have been killed. The series originates with this event and then transitions to an emphasis on the challenges and rewards of motherhood as Ava finds herself the sudden guardian of three adolescents recently arrived from Kansas. (In this way the series regionalizes its sense of the value of traditionalism in a fashion that is reminiscent of *Providence*). In a virtually verbatim plotline (although set on the East Coast rather than the West Coast), the feature film *Raising Helen* (2004) showcases a rapidly rising junior executive in the fashion industry whose sister and brother-in-law are killed and who also bequeath to her three orphaned children.

In many of the accounts of redemptive, transformative motherhood that circulate in the popular culture landscape, women repeatedly discover themselves when they experience an immediate and powerful sense of enchantment with their newborn. In Caitlin Flanagan's *To Hell with All That: Loving and Loathing Our Inner Housewife*, for instance, Flanagan writes that she always considered herself a failure until she gave birth to twin sons at which point she was transformed: "I had, at long last, done something right" she observes in postpartum wonder (106). (Flanagan even repeatedly uses the language of religious epiphany and deliverance in describing her children's birth.) In an account such as that of Katherine Ozment writing in the *New York Times*, motherhood resolves depression and suicidal ideation. In a style section essay, the author recounts her lifelong struggle with depression and the immediate clarification of her illness on the birth of her son, noting that the first days with her child "were as much the beginning of life for me as they were for the baby he was then" (9). Susan Cheever discusses the revelation of holding her newborn in similar terms: "The moment I held her in my arms, I became a different person. You could say that I joined the human race" (40).[6]

Such configurations of motherhood as salvation are also, of course, to be found in the testimonials of countless celebrity mothers. When Britney Spears decided to make known a change in her religious status, she used her Web site to announce, "I no longer study Kabbalah. My baby is my religion."[7] Angelina Jolie has attested that adopting her son Maddox "made her a woman" (Sales, 83), while Celine Dion has sung of her feelings of triumphant self-discovery on the birth of her son Rene-Charles. The commercial crossover possibilities of motherhood are apparent in the Dion's hit, "A New Day Has Come," which underscores the creative concept name for the star's Las Vegas show while linking her reemergence after a professional hiatus to the rejuvenating effects of motherhood. The song's lyrics include the lines:

> Where it was dark, now there is light
> Where there was pain, now there's joy
> Where there was weakness, I found my strength
> All in the eyes of a boy.

In advertising directed to women, private motherhood is often symbolically, commercially universalized. In 2003 DaimlerChrysler paid Dion about $14 million to sponsor a broadcast of the star's "A New Day" concert on CBS, to have her appear in print and broadcast ads, and to make public appearances (Kiley). The ads tended to explain and source Dion's music as expressive of a broad maternal sensibility; for instance, as part of the campaign Dion cuddled her son while riding in a Chrysler minivan to the strains of "Have You Ever Been in Love?" Dion's bid for status as universal mother was further substantiated by a series of Anne

Geddes photos that paired the star with a variety of ethnic and racially marked babies whose racial otherness was meant to contrast with Dion's whiteness (in some of the photos the babies wore colored caps so that their "hair" would match the star's outfit and in one case this required an infant to appear to have green hair). This spiritualized presentation of the infant as style accessory and Dion as "global maternal" carried a specific commercial valence given that Dion had recorded a CD of lullabies called "Miracle," which had been cross-promoted on an episode of the *Oprah Winfrey Show* (titled "Miracle Babies") in which the two stars cooed over infants born prematurely.

In a similar vein, new narratives of female celebrity benevolence often draw on public knowledge of a star's maternity, suggesting that their capacity to feel for others in need is an extension of a full humanity facilitated by mothering as was the case in Dion's emotional pleas to support the victims of Hurricane Katrina and in Jolie's ongoing efforts to draw attention to third-world poverty. The lionization of motherhood in celebrity representations always teeters on the brink of open exploitation in which children are crudely presented as forms of capital. At the August 2006 Emmy Awards, celebrity swag bags included T-shirts by the clothing company I Dream of Johnny that read, "My Bling Is My Baby," and for infants and children, "I'm the Bling."

The social currency of motherhood in postfeminist culture is hinted at in the extension and application of the term "mom" well beyond the family context in which it originated as a shortened and informalized version of "mama." Ben Yagoda has recently argued that "'mom' is indisputably the word of the moment in the culture at large," citing the more than 320 million Google hits on the word as opposed to 192 million for "dad" and the more than 3,000 books with "mom" in the title on the Amazon Web site. Yagoda draws attention to a subtle but significant change in the social usage of "mom," with the term now self-applied by a large number of women (as in "I'm John's mom," or "Speaking as a mom") and increasingly used in reference to particular women by people outside their families ("How's your mom?").

"Mom," with its casual and intimate connotations, gives off the impression that maternal status now factors outside the family to an increasingly greater extent. Demographic categories such as "soccer mom," political ones such as "security moms," and terms such as "working mom" (whose warm sound would seem to alleviate the rampant ideological uncertainty about how this state is to be achieved) seem to reflect an understanding that the sentimentalization of motherhood is universal. As Yagoda aptly observes, "mom" is the ideal term for a postfeminist era for "it finesses the feminist challenge to American motherhood. . . .

It cannot be a verb. It's just an identity, something we all seem to be looking for these days."

Roberta Garrett has noted, "the 1990s could be characterized in the history of reproductive technology as a decade in which the institution of motherhood was publicly declared in crisis. Since the birth of the first test-tube baby in 1978, pregnancy's categorization as a 'natural' act has been contested medically and scientifically" (167). The terror that new technologies might shift the burdens of parenting and blatantly contradict the "self-evident" fact that mothers should be the natural priority (and near exclusive) caregivers of children helps to explain the emergence of the new bravura mothering in which postfeminist motherhood is equated with ultimate clarity and the will to achieve or endure. Flanagan concludes her book by relating her battle with breast cancer and concluding an account in which her own doubts, fears, and uncertainties are continually emphasized by stating confidently, "Here's what I know: When I woke up from the final surgery, I didn't want to see the article I've written or the editors I've worked for. I wanted to see my sons and my husband. And I wanted to go home." (2006, 239) Such certitude is very much in the mode of Oprah Winfrey's sloganistic, "What I Know for Sure," the title of her closing column in each issue of *O* magazine and a mantra the star is careful to synergistically repeat from time to time on her television program. Such formulations appear to cut through postmodern ambiguity and ambivalence, giving credence to female intuition as a higher order epistemology.

Temporal disorder and maternal righteousness are dramatically brought together in a film such as *The Forgotten* (2005) in which heroic supermother Telly's (Julianne Moore) capacity to connect with her son and sustain his memory empowers her to defeat a vague supernatural conspiracy that is testing whether parental love can be eradicated. Although nearly every logical sign shows Telly that her son is dead, the film's commitment to the power of private maternal certitude is such that she will move heaven and earth to recover him, leading to a joyous reunion at the film's close. With mothers now called on to cultivate every iota of talent in their children, to protect them from the predators that are imagined to be all around, to guard their health (particularly in terms of the new food allergies, asthma, and other ailments on the rise), and even (in an increasing number of cases) to bear the full burden of their education through homeschooling, cinematic narratives of bravura mothering may well register as realistic no matter how fantastical the genre in which they appear. Under the new bravura terms of motherhood, mothers are not only cast as expert decoders of all human behaviors but they are also frequently depicted as higher level readers of illness and disability.

In recent years media reports on the autism epidemic in the United States have frequently included a crusading supermother who not only attends to her child's needs but also interprets her autistic child's value to society as a whole. The strains of such an interpretation are sometimes in evidence as in a 2005 *USA Today* profile of a family in which five of six children suffer from autism. The piece chronicled in detail the challenges of everyday life in such a family and the father's sense of stress and anger, but concluded with the children's mother attesting, "They're here to teach me something I'm sure" (Jayson, 9B). While such accounts of interventionist and advocate mothering embed a disturbing romanticization of disability, they nevertheless are grounded in a recognition that without advocacy, educational and social systems may well overlook and disenfranchise the disabled. In the new social constructions of autistic and other disabled children who are spiritual beacons to their mothers, families, indeed their communities at large, mothers are important social intermediaries. Stories of this kind emerge from a cultural milieu in which femininity is resanctified by its association to children as "angels," figures of purity and innocence in a corrupt world.

The new terms on which motherhood is enobled are not just ideological; they are of course economic as well. After all, the display of hypermaternity among elite white women is both a form of conspicuous consumption and a rationale for it. The supersizing of American cars and houses has taken place in exactly the era in which as Susan J. Douglas and Meredith W. Michaels observe, "the new momism has become the central, justifying ideology of what has come to be called 'postfeminism'" (24). In this period not only has the ante been substantially upped on what are considered consumer "necessities" for babies and children, but a large luxury market for children, babies, and mothers has also sprung into being that scarcely existed before.[8] As one commentator has observed (although somewhat ungrammatically) "many upwardly mobile parents have grown to accept that their child needs $1,000 cribs, $800 strollers and $30 booties for infants who cannot walk" (Chura, 6). It is important, then, to bear in mind all the ways that "family values" operates as a consumerist script.

Conclusion

The various manifestations and permutations of postfeminist hegemony with regard to time and aging proscribe heterosexual female identity in punishing and heavily regimented ways. As I have argued, postfeminist culture keynotes a set of themes deemed central to contemporary women's experiences and concerns and one of the most striking recurrent elements is the celebration of a New Age flexibility in which traditional distinctions between youthfulness and adulthood are seen to be dissolving (even while the disapprobation accorded to the "aged" female body has intensified). Postfeminist media culture aggressively tropes femininities with a predilection for typologizing them into (a frequently extended) girlhood or maternity. Age friction is certainly a regular feature of postfeminist representational culture with countless contemporary chick flicks depicting the older female professional as a bad woman, an antirole model for the protagonist and a figure of calculation, deceit, and insecurity, thus doubly defying postfeminist precepts that insist on demographic propriety and the dichotomization of women's experience into premotherhood and motherhood.

Postfeminism has fully restored the (only very slightly dented) respectability of the young woman/older man couple through such legitimizing discursive terms as "trophy wife" and "starter marriage" and indeed has turned of late to celebrating the virility of the senior citizen patriarch (Freydkin).[9] Other paradigms of retromasculinity currently circulating include the harem style male patron (Hugh Hefner) and the swinging male bachelor (even if lightly critiqued as in the *Austin Powers* franchise [1997, 1999, 2002] and recent remake of *Alfie* [2004]).[10] Meanwhile other aspects of the popular culture landscape reveal the intransigence of paradigms of disgust and moral condemnation with regard to midlife female sexuality "run amok." For instance, the romance of the older female teacher/male student has become an overreported template for moral panic by U.S. broadcast media; the standard-bearer here is the now decade-old case of Mary Kay Letourneau, the Seattle elementary-school teacher who fell in love and had two children with her young student, a case that has maintained an unlikely longevity in print and broadcast journalism. Meanwhile public scandals over older women–younger men relationships such as the case of Debra Lafave, a Florida schoolteacher charged with having sex with a 14-year-old student, continue to be featured with some regularity.[11]

Postfeminist representational culture is acutely age conscious; a variety of chick flick fictions from *Bridget Jones' Diary* (2001) to *13 Going on 30* and *Sex and the City* (1998–2004), which even in its cancellation exerts strong cultural influence, have shown themselves to be exceedingly precise about the ages of their twenty- and thirtysomething protagonists. Meanwhile, the cult of youth is being technologically facilitated on a variety of fronts with myriad reality television shows dedicating themselves to rejuvenating transformations and the fantasy that aging can be managed away through plastic surgery, exercise, and diet. By emphasizing rituals that anchor and mark time, by fictionally highlighting the experience of temporal dislocation, and by promising that commodity culture can erase the impact of time, popular culture operates as a zealous timekeeper for women. Ritualizations attendant to sexual maturity, marriage, and motherhood have risen in prominence as women are cued to understand that "exemplary time" is biological, emotional, and consumerist. A new exhibitionism of pregnancy and motherhood may work to compensate a generation of women raised with feminist expectations for the actual setbacks in women's public stature and labor force status.

Even as it hyperidealizes marriage, pregnancy, and motherhood, postfeminist popular culture links all three to various archetypes of time-beset femininity. In this way women are subject to a contradictory discursive complex of exhortation and reproach with regard to how they spend, manage, or "defy" time. Postfeminism can seemingly celebrate some women for their time victories while (implicitly or directly) castigating others for their failures. This account of the strict ideological control postfeminism seeks to maintain over the female life cycle and its pervasiveness in popular culture reminds us of the considerable impediments in place that prohibit a productive "queering" of the heterosexual economy of dominant representational paradigms.

Notes

1. Barker (2004) notes a trend toward young celebrity brides indicating "a recent spate of nearly child brides" among film, television, and popular music stars.

2. Bellafante reports clinicians who attribute the rise of eating disorders and overexercise among midlife women to "not just anxiety about aging, but a fear of aging in a culture that is 20 years into a fitness obsession" (4) and a culture where "the cultural pressure to look 23 at 45 has never been so palpable" (9).

3. Worth noting, too, is the ubiquity of time-travel themes in popular print fiction as well, as exemplified, for instance in the best-selling *The Time Traveler's Wife* (soon to be adapted into a film).

4. That the postfeminist maternalization of femininity rests on race and class privilege is suggested by the urban slang term "baby mama," which points toward the kind of mothering experience of which postfeminist culture is strikingly unaware—the single black mother.

5. They certainly did not do so in strictly uniform ways, although (not surprisingly) a threat of Oedipal anxiety runs through the majority of such films. In *8 Mile*, Rabbit is deeply troubled by his mother's sexual relationship with a man his own age and one of his rap lines refers to sleeping with a competitor's mother. Worth noting is that Kim Basinger has also played older women involved with younger men in both *L.A. Confidential* (1997) and *The Door in the Floor* (2004).

6. Cheever's account gains greater depth than the others I cite here as she reflects on the hostility she experienced toward other people's public selfishness

as parents, her complete disregard for such feelings when she herself became a mother, and her subsequent regaining of such resentments as her children grew toward adulthood.

7. From www.britneyspears.com, May 15, 2006.

8. In Flanagan's well-known 2004 *New Yorker* article, "Bringing Up Baby," she notes that "Americans spend six billion dollars a year on gear for their babies" (46) and chronicles a variety of high-end strollers, baby monitors, cribs, and even baby wipe warmers.

9. Freydkin notes the late-in-life fatherhood of Larry King, Rod Stewart, and Donald Trump, all of whom in 2005 were parents of five or six children and had either very young families or babies on the way. In this context, also worth noting is a high-profile Hollywood film currently in preproduction entitled *Father Knows Less* starring Dustin Hoffman as a man whose trophy second wife leaves him, forcing him to call on the children of his first marriage for help in raising the children from his second.

10. While my focus here is on postfeminist conceptualizations of normative femininity, there would be much to say as well in regard to new conditions of normative masculinity and the heightening and de-stigmatizing of social discourse regarding male sexual capacity. In her study of the socioeconomic impact of Viagra, Meika Loe provocatively contends that "since Viagra's debut, 'normal sex' in America is more and more narrowly defined and difficult to achieve. Then again, normal sex is a seeming requirement for normal personhood" (19).

11. Levy (2006a), discusses the recurrence of stories about female teacher/male student sexual involvement in the media.

10

KEVIN HEFFERNAN

"Are You Saying My Son Is a Bitch Boy?"

The Perilously Achieved Hegemonic Masculinity of Ben Stiller

IN THE 1996 UPN TELEVISION SPECIAL *Star Trek: 30 Years and Beyond*, actor Ben Stiller, then transitioning from television star to Hollywood leading man, found himself speaking to host Ted Danson about his own life as a longtime *Star Trek* fan. "When I was a kid they called me a nerd," he proudly declared. "But now, here I am—on stage with Kenny G and the cast of *Star Trek*! Who's the nerd now, huh?!" This declaration of redeemed masculinity, both defiant and ironic, points to some of the most remarkable elements that came to characterize the star persona of Stiller in numerous Hollywood romantic comedies in the years bracketing the new millennium. The romantic comedy, whose narrative and ideological goal is the formation of an ideal heterosexual couple out of two opposed, bewildered, antagonistic, and far from ideal characters, allows the tentative and embattled masculinity of Stiller's characters to assume, pretend, reject, embrace, and flee multiple guises of heterosexual desire. Also, the intersecting plotlines of the romantic comedy place the relationship between Stiller and his inamorata in juxtaposition with other forms of sexual desire, some idealized, some pathological. The hitchhiking serial killer in *There's Something about Mary* (1998), the bickering Jewish step-parents in *Flirting with Disaster* (1996), the J. Crew–clad WASP couples in *Meet the Parents* (2000), and the sociopathic lothario in *Your Friends and Neighbors* (1998) all hold the mirror up to the Ben Stiller "nerd" as he pleadingly, angrily, cautiously, and impulsively struggles to assume the mantle of straight male privilege.

These two elements, the transformation of the comic protagonist into a suitable romantic partner and the plot's series of doublings and parallels are among the defining elements of the tradition of New Comedy, which begins in the ancient world with the Greek Menander and the Romans Plautus and Terence. New Comedy was a reaction against the scabrous social satire and ebullient grotesquerie of the plays of Aristophanes. For the animalistic desires that drove the protagonists in Aristophanes, Menander substituted a desire for monogamous heterosexual union. Many of his stock characters and plots are still with us, from the misplaced letter (or MCAT scores) to the harsh father and romantic leads' wisecracking confidant(e)s. It is also present at the birth of the modern sensibility in the plays of Shakespeare and threads through the work of Wycherley, Congreve, Musset, and Marivaux before forming the dominant mode of romantic comedy the classical Hollywood cinema and its poststudio variants employed.[1]

But the New Comic transformation of "Ben Stiller" into a fitting heterosexual partner to the female lead can only be experienced in relation to other, queered sexualities against which he struggles for recognition. The more he struggles against them, the more he needs them to define himself. In his 1995 book *The Invention of Heterosexuality*, Jonathan Ned Katz recounts:

> In 1923, "heterosexuality" made its debut in Merriam-Webster's authoritative New International Dictionary. "Homosexuality" had, surprisingly, made its debut fourteen years earlier, in 1909, defined as a medical term meaning "morbid sexual passion for one of the same sex." The advertising of a diseased homosexuality preceded the publicizing of a sick heterosexuality. For in 1923 Webster's defined "heterosexuality" as a "Med." term meaning "morbid sexual passion for one of the opposite sex." Only in 1934 does "heterosexuality" first appear in Webster's hefty Second Edition Unabridged defined [as] a "manifestation of sexual passion for one of the opposite sex; normal sexuality." Heterosexuality had finally attained the status of norm. (85)

The trials the Ben Stiller character must undergo in pursuit of this norm are remarkably consistent across four very different films. Mel Coplin in *Flirting with Disaster*, Greg Focker in *Meet the Parents*, Ted Stroehmann in *There's Something about Mary*, and Jerry in *Your Friends and Neighbors* each must perform (in Judith Butler's sense of "gender as performativity" [24–25]) repetitive assertions of masculinity, which inevitably lead to violent competitions with other characters over who is the better heterosexual male. But because, as Butler demonstrates, no stable identity undergirds these performative acts, the stage fright and self-hatred both Stiller's character and those around him experience is often funneled into rage. Here, forgetting one's lines in the high-stakes heterosexual war of words and actions (or *agon*, in the phrase of ancient Greek and Roman drama) becomes synonymous with actively exhibiting queer sexuality. Finally, each film is loaded with jokes exposing the absurdity of what Michael Warner (1999) has termed "male heteronormative behavior." Competition, the white, middle-class order that has always constituted a crucial component of "normal" heterosexuality, the mentor relationship, and the ideology of "bro's before ho's," inevitably explode in the faces of the films' characters. But the joke is not always on the same character, and each of these films takes a highly distinctive view of the crippled masculinity on display and what it means.

Magnanimous in Victory: *Flirting with Disaster* and the Heteronormative Family

Flirting with Disaster, written and directed by David O. Russell, tells the story of Mel Coplin (Stiller), a thirty-year-old first-time father who is unable to name his male son or have sex with his spouse because he is haunted by questions of his origins, never having met his birth parents. His Jewish adoptive parents, Ed and Pearl Coplin (George Segal and Mary Tyler Moore) are horrified and threatened by his search, his wife Nancy (Téa Leoni) struggles to be supportive, and recently divorced Tina Kalb from the adoption agency (Patricia Arquette) is documenting Mel's process of reunion as part of her doctoral dissertation. Of the four films, only *Flirting with Disaster* is obsessed with procreation, the biological process that has historically born much of heteronormative ideology on its rickety legs. The film begins with Mel's voice on the soundtrack imagining what his mother could be like as we see women in their sixties on the streets of Manhattan illustrating his speculations, from the idealized to the grotesque. A similar accelerated montage accompanies his speculations on his father (a shirtless, mentally ill street person seems the most likely candidate at one point), and finally we see an even more frenetic montage of all of the women with whom Mel could have possibly married and started a family. "The mystery of your unknown self is about to unfold," states the leggy, elegant, and glacial Tina Kalb as the computer spits out the (incorrect) name and address of Mel's birth mother, Valerie Swaney of San Diego.

"Why is he doing this—*Roots* thing? Weren't we good enough parents?" asks a tearful Pearl Coplin before Mel departs for San Diego. Her anxious question brings to the foreground another key aspect of conflicted masculinity at the heart of Stiller's work in the romantic comedy, namely the contradictions inherent in whiteness itself. In *Gender Trouble*, Butler elucidates the complex and shifting historical backgrounds against which gender is performed and finds that race and class markers have been paramount in costuming the charade. *Flirting with Disaster* constantly conflates Mel's discomfort of social class markers with his ill-fitting heteronormative suit. The cocktail swilling, Sunbelt Republican Valerie Swaney (a framed charcoal portrait of Ronald Reagan hangs in her foyer); former biker, truck-driving Fritz Boudreaux (he greets Mel first with a vicious attack then with an affectionate, "You little shit! Look at this turd face, Mitch. This is my son!"); and the seemingly ideal WASP Schlichting family all represent various guises and experiences of whiteness that the clueless Mel attempts to adopt and accommodate. "This is amazing. I've never shared physical traits with family before," he states to Valerie. Ed and Pearl Coplin, the high-strung Jewish adoptive parents provide yet another model of whiteness for Ben to assume: "They gave you kind of a Hebe look, kid," says Fritz's friend Mitch right before Mel's disastrous truck-driving lesson.

During Mel's first two failed reunions with mistaken parents Valerie and Fritz and later in the cross-country journey to New Mexico, he is taken for a pervert, a weakling, and an androgyne. Valerie's impossibly beautiful twin daughters, Jane and Sandra, searching for a family resemblance between Mel and their kin, remark that he bears an uncanny similarity to their Uncle Freddie, currently in jail for fraterism, the act of rubbing up against people in public places. His bout of Indian wrestling with Tina in the Swaney living room sends him careening into Valerie's glass case of knickknacks. Later, on the "muy macho" Gundall, Michigan, home turf of Fritz Boudreaux, Nancy's concern for the baby's safety during Mel's truck driving lesson is immediately met by Fritz with, "Are you saying my son is a bitch boy?" and Mitch chimes in, "He's pussy whipped." In one of the film's many parodies of patriarchal masculinity, Fritz attempts to teach Mel to drive his rig, and the lesson leads to the destruction of the tiny Gundall post office.

The introduction of agents from the Bureau of Alcohol, Tobacco and Firearms, Paul Harmon and Tony Kent in the next scene exponentially increases Mel's anxiety. Paul and Tony, revealed as a bickering gay couple when they take Mel and Nancy to dinner, comprise one of the film's richest comic elements. Tony is a former high school classmate of Nancy's, a handsome former football player who will prove to be comically, grotesquely, and absurdly well-informed about breastfeeding, circumcision, and infant care throughout the film's middle acts. As the wildly inappropriate attraction between Mel and Tina Kalb blossoms, so does the desire between Nancy and the bisexual Tony. The nervous, bitter "fifth wheel" Paul openly speculates about the imminent tryst between Tony and Nancy, and when his company proves unbearable to the two of them he is asked to ride in the other car with Mel and Tina, to whom he angrily refers as "illicit couple number two."

At a roadside bathroom break, Nancy loses the keys to her rental car, and the two couples are forced to ride in the same cramped Ford Taurus. Now the threat Tony poses to Mel takes on multiple, reinforcing, and contradictory elements. First, Tony is the next in a line of masculine role models against which Mel may fail to measure up. He is athletic, handsome, and has an encyclopedic knowledge of the many bewildering skills incumbent on a new father. Child care is not Tony's only field of expertise, however. "Nancy mentions that you have some problems around the issue of oral sex," Tony blurts out to Mel, who sinks behind the steering wheel. Tony suggests humming to relieve the stress: "That really helps me to relax and enjoy the fellatio." When Mel suggests changing the topic, Nancy accuses him of homophobia and listens with interest to Tony's revelation that he does not enjoy anal sex. As Mel winces and wishes he were somewhere else, Paul helpfully chimes in, "Nancy's just testing the risk factor for sex with Tony, Mel."

When the foursome finds their destination, Antelope Wells, they find it has been closed due to radiation poisoning (ironically, the very thing the paranoid Ed had warned them about), Paul and Tony are forced to accompany the Coplins all the way to the home of Mel's birth parents, Richard and Mary Schlichting (Alan Alda and Lily Tomlin). Mel is beside himself and imagines introducing them to his parents by saying, "Nancy invited these two gay guys just for fun." A justifiably offended and angry Tony responds by calling Mel "neurotic guy," and the escalating argument leads to Tony standing inches away from Mel asking, "Do you want to get intimate? Is that what you're saying?"

The home of Richard and Mary Schlichting, a historic Queen Anne structure seemingly transported slat for slat from Pacific Heights in San Francisco to the middle of the New Mexico desert, appears to provide Mel with an almost idealized origin. The lachrymose hugs of Valerie Swaney and the vicious attack of Fritz Boudreaux are nowhere to be found in Richard and Mary's welcoming of Mel into their home: They quietly and with great warmth and dignity shake his hand and invite the entire retinue in for dinner. For once, the class and education markers of heteronormative masculinity appear to be working in Mel's favor. Then, Mel shudders when Richard gestures to the off-screen group and asks matter-of-factly, "Is this some kind of swapping thing you have going?" As Nancy and Tony retreat upstairs, the Schlichting's sullen and rage-filled son Lonnie serve Mel and company dinner , and Lonnie spikes Mel's dinner with a massive dose of LSD, but the repressed Paul is moved to Mel's chair and consumes the drugged quail. The film then intercuts the adulterous fumblings of Tony and Nancy—he asks if she would like to take a shower together, and she responds, "Okay, let me go get my shower cap"—with Richard and Mary's telling Mel the story of giving him up for adoption after they were arrested for dealing LSD in the 1960s. Paul begins to feel the effects of the LSD, and under the stress of this experience, Richard, Mary, and Lonnie are revealed to be yet another resentment-filled, argumentative, neurotic heterosexual family.

In this most classical of New Comedies, the dutiful parents Ed and Pearl show up at the Schlichtings' house just as the family flees for Mexico on Paul's attempts to arrest them while he is freaking out. The forces of heteronormative order reach maximum instability at this point with a tripping federal agent, imminent adultery, and Jewish parents busted for drugs because a mistaken switch of cars, another New Comic plot staple, leads to the police discovering the Coplins with huge quantities of LSD in the trunk of their car just as Mel discovers Nancy and Tony together engaged in the unusual foreplay technique of armpit licking. Mel finally decides to "stop this craziness," and the chastened protagonist listens to Nancy's stipulations for their continued relationship, including the naming of their son. Pearl and Mel are released from jail on the intervention of Paul and Tony, and the final image before the credits roll is a cracked "family portrait" of the Coplins, Mel and Nancy, and Paul and Tony standing outside of the police station. Pearl remarks to Ed, "I think those two are homosexuals." Ed chimes in, "And they want to adopt a kid. That's so sick," to which Pearl replies, "Can you imagine the neuroses that child will be exposed to?"

In the war over heterosexuality, *Flirting with Disaster* represents a magnanimous and sympathetic look at the universal human experience of feeling unworthy, anxious, alone, and afraid; it also points to the necessary (but often deeply unsatisfactory) palliative role sexual and family relationships play in people's responses to this feeling. The character of Mel, by turns earnest, deceptive, selfish, sympathetic, credulous, and skeptical, desperately seeks some model of heterosexual masculinity on which to base his own tenuous patriarchal authority, exemplified in this film by the naming of his son. The other relationships that swirl and pulse around him increase rather than diminish his sense of disorientation and loss, until he finally makes peace with the imperfections in his adoptive parents, his marriage, and ultimately himself.

Pax Romana: Meet the Parents and Proving Your Masculinity

An entirely different economy of heterosexual desire and patriarchal authority suffuses *Meet the Parents*, which Jay Roach directed. Like *Flirting with Disaster*, *There's Something about Mary*, and *Along Came Polly*, *Meet the Parents* pairs the high-strung, verbose, and diminutive Stiller with an idealized blonde *shiksa*, in this case Pam Byrnes, a New England–born schoolteacher played by Teri Polo. Stiller's character, Greg (né Gaylord) Focker, a male nurse in Chicago, spends a weekend among the lush fall leaves of suburban New England and the WASPs who live under them to ask permission to wed Pam from her possessive, suspicious, and paranoid former CIA agent father Jack, played by Robert de Niro, another in a long line of threatening New Comedy father figures. On the same weekend, Pam's sister Debbie is marrying "Dr. Bob" Banks, an accomplished second-generation surgeon, in a highly formal backyard wedding ceremony. The mere presence of the outsider Greg, the suspicion this arouses in Jack, and Greg's wildly inappropriate attempts to impress Jack result in the physical destruction of almost every symbol of the traditional heterosexual wedding over the course of the nightmarish weekend. Again, the Ben Stiller character finds himself both in (largely unwanted) competition with other heterosexual men and as an unwilling repository of motivic and character traits the film explicitly codes as characteristic of queer and other "aberrant" sexualities.

Meet the Parents begins with Greg, dressed in surgical scrubs, earnestly, almost tearfully proposing to his off-screen love, ending his plea with, "Will you marry me?" An eyeline match reveals the listener to his proposal, a bedridden old man, who answers, "Yes." We then discover that he is practicing his proposal to the patient, who praises his gentle touch even as Greg attempts to remove a catheter from him, prompting him to emphatically beg, "No, no," an outburst that Greg interprets as wise counsel to a question about marriage he has asked.

Figure 11. Jack (Robert DeNiro) gauges the appropriateness of Greg/Gaylord (Ben Stiller) as his daughter's fiancée in *Meet the Parents* (2000). *Author's personal collection.*

In the same way that Mel Coplin must compete with the handsome, tattooed Tony in *Flirting with Disaster*, so Greg Focker must enter into various arenas of heterosexual, masculine struggle. In addition, his Jewishness further marks him as an outsider: Pam's former fiancé Kevin (Owen Wilson) regales him with stories of the centrality of Christian faith in his life, and Pam's brother Denny's derisive observation that Gaylord Focker is "not a normal name, ya know?!" refers to Greg's status as both ethnic and sexual outsider. In this, Greg is exemplary of the twin outsider groups David Lugowski described earlier in this volume—gay men and Jewish men both capable of "passing" and under pressure to do so. Throughout the weekend, the impossibly white, impossibly WASP alpha male surgeons, former CIA men, and Wall Street investors react with barely concealed contempt for Greg's profession as male nurse. Kevin hosts the rehearsal barbecue, and his tall, blonde WASP good looks; fabulous wealth from investing in biotech futures; athletic prowess (we see numerous photographs of him skiing with Pam); woodworking skills; and implied sexual stamina (Pam characterizes their past relationship as "a stupid sexual thing") provide a model of straight male sexuality up to which Greg can never hope to measure. Lent a swimsuit by Kevin, Greg hesitates in the bathroom, terrified to put on the Speedo thong. Emerging virtually naked, Greg is drawn into a Kennedyesque game of highly competitive water volleyball and is contemptuously called "Florence Nightingale" by the world famous surgeon and father of the groom Larry Banks when he misses a shot. Anxious to prove his mettle, Greg viciously spikes the ball over the net and accidentally breaks the nose of bride-to-be Debbie. When Jack finds out that the lost beloved family cat Jinxie "found" by Greg was a fake from the local animal shelter, Greg attempts to beat Jack home by driving Dr. Larry's sports car. This results in a hilariously incongruous scene of street racing between father and hopeful son-in- law, the angry and fretful Greg hissing, "You wanna play, Pops? Let's play."

But Greg's masquerade is unsuccessful. He is dogged throughout the weekend with evidence of his insufficient straightness. His birth name, Gaylord, he had changed to Greg after what the movie implies was savage harassment by grade school classmates. His escalating lies about owning cats and growing up on a farm inexplicably result in Jack's suspecting him of bestiality in the form of trying to milk female cats. Worst of all, the airline has misplaced Greg's bag, which contains the engagement ring he bought for Pam. When the (wrong) bag is finally delivered to him at the Byrnes house in yet another mistaken identity plot element from Roman New Comedy, he assures the increasingly suspicious Jack, "There's something in this suitcase here that I'm planning to give her which I think symbolizes the level of my commitment to her." Later secretly picking the suitcase lock in the guest bedroom, Jack finds leather lingerie, a whip, and worst of all, a "Canadian Mountie" strap-on dildo.

Greg's attempts to simultaneously track down the escaped cat Jinxie and sneak a cigarette on the roof results in a massive fire, which destroys the backyard trees and Kevin's ornate carved altar ("or choppa [*sic*] as you might call it," he says to Greg). His flushing of the downstairs toilet, violating Jack's direct orders, causes the septic tank to explode, covering the backyard and all of the wedding rehearsal participants with the collected feces of the Byrnes family. Later, a stray cat Greg has substituted for the missing family pet eats Greg's nicotine gum and destroys Debbie's wedding dress in its drugged frenzy. The mirth all this destruction brings to the audience is based in both Greg's humiliation as an outsider to all these august institutions and in a nihilistic delight at the spectacle of Jack's meticulous plans destroyed in rising flames, the rage of a drug-crazed stray cat, and a tide of human waste.

Unlike *Flirting with Disaster*, however, *Meet the Parents* treats the supposed masculine deficiencies of "Ben Stiller" as simple misrecognition. We know that Greg Focker is a loving, loyal, and supportive partner to Pam and is respectful of the traditions of East Coast WASP courtship, even though they are as bewildering to him as they would be to a recent arrival from another planet. The more he attempts to demonstrate his worthiness, the more he seemingly reveals himself as an effeminate, duplicitous, pot-smoking, Godless pervert, leading to his ultimate ejection from the Byrnes home as he is unmasked as a "gay fucker": Here, heteronormative patriarchy offers unqualified support and acceptance to those worthy of its embrace, and much of the subversive force of the movie's satire is contained by our knowledge that the most of the jokes are on Greg, who we know, after all, is "normal."

A characteristic element of classical New Comedy is character transformation through conflict and distress, and both Greg and Jack undergo change in the wake of the destruction wrought by Greg over the course of the disastrous weekend. Greg realizes that his efforts to impress Jack as worthy of his daughter are doomed to failure, and Jack comes to understand that his controlling and paranoid behavior is a curse on the two women he loves. These dynamic male characters are set off from the largely static, constant women who circle around them, and the reconciliation between Jack and Greg resolves the narrative conflict in *Meet the Parents*. Jack learns from a fax from Greg's parents that he scored high on the MCAT exam under the name "Gaylord," and Jack uses his patriarchal authority to reunite the couple in the film's final act. When Greg is detained at the airport after his violent outburst on the return flight to Chicago, Jack "takes over" the investigation of him at the airport security center. He holds Greg's arms, monitoring his muscle movement and pulse as a "human lie detector." Finally, Greg answers all of his questions honestly and unself-consciously, and Jack accepts his responses. Then, replaying the same-sex marriage proposal from the opening of the film, Jack presents Greg with his own engagement ring and asks, "Greg Focker, will you be my son-in-law?"

The film ends with the orgy of heterosexual iconography characteristic of endings in New Comedy. Greg proposes to Pam, and Debbie and Dr. Bob are married in the Byrnes's backyard. The bride and groom kiss, the assembled guests applaud, the Byrnes and the newly engaged Greg and Pam look on and smile, and a craning camera reveals flowers covering the charred altar, the wounds to the institution of heterosexual marriage beginning their process of healing. The ending of *Meet the Par-*

ents resolves the war over heterosexuality in a magnanimous *Pax Romana*, extending membership to the unconventional but suitably normal Gaylord Focker in exchange for his pledge of constance and obedience.

Guerilla Warfare: *There's Something about Mary* and "New Old Comedy"

There's Something about Mary, directed by the Farrelly Brothers, was the breakout box-office hit which established Ben Stiller as a versatile and distinctive leading man and catapulted Cameron Diaz to first rank of movie stardom. It is also one of the most subversive romantic comedies yet to emerge from the New Hollywood. Stiller plays Ted Stroehmann, a grown man still obsessed with his high-school crush, Mary Jensen (Cameron Diaz), with whom he had one interrupted date at the senior prom. Following the advice of his friend Dom (Chris Elliott), Ted hires Pat Healy (Matt Dillon), a sleazy private investigator, to track down Mary hundreds of miles away in another city, where she is a successful surgeon and cares for her mentally challenged brother Warren (W. Earl Brown). The duplicitous Healy then begins to court the beautiful Mary despite the warnings of her bookish, disabled friend Tucker (Lee Evans). During its middle two sections, the film juxtaposes Mary's relationships with the three men, Healy, Tucker, and Ted. She talks about (but we never see) two of her previous boyfriends, the kind and supportive Brett and the deranged stalker Woogie, whose threatening behavior had forced her to change her name and move to a different city. After his progress with Mary is blocked both by Tucker's warnings and her deepening relationship with Ted, Healy discovers that Tucker is Norm Phipps, a fully able (although emotionally arrested) pizza delivery boy still living at home with his parents. Then, he reveals to Mary that Ted hired a private investigator to track her down. In an astonishing, literally farcical climax, every male suitor Mary has ever had bursts into her living room at once: Healy and Norm demand that Mary choose between them, and a newly chastened Ted admits defeat. The stalker Woogie is unmasked as Ted's friend Dom, who had used Ted to find Mary's new identity and address. Finally, the mysterious Brett appears and is revealed to be NFL All-Pro quarterback Brett Favre, who quietly and earnestly professes his love for Mary in some of the most wooden line readings ever delivered by a muscular nonactor outside of a gay porn film. Ted leaves the apartment in tears, and Mary chases after him, realizing in his willingness to give up his obsession with her as the sign of true love.

"I'm not a stalker," Ted defensively asserts to Healy early in the film. In fact, his actions and psychological profile reveal just the opposite.

We never see or even refer to his parents or any event from his life that precedes his obsession with Mary. He remains the humiliated high school boy whose sense of himself rests entirely on possessing the unattainable romantic object, and he uses stealth and deception to find her and gain her trust. At the core of Ted's obsession is an almost bottomless self--hatred, which incessantly replays itself in images of castration, deficient masculinity, and the most humiliating expressions of same-sex desire. The defining moment of Ted's life is his humiliating genital trauma in Mary's bathroom on the night of the senior prom, eventually led away in an ambulance with both his "franks" and "beans" caught, bleeding and strangled, in the zipper of his rented tuxedo. This moment is reprised when he unwittingly finds himself caught in the middle of a huge bust of dozens of male couples engaging in anonymous sex at a roadside rest area and is led away in a paddy wagon, this time captured for a live television audience on an episode of *Cops*. Earlier, he had given a lift to a hitchhiker who, we find out, was a serial killer with a dismembered body in his duffle bag. Interrogated by the police, he believes himself facing charges of picking up a hitchhiker when in fact he is under suspicion for murder. His matter-of-fact answers to the questions asked by the investigating officers enrage the cops, who believe themselves in the presence of an unapologetic and murderous sociopath. When Dom eventually bails Ted out of jail, he is discovered spooning with a frightening, tattooed prisoner on the bottom bunk of his cell. As in *Meet the Parents*, the queer sexuality with which the Stiller character is associated is of the most threatening kind, in this case anonymous public sex and the often coercive and brutal sex of the homosocial prison environment.

The two main antagonists in *There's Something about Mary*'s masculine arena are Ted and the private investigator Pat Healy. Early in the film Healy calls Ted a stalker, and Healy's discovery of Mary in Miami Beach signals the beginning of the film's second act. Healy is Ted's most serious rival for Mary's affection, and Ted's ultimate realization that he is no different from Healy forms the basis of his redemption. At the beginning of the film, we watch the school-age Ted gazing longingly at Mary from afar, and his point-of-view shots, combined with the swirling romantic music, emphasize his infantilized, almost de-sexualized adoration of her. Healy expresses the omnipresent other side of this "pure" rapt voyeuristic pleasure, eavesdropping on Mary's conversation with her friends, guffawing at her private joke about her vibrator, and spying on her with binoculars as she undresses upstairs in her bedroom. Healy narrates his own porno film starring Mary as lounge music plays in his head and he snarls, "Here comes the money shot," when she begins to unhook her bra. Heterosexual male viewers are both complicit in this act of voyeurism and smugly superior to this cretinous degenerate and his actions. Reaching for higher power binoculars, Healy zooms in on the upstairs window. The music stops, and he (and the viewer) see an extreme close-up of obviously prosthetic sun-scarred breasts, which we then see belong to Mary's roommate Magda (Lin Shaye). A quick reframe shows the barest glimpse of Mary's breast as she pulls on her T-shirt and the lounge music resumes on the soundtrack. Ted's look of aroused astonishment precedes a slow fade to black, and the film's main romantic rivalry has been established.

These and other scenes in *There's Something about Mary* revel to an extraordinary degree in animal physicality and infantile erotic desire. At times, the narrative's emphasis on courtship and comic transformation of the protagonist seems to struggle with the upswelling of these more grotesque elements, reflecting the influence of a strain of male-oriented, "gross-out" comedies of the 1970s and 1980s such as *Animal House* (1978), *Caddyshack* (1980), *Porky's* (1981), and the Farrelly Brothers' own earlier films such as *Dumb and Dumber* (1994) and *Kingpin* (1996). According to William Paul, these films look back to the pre–Roman Old Comedy plays of Aristophanes in their exuberant immersion in body processes and equally enthusiastic deflation of both authority figures and sentimentality (85–112). In *There's Something about Mary*, Ted's courtship of Mary initially proceeds in just the sentimental and chaste fashion Aristophanes mocked in *Lysistrata* and *The Birds*. However, he is eventually forced to confront the physicality of his attraction to Mary in humiliating moments throughout the film. His genital injury from the zipper on prom night is later replayed when Magda's dog, Puffy, crazed from amphetamines Healy administered, flies across the room and viciously clenches Ted's crotch with her teeth. Then, in the signature moment of the film, he takes the advice of his scheming friend Dom—another burlesque of the male mentor relationship—and masturbates before his date with Mary because, Dom asserts, in his post-orgasmic state he will "think the most like a chick." The copious ejaculate, in another film genre the ultimate expression of masculine power and virtuosity, winds up, unbeknownst to him, dangling from his ear, and Mary, believing the substance to be hair gel, uses it to spike her bangs up over her head in a hideous parody of 1980s hair design.

Providing musical interludes and acting as Greek chorus to the story is singer and songwriter Jonathan Richman, an eccentric musical figure who became a sort of poet laureate of dweebs, nerds, and losers. Fronting a constantly changing group of musicians under the name Jonathan Richman and the Modern Lovers in the 1970s and 1980s, Richman transposed the three-chord rock and slice-of-life lyrics of his idol Lou

Reed to the world of the suburbs, substituting for Reed's New York stories of drug addiction and sexual paraphilia lyrics about the ice cream man, supermarket logos, and pride in New England. Performing directly into the camera from various locations in the film just out of eye and earshot of the characters, Richman is shot to death in the film's final moments by Magda's boyfriend Herb (Herbie Flynn), who was aiming his hunting rifle at Ted because he, too, was obsessed with Mary.

Even more outrageous than the movie's premise of a romantic comedy told from a stalker's point of view is the complete absence of anything like a healthy model of heterosexual masculine identity anywhere in *There's Something about Mary*. The figure of Brett is an impossible masculine ideal who exists only to underscore the wounded pathology of Mary's other suitors, and what a grotesque lot they are. Dom (also known as "Woogie") became so threatening to Mary that she took out a restraining order on him and changed her name. His current life of suburban normality (he has beautiful children and a devoted wife who fellates him as he drinks beer and watches *Cops* on television) is intolerable to him. As the movie progresses and he gets closer to Mary, he erupts into almost leper-like boils and skin lesions. Norm (also known as "Tucker") was so obsessed with Mary that he badgered a friend into beating him with a baseball bat to become one of Mary's surgical patients. Healy pretends to be an architect who dreams of retiring to Nepal and living a life of quiet contemplation.

In the battle over heterosexual desire, *There's Something about Mary* is characterized by guerilla warfare. With the exception of football star Brett Favre, the film has no uniformed troops, no chain of command, and no military training. Nowhere is there a workable model of heterosexual male desire for the characters to emulate, modify, or even reject. The male characters are trapped in a perpetual adolescence of uncontrolled ids and wounded egos, and their neurotic sense of incompleteness is associated with physical infirmity and degeneration, from Ted's mangled genitals to Norm/Tucker's disability (first very real, deliberately self-inflicted with a baseball bat, then pathetically although convincingly faked) to Dom/Woogie's rash, twitches, and Job-like boils.

Scorched Earth: *Your Friends and Neighbors* and the Absence of Heterosexuality

Your Friends and Neighbors, written and directed by Neil LaBute, is a more cerebral variation on conventions of the romantic comedy as tweaked by Woody Allen and others in films such as *Hannah and Her Sisters* (1988) and *Husbands and Wives* (1992). None of the characters is mentioned by name in the film, underscoring the almost-allegorical status they hold as "typical" middle-class Americans the title implies. Also, the story unfolds in relentlessly, flawlessly, depressingly upscale surroundings with the six principals decked out in the trendiest urban fashions; living in elegant urban digs; and eating, drinking, and trysting at the nicest hotels, bars, used bookstores, and art galleries.

The unifying thread of the story is a question making the rounds of the loosely affiliated group of six protagonists, "What was your all-time best fuck?" Barry (Aaron Eckhart) is married to Mary (Amy Brenneman), but he can only sustain an erection while masturbating (his "all-time best," he confesses, has always been himself). Mary is so bewildered by the question that she undertakes a freelance article to ask other women for their responses. Jerry (Ben Stiller), a college theater professor, is living with Terri (Catherine Keener), an advertising copywriter, and the two are friends with Barry and Mary. At the conclusion of a Sunday afternoon visit, the seemingly shy and owlish Jerry asks the sexually unsatisfied Mary for her number, and shortly thereafter, the two begin an affair. Terri, who has long been annoyed by the verbose and self-centered Jerry, meets Cheri (Nasstasja Kinski) at a local art gallery and the two begin to meet afternoons for wine and lovemaking. Barry's friend Cary (Jason Patric) is a cold, rage-filled misogynist who verbally harasses their mutual friend Jerry and who confesses, in the film's most famous scene in a gym steam room, that his "all-time best" was during the gang rape of a younger male high school classmate years ago. Eventually, the two heterosexual couples shatter, Jerry begins to sleep with one of his female students, Barry is no longer even able to arouse himself, and Mary and the frightening Cary lie in bed, expecting a child together.

Like LaBute's previous film, the Sundance–award winning *In the Company of Men* (1997), much of the dramatic power of *Your Friends and Neighbors* lies in its stark, quietly effective performances with scenes shot on location in an unobtrusive style, reflecting LaBute's background in theater. Specifically, *Your Friends and Neighbors* draws on English Restoration comedy, in particular William Wycherley's *The Country Wife* (1675), a play that Jerry is staging with his college class. The pervasive cynicism and selfishness of the characters in Wycherley's play, along with the seeming ubiquity of adultery, is expressed in a line that could well serve as an epigraph to LaBute's film: "Keeping a cuckold company, after you have had his wife, is as tiresome as the company of a country squire to a witty fellow of the town, when he has got all his money."

In this play-within-a-play, Ben Stiller plays Jerry who plays Mr. Horner, a libertine who pretends to be newly impotent and disdainful of the company of women to gain trusted access to numerous married and engaged women in the days surrounding the wedding of Mr. Sparkish and Miss Alithea. Of course, Jerry himself has learned to play the role of the shy, sensitive bookworm, a cloak under which he hides his lustful, aggressive, and territorial designs. (He woos Mary by musing, "Shakespeare is a gift, really.") The "best fuck" discussions among the men become yet another arena of masculine competition, and Jerry refuses to play until the end of the film. Sporting a graying goatee and owlish glasses (perhaps a disguise to protect the more likeable "Ben Stiller" comic persona), Jerry would rather discuss sexual matters with seeming Olympian detachment in front of his students, one of whom plays the title character of Wycherley's play and with whom he is sleeping at the film's conclusion. But like Mr. Horner (and like every other male character in the film), his heterosexual desire is knowable only through its negation in impotence, emasculation, and "aberrant" sexual practices. We first see him simulating anal sex onstage with the student in rehearsal crying out Mr. Horner's line, "I'll get into her the back way and so rifle her for it," and soon the film cuts to a scene of anal sex between Jerry and Terri as he acts out the desire aroused in him by rehearsal, mouthing hilariously incongruous erolalia such as, "That's it, baby, absolutely. . . . You and I are in complete harmony." Then, during his second hotel tryst with Mary, he is unable to sustain an erection. As she stares into space incredulous about repeating her unhappy history of sex with Barry, he pleads, "This is not me. I'm much more hard and firm than this!" She shakes her head and puts her wedding ring back on. The eventual fate of his relationship with Terri is, of course, threatening to his masculinity on multiple levels. She is obviously unsatisfied with the verbose anal sex he prefers, and his failure as a lover and partner drives her, in his eyes anyway, into the arms of another woman.

If Ben Stiller's Jerry represents the supposedly "sensitive" male and Aaron Eckhart's Barry the putative "regular Joe," Jason Patric's Cary is the unyielding remorseless alpha male whose motto is "revenge fucks are always the best" and who brings out the worst in the characters around him—Jerry tells Barry, "Whenever we get together with this guy it's like somebody slipped you an asshole pill." The self-hatred and wounded masculinity at the core of Cary's personality has been siphoned into a boiling rage at women and "pussy" men. He has a particular aversion and hostility to women's reproductive capacity. We see him in his hospital scrubs miming football moves with a detachable fetus model while asking a colleague about a woman he plans to date; later, when that woman gets her period on his "three-hundred-eighty thread count" bedsheets, he screams at her and accuses her of doing it on purpose while she cowers in the bathroom. As he uncoils on her, he stands in front of an expressionist painting of a dimly lit, blurry figure howling in agony. Later, when pressed on the question of his "best lay" in the gym's steam room with Barry and Jerry, he quietly and fondly remembers Timmy Carter, a younger boy in high school who had told the gym teacher of the older boys' misbehavior. The older boys then cornered Timmy in the abandoned boys shower and raped him. Cary grows sentimental telling the story, referring to the rape as "making love" as Jerry and Barry look on, speechless. At the end of his story, he takes a sip of water and muses, "It's never been like that with a woman." After this door into the abyss has been quietly shut, Cary and Barry badger Jerry about his answer to the question. When the subject of Terri's "femininity" is brought up, Jerry loses his temper and says to Barry, "The best fuck I ever had? That'd be your wife." He turns and leaves the locker room, Barry is dumbfounded, and Cary matter of factly states, "That beats my story."

At the end of the film, Jerry's production of *The Country Wife* is in dress rehearsal, and Barry comes by to speak to him. The two men sit together, the supposedly normal Barry in his business shirt and tie, the fey Jerry in full English Restoration foppery, with wig, powdered face, and beauty mark. Then, with the "best fuck" contest fought to a bitter draw, the denouement finds Jerry in bed with the still-silent undergraduate student, sneaking off to the bathroom to call Terri. Terri is in bed with Cheri, refusing to answer her entreaties to speak. Barry is in bed by himself, unable to sustain an erection with a phone sex operator, and Cary and Mary are expecting their child. These characters and their fates bring us back full circle to Webster's 1923 definition of heterosexuality as "morbid sexual passion for one of the opposite sex."

I have tried to show that the star persona of Ben Stiller in one genre, the romantic comedy, relies for much of its kick on the contradictions inherent in the popular cinema's articulation of heterosexual masculinity in the new millennium. Specifically, these movies highlight the performative nature of heterosexuality and delight in peeking behind the mask at the void underneath. The Hollywood star system, which has always emphasized the carefully crafted, highly individualized serial performances of actors, now must find a way to unite narrative conventions as old as drama itself, such as masculine struggle, anxiety about the body, the threat to the social order desire poses, and the channeling of desire into acceptable expression with the begrudging acknowledgment of a proliferation of sexualities that threaten to render much of the romantic comedy quaint and anachronistic. The Ben Stiller persona has been very successful in holding these seemingly opposite tendencies in dynamic equilibrium. This comic persona varies widely in the uses it can serve, from the existential everyman in *Flirting with Disaster* to the oddball under the big tent in *Meet the Parents*. Darker undercurrents of the embattled straight man are found in *There's Something about Mary* and, in a sort of limit text, *Your Friends and Neighbors*. Each of these films in its own way demonstrates the symbolic centrality of alternative sexualities to the experience, even the very definition, of heterosexual desire in contemporary popular culture. The minefield of "deficient" or "aberrant" desire on display or hinted at in these films is now a part of the landscape even the most unreconstructed hetero male must carefully tread. Not that there's anything wrong with that.[2]

Notes

1. For a discussion of comedy in the ancient world, see Hunter.
2. I have stolen the punch line of this chapter from Wiles, who inspired many of the approaches I have taken.

11

Allan Campbell

"Fuck Boy Meets Girl"

Heterosexual Aspirations and Masculine Interests in the World of Quentin Tarantino

> When I'm getting serious about a girl, I show her *Rio Bravo* and she better fucking like it.
>
> —Quentin Tarantino (Wild, 133)

NOT WIDELY IDENTIFIED AS GAY OR bisexual, Quentin Tarantino is hardly what most people would call a queer filmmaker, but the representations that constitute him and his work render heterosexuality nominal and somewhat elusive. His actual sexual orientation is less relevant here than the interpretive possibilities that come from a range of representations organized by both his stardom and his direct participation, dealing with what Chris Straayer has called the sexually hypothetical, a description she uses when making homoerotic inferences about characters in films, but which at the same time renders assumptions of heterosexuality fragile and suspect (9–22). This chapter analyzes the public representations of and by Tarantino in terms of their disjunction between heterosexual aspirations (the prospect for sex and romance between the sexes) and masculine interests (pursuits that traditionally have tended to unite men and leave women behind), a contradiction exemplified in the epigraph by the standard he holds for his ideal "girl," who simply must like his favorite Hollywood Western to be worthy of him.

Tarantino's world casts heterosexual romance as an unsuccessful rival interest to rituals associated with men, especially but not exclusively involving acts of violence. Male protagonists give way to female protagonists in the later films, but the preoccupations and priorities remain surprisingly constant, different sexes but similar kinds of homage to male-identified culture and genres with heterosexual fulfillment seldom a basis for narrative closure. Media coverage, of which the writer-director has been a willing part, tends to enhance those themes, focusing on a bachelor with a huge film library and many fond boyhood memories.

Indeed, more than any other American director since Woody Allen, Quentin Tarantino's celebrity is a key component in the intertextual relations that shape the reception of his films. The widely known video-clerk-makes-good story of his life underscores the obviously citational aspects of his movies, the self-conscious rummaging through popular culture's past, which in turn suits his often loud, hyperactive personality, sometimes featured in the role of a passionate fan, a version of himself. Unlike Allen, however, Tarantino has never played the lead in his own movies, and besides small roles in *Reservoir Dogs* (1992), *Pulp Fiction* (1994), and the *Death Proof* portion of *Grindhouse* (2007), his on-screen exposure has been elsewhere—cameos in other people's films, guest-starring roles on television, a brief stint as a judge on *American Idol* in 2004, and, of course, many talk-show appearances, including one on a special 2006 Oscar-night edition of ABC's *Jimmy Kimmel Live* in a year when he had no nominations. The extras that can be accommodated on digital versatile discs have the potential to give him an opportunity to be seen and heard more directly in his own work, inevitably granted with the releases and rereleases in that format.[1] His availability to the media also has assisted in the marketing of him as a prominent auteur, as has, to a lesser extent, the publication of his screenplays (Tarantino 1994, 1997, 2000a, 2000b, 2000c, 2007). While scholarship on him has been infrequent, one university press has collected some of the press coverage in a book for its *Conversations with Filmmakers Series* (Peary), putting him in the company of canonical favorites such as Allen (Kapsis and Coblentz),[2] Jean-Luc Godard (Sterritt), and Alfred Hitchcock (Gottlieb).

Because the director has yet to identify himself as part of a historically oppressed group, that canon's non–gay-identified white-male hegemony can assimilate the likes of Tarantino without the worry of relegation to a ghetto of special interests or area studies.

Yet unlike his forebears, Tarantino came to prominence as a filmmaker when that hegemony was undergoing some considerable challenge. His debut film, *Reservoir Dogs*, was released at a time when some have perceived, both then and in retrospect, as "a watershed year for the independent gay and lesbian film and video" (B. Ruby Rich, 164), enough to merit the term New Queer Cinema. With a dozen years hindsight, Peter Biskind has written about Tarantino's impact on independent cinema with his first motion picture:

> Despite the success of *Poison* (the 1991 Todd Haynes film), the New Queer Cinema peaked in 1992, almost as soon as it began. There were many reasons for this, but not the least of them was that Tarantino had stolen its thunder. (*Reservoir*) *Dogs* was as unsettling as *Poison*, without having to shoulder the queer baggage. (121)

Biskind sees Tarantino's first completed feature as "an anti–art film art film, a canny amalgam of outsider and insider art" (121). At least on the surface, it can be described as an apparent retreat from the queer moment found not only in independent film at the time but also in film scholarship addressing issues of power and ideology. Yet even if the texts surrounding Tarantino are not gay exactly, to what extent can they be characterized as heterosexual?

As Dana Polan has pointed out, little academic writing has been done on this filmmaker, especially when compared to the several volumes on him that trade publishers have produced and to the many Web sites fans have created (2000, 7–18, 64–65). In one scholarly intervention, Sharon Willis places Tarantino's films within what she calls "a hyper-oedipalized play with popular culture artifacts" that "embed[s] a nostalgic reading of the 1960s, through 1970s popular culture versions of masculinity," which displace the historical struggles of blacks, women, and gays (66–67). In a subsequent analysis, this time focused almost solely on *Pulp Fiction*, A. Samuel Kimball uses the dialogue and descriptions from Tarantino's published screenplay as a guide to the picture's salient points of interest, arguing that the filmmaker's figurative emphasis on certain body parts underscores the homophobic development of the film's narrative, particularly the notorious rape-revenge scene, which enables one of the male characters (the appropriately named Butch) to reunite with his female lover, Fabienne. Backing off from such heavily determinate readings, Polan himself suggests that *Pulp Fiction*'s eclectically stylistic pastiche renders deep engagement with the film's content almost beside the point. Letting a description of the ending almost speak for itself, Polan concludes his monograph by writing:

> Amazed bystanders. Two hip guys who can maintain cool (even with inappropriate dress). Style winning out over substance. This is how the film ends. More than any explicit message, this is the point of *Pulp Fiction*. This is why it's a phenomenon. (2000, 86)

But in distancing himself from interpretations that "see the film as hiding some real political issues" (7), he risks minimizing the concerns that give rise to these readings.

These scholars all make valuable points, and Willis offers hers as part of an ongoing dialogue in and about ideological struggle, where I hope my own intervention can make a productive and progressive engagement. Sharing her and Kimball's political concerns, I am in awe of their wide-ranging look at the films' more reactionary implications, but I nevertheless want to focus on the world of Tarantino in terms of its ideological contradictions, which, despite the extras featured on DVD releases of his own films, is perhaps best exemplified by the writer-director's cameo in someone else's movie—*Sleep with Me* (1994), a contemporary homage to queer film criticism, as delivered by one man to another about an action movie in the aftermath of a failed heterosexual courtship.

Dating Pauline and Fucking Elvis

The texts surrounding Tarantino—the early ones more directly, the later ones in a more displaced fashion—call attention to what Eve Kosofsky Sedgwick (1985) has described as the male homosocial discontinuum within heterosexist patriarchy, whereby men are torn between alliances with other men and sexual obligations with women. *Top Gun*, the deceptively conventional 1986 action film directed by Tony Scott, was released on DVD in 2002 with few special features, but Tarantino's diegetic interpretation of that film in *Sleep with Me*, issued in a similarly skimpy DVD in 2004, functions as a revealing supplement sold separately.[3] Playing the screenwriter Sid, hanging out at a party thrown by two of the film's principal characters, Tarantino suggests to another man that *Top Gun* should be celebrated for its "subversion," arguing that its progression of a nominally heterosexual romance is predicated on Kelly McGillis's character dressing like Val Kilmer's Iceman to win over Maverick, the protagonist Tom Cruise plays, and enthusiastically points to the film's "real ending," where Kilmer and Cruise warmly offer each other the chance to be his wing man.

In his analysis, Kimball reduces Sid's interpretation to an epigraph and only quotes the portions that describe the indecision of Cruise's character between homosexual and heterosexual object-choice, a selective transcript that implies a continuation of the same homophobia the scholar finds in *Pulp Fiction*. Although Kimball wants to present Tarantino's sexual politics as overdetermined, his cameo in *Sleep with Me*, at least as much as the media coverage or the supplemental features of some of the DVD editions of his own films, calls for a more dialectical consideration, one that further illuminates the contradictory dynamics of gender and sexuality found not only in *Top Gun* but also in the representations that cumulatively make all that is "Tarantino."

The filmmaker's cameo appearance in *Sleep with Me* itself exemplifies the disjunction between his heterosexual aspirations and his competing masculine interests, as Sid's conversation with another man is occasioned by his failure to connect romantically with a female guest. His remark, "Fuck boy meets girl," can be seen both as exasperation with the banal cliché of heterosexual romance in Hollywood cinema and as expressed disappointment in his failure to hold a woman's interest just moments earlier, even as the sudden opportunity to discuss action films with another man provides some compensation. Both men gleefully quoting lines from its ending, their shared passion for the Hollywood action movie gives them a bonding moment.

Tarantino's feature-length commentary on the 2002 DVD release of *True Romance* (1993), which *Top Gun*'s Tony Scott directed from the young writer's early screenplay, helps push sexual ambivalence to the forefront. The pre-credits sequence of the film features the male protagonist Clarence failing to pick up a woman at a bar after he asks her to see some action films with him, a Sonny Chiba triple feature, and then soon after the opening credits are over, he meets up with another woman, Alabama, who is willing to accommodate his interests in popular culture totally, introducing herself at the theater featuring the action movies, kissing him at the comic-book shop, and sleeping with him near some noticeable pictures of Elvis Presley in his bedroom, all before their marriage the next morning. While overall a stark contrast to that amazing hookup, what is striking about the film's opening scene is he and the first women find their one momentary emotional contention when admitting their mutual willingness to sleep with Elvis Presley (subsequently played in the film's platonic fantasy sequences by Val Kilmer, the aforementioned representative of "the gay way" in *Top*

Gun). The subsequently published screenplay here matches the film's dialogue nearly verbatim:

> I'd watch that hillbilly [Elvis] and I'd want to be him so bad. Elvis looked good. I'm no fag, but Elvis was good-lookin'. He was fuckin' prettier than most women. I always said if I ever had to fuck a guy . . . I mean *had* too [*sic*] 'cause my life depended on it . . . I'd fuck Elvis. (Tarantino 2000c, 5)

On the DVD, Tarantino's commentary track first reveals that he originally made that confession as an actor in his early, unfinished film *My Best Friend's Birthday*, and goes on to tell us that the main male character in *True Romance* was largely based on him at the time he wrote the screenplay, particularly in terms of his limited experience with women. When the narrative moves to the theater where Alabama aggressively pursues Clarence, Tarantino points out that this moment in a supposedly Detroit cinema was actually shot at the Vista in Los Angeles, which he informs the viewer, years ago used to screen pornography for gay men. What is fascinating about this historical aside is that pornographic film venues often serve as cruising grounds for men who want to pick each other up (similar to some restrooms, if not the one where Cruise's Maverick first propositions McGillis's character in *Top Gun*). In *True Romance*, a man with masculine interests—action movies and comic books, not to mention the chance for easy sex—finally has the opportunity to meet the right woman, even if she is not Elvis.

The 2002 DVD release of Tarantino's directorial debut *Reservoir Dogs* shares its feature-length commentary with several contributors to the film and provides three brief commentary tracks from professional film critics on select scenes. Only one character in that film, Mr. Pink, is explicitly marked as gay, being called a homophobic epithet after he protests the name he has been assigned, and only responding to the remark by asking if he instead could be called Mr. Purple (an approximation of lavender). During the feature-length commentary, Tarantino says that he originally intended to play Mr. Pink himself, but was impressed enough with actor Steve Buscemi's work, particularly his performance in the film *Parting Glances* (1985), where Buscemi also happens to play a gay character, that the director instead gave the role to the acting veteran. The most prominent human bond in the picture, however, is between two other male characters, Mr. White and Mr. Orange, the former willing to kill his fellow accomplices to save the other's life, the latter feeling finally obliged to come out as an undercover cop.

Despite Sid's confident queer reading of *Top Gun* in *Sleep with Me*, Tarantino in the commentary track for his own film declines to discuss "subtexts," perhaps as an artist's prerogative, but he does discuss the film's commercial breakout success by contrasting it with what else constituted independent cinema at the time—what he calls "Sundance 'save the farm' regional films and Sundance gay films"—and says that ordinarily a successful independent film is what plays more than a week at the Sunset 5, which happens to be a West Hollywood multiplex that screens many explicitly gay pictures. Still, two of the critics on the DVD spend considerable time discussing the relationship between Mr. White and Mr. Orange. Amy Taubin suggests a sadomasochistic bond, which she also describes as loving; Emanuel Levy thinks their tenderness is similar to that between a father and a son, but in outright rejecting the hypothesis of a homoerotic bond, he nevertheless makes that issue explicit. The third critic, Peter Travers, notices Mr. Orange putting on a wedding band before he goes out to meet the criminals and wonders whether the character might be married or divorced. An unspoken question is whether the ring is part of his cover, heterosexuality as a meticulously crafted identity.

What particularly distinguishes *Reservoir Dogs* as an independent film, suggests Tarantino on the DVD, is its emphasis on violence rather than sex, a claim that can be extended to his other films. Among the rare moments of sex in Tarantino's work, *Pulp Fiction* features the initiation of subsequently off-screen oral encounter between Butch and Fabienne, but Butch's attention to her is soon diverted by his need to risk his life retrieving a watch passed down among generations of men, all but Butch (who instead becomes a boxer) having served in war overseas. Butch's female lover, Fabienne, forgets to pack the watch for their getaway, not understanding its significance to men handing it down to one another and, in some cases, hiding it up the ass for safekeeping, at least according to a surviving war veteran, who served with Butch's late father.

A memento of male camaraderie and an apparent rival to Fabienne, the watch's hiding place intimates both the possibility of homoeroticism and a barrier denying its more explicit realization, foreshadowing a homophobic scenario when Butch and his momentary adversary Marsellus, whom he just earlier tried to knock off with his girlfriend's automobile, are kidnapped by other men wanting to rape them. After he breaks free from captivity, Butch decides not to return immediately to Fabienne but instead to go back and save Marsellus, already being anally penetrated by one of his captors. After careful deliberation over weapons with which to strike, Butch chooses a long samurai sword, a phallic instrument to end the explicitly sexual assault by other men against Marsellus, who, after Butch kills the other captor, ultimately shoots the rapist in the crotch. The brutality against the captors that enables Butch to return to Fabienne also allows for a truce with Marsellus, provided that Butch says nothing about his former enemy being literally fucked, an alliance between the two men based on explicit disavowal of homosexuality.

Yet the uneasy heterosexist resolution of this segment, Butch and Fabienne riding away on the shot rapist's "chopper"—a term that recalls the samurai sword that he uses to rescue Marsellus—hardly provides the terms of the entire film's narrative closure. While the reunion of the couple is the last of its chronological events, *Pulp Fiction*'s non-chronological narrative reaches its conclusion with the decision by another character in the ensemble cast, Jules, to leave the underworld and go on a series of adventures by himself, with the martial-arts television Western *Kung Fu* (1972–1975) serving as his model. A man's romance with male-identified popular culture renders any other kind secondary.

Besides his films, biographical disclosures in the media signal heterosexual pursuits as a low priority for the writer-director. In an early book on Tarantino, film critic Jami Bernard describes his brief courtship with fellow filmmaker Alison Anders as one involving invitations to play board games and alphabetize videotapes but not much in the way of sex:

> "I can tell you that he's a good kisser. A very good kisser," says Allison. "And that, yes, he talks about movies during the make-out session." (218)

Since then, Tarantino has been linked with other female celebrities, including actress Mira Sorvino (the inspiration for the Mighty Mighty Afrodite Productions credit in *Jackie Brown* [1997]) and comedienne (and self-described "fag hag") Margaret Cho, although he is on the record denying any romantic involvement with his muse, Uma Thurman (at least according to the web entry "Quentin Tarantino—Wikipedia, the free encyclopedia"). Yet with the possible exception of Thurman, no particular relationship with a woman has made a significant contribution to his star image.

If one turns to the aforementioned *Interviews* book (Peary), one can find an annotated list of Tarantino's favorite films (Wild, 133–135), which includes the director's revealing comment about his ideal women having to share his fondness for the Western movie *Rio Bravo* (133). Preserved for posterity in the university publisher's anthology, the 1994 *Rolling Stone* profile that precedes the list hints at the alternatives to him not meeting the right woman with what can be called its either loaded or coded descriptions of the filmmaker:

> [Tarantino on Madonna and her song "Like a Virgin":] "She signed my *Erotica* album: 'Dear Quentin, it's about love, it's not about dick. Madonna.'" [And then in the very next sentence, one reads:] In *Sleep with Me*, Tarantino nearly steals the show with a cameo as a partygoer lecturing passionately on the homosexual subtext of *Top Gun*. (127)

> Tarantino—who doesn't have a girlfriend at the moment and who has apparently failed to develop the habit of having torrid affairs with his actresses. . . . (133)

> Tarantino, who was thanked by Kurt Cobain in his liner notes. . . . (133)

Granted, Tarantino can be lauded as quite professional for not becoming too emotionally involved with anyone at work, and while Madonna and Kurt Cobain have courted both public sexual ambiguity and gay fans, heterosexually identified men also buy their albums, and the shared status of all three as celebrities can be said to help put them in contact with one another. Still, the writing about Tarantino here is suggestive, especially the nearly redundant description of his abode—"Tarantino's West Hollywood, California bachelor apartment" (124–125). At the same time, the filmmaker's lack of public response to the piece betrays none of the defensiveness that one would expect from the likes of Cruise or Kevin Spacey. A 1996 interview from *Details* magazine provides Tarantino's reaction to being told that he is the subject of gay rumors: "Really? That's cool, man. I totally dig it" (Udovitch, 174). Of course, given the original publication context, maybe he was just aware of the market he would have been addressing; or perhaps he was too involved with his stated primary love to care. Years later, Quentin Tarantino told *Entertainment Weekly* that his dream date on a desert island would be the late film critic Pauline Kael, born more than forty years before him, "if we'd have enough movies to watch and talk about" ("QT's Dream Team," 28). In such a fantasy scenario, the hypothetical coupling between the sexes does not require heterosexual consummation, just a mutual fondness for similar cultural artifacts.[4]

While Tony Scott's *True Romance* includes a sex scene, Tarantino generally has shied away from depicting much in the way of sex in the films he has directed himself, especially since *Pulp Fiction*. Adapted from an Elmore Leonard novel with his longtime idol Pam Grier—an action film veteran from the blaxploitation era—in the title role, *Jackie Brown* shows Tarantino stretching out with a strong female character, but it is telling that another woman, the one featured in the film's brief sex scene, ends up killed. Based on an original screenplay, *Death Proof*, Tarantino's contribution to his and Robert Rodriguez's double-feature *Grindhouse* homage, elaborates on the terms of victim and victor. All the female characters in *Death Proof* converse with one another about heterosexual romance, specifically the need to hold out on gratifying male heterosexual desire until trust and the stability of a true relationship seem sufficiently promising. The first group of women stalked by serial killing driver Stuntman Mike all die, their lack of vigilance foreshadowed by one woman being successfully dared into giving her future killer a lap dance, the most erotic scene—comparatively, and without any nudity—in a film that otherwise relegates sex to dialogue, and, perhaps unsurprisingly for Tarantino, the one not seen by U.S. audiences until the film's release later that year on DVD. In the theaters, it was substituted with the intertitle "Missing Reel," but after Arlene already agrees to do it. In both versions, we see her fatal end.

In addition to being even more chaste on-screen, the second group of women depicted in *Death Proof* are luckier than the first, in part because two of them are stuntwomen themselves and, not so incidentally, fans of the car-chase suspense genre that they diegetically inhabit. Four women in the film industry temporarily in rural Tennessee, Kim and Zoë (the latter played by real-life stuntwomen Zoë Bell, who had earlier worked as Uma Thurman's stunt double during the filming of *Kill Bill* [2003–2004]) speak fondly of action films, while "pretty young starlet" Lee and Abernathy—"(makeup and hair)"—to crib descriptions from the published screenplay (Tarantino 2007, 80)—instead express preference for romantic teen comedies such as John Hughes' *Pretty in Pink* (1986). Deciding to ride in a white 1970 Dodge Challenger (the same kind, it is acknowledged, as the one featured in the 1971 film *Vanishing Point*) with "the cool kids"—that is, with the stuntwomen wanting to live out traditionally masculine fantasies—the otherwise seemingly feminine Abernathy eventually joins self-described "gearheads" Kim and Zoë in dealing the final fatal blows to their would-be killer. Earlier in the film, Lee, wearing a cheerleader's outfit (hints of a more explicitly sexualized film genre from the 1970s), is last seen left behind with the car's male owner, whom Abernathy has intentionally misled to expect sex from her in the effort to convince him to let the other three take the car unsupervised. That, of course, leaves Lee and the car owner unsupervised. The superimposed words "The End" over the shot of the three women prevailing over Stuntman Mike provides no reassurance about Lee's undisclosed fate. For once, *Death Proof* is a film directed by Quentin Tarantino with a chronological plot.

True Romance's male protagonist Clarence, who has sex with Alabama, would have faced death if Tony Scott kept Tarantino's original ending. In Scott's version of the earlier film, the male protagonist survives with the loss of an eye—the symbolic value of which would find its way back into Tarantino's own later work—and also the appearance of an acceptable male object of his love, a son named Elvis. For all the talk about dating men, the relationship between action-film buffs Zoë and Kim in *Death Proof* hints briefly at other possibilities, the latter agreeing to let the former do stunts with the borrowed Challenger in exchange for these favors: "You crack my back, you give me foot massages, and after a shower, you put moisturizer on my butt." Yet Kim's gun, which she calls Roscoe, seems her most constant companion—indeed the one that marks the key turn in the women's battle with Stuntman Mike. With its female protagonist reduced to a single kiss with her bail bondsman before skipping the country without him, *Jackie Brown*'s most erotic moment arguably comes during the diegetic showing of the infomercial *Girls Who Love Guns*, bikini-clad female beauties alternating between the firing of artillery and sliding their hands across the phallic objects they profess to adore. The two volumes of *Kill Bill* take their cue at least as much from that moment in *Jackie Brown*, albeit with weapons more an extension of the subject than a possible fetish object, as they do from any of the human relationships in Tarantino's other films.

Father Roles and Secret Identities

Kill Bill can be seen in many respects as the culmination of Quentin Tarantino's preoccupations. Split into two volumes, released months apart, the film's nominally heterosexual matrix, the female protagonist initially identified as the Bride, unfolds to suggest an Oedipal conflict, with protégé assassins of either gender serving as sons, and their masters as family heads. Assuming the name Arlene, the Bride even introduces Bill to her new suitor Tommy as her father, an ostensible cover that pushes subtext up to the surface. Moreover, the Bride's real name is Beatrix Kiddo, by whose apt surname Bill calls her. Besides its leader, the only male member of the Deadly Viper Assassination Squad is a blood relative of Bill's, and the inscription on his sword—a samurai sword recalling the one used in the rape-revenge scene from *Pulp Fiction*—draws a fine, if wobbly, line between homosocial desire and another kind of bond between men, "To My Brother Budd, The Only Man I Ever Loved.—Bill." The brothers' names evokes Melville, specifically his tale of a handsome sailor both loved and killed in a setting far away from heterosexual entanglements, while the narrative alludes to Freud's favorite Sophocles tragedy, Budd threatening at one point to blind the Bride, and another of her old colleagues, the androgynously named Elle Driver, missing one eye after another for her defiance of another master, Pai Mei.

Although the gender roles are often blurred in *Kill Bill*, Sharon Willis's view of Tarantino's work as "a hyper-oedipalized play with popular culture artifacts" a decade earlier is prescient here. The actor Sonny Chiba, whose star power helps bring Clarence and Alabama together in *True Romance*, appears in the first volume of *Kill Bill* as the character Hattori Hanzo, a legendary maker of swords, effectively helping give birth to the samurai who seeks to displace the father by killing him. Before being featured in either volume, actor Gordon Liu had fought the character Pai Mei in earlier film roles, as the viewer of the DVD of *Kill Bill, Vol. 2*, can learn by viewing the making-of documentary found among the extras. In the movie itself, Liu finally has taken the place of Pai Mei, himself brought down by Elle Driver, but not before imparting the knowledge that enables the Bride to become the eventual killer of Bill. In the Bride's trajectory, Hanzo can be said to play a mother, who, in this case, gives birth to the swords that help define the assassins; Pai Mei, both a father, whom Elle Driver kills after losing an eye, and, in some respects, a mother, coparenting with Bill; and Bill himself, the primary father, portrayed by another figure from popular culture's past, David Carradine, best known for the American television series *Kung Fu*, with which Tarantino claims in the aforementioned making-of documentary to have grown up watching, and, of course, after which Jules plans to model the rest of his life by the end of *Pulp Fiction*. Yet Bill is also the parental figure with whom "Kiddo" sleeps before killing him. In the effort to honor as well as displace the cultural icon Carradine from his childhood, Quentin Tarantino recruits actress Uma Thurman.

Readers of a 2004 *Entertainment Weekly* interview find *Kill Bill*'s writer-director expressing strong affinity with his protagonist:

> I love the Bride. I *love* her, all right? I want her to be happy. I don't want to come up with screwed-up scenarios that she has to fight the whole rest of her life. I killed myself to put her in a good place at the end of this long journey. (Schilling, 26)

Her gender enables Tarantino to use the verb *love* without inhibition, but he does not suggest that he wants to marry her as much as equate her fate with his. In her essay "Her Body, Himself," Carol J. Clover suggests that female film characters in danger can be sources of identification for male viewers. While Clover is writing on the topic of slasher films, *Kill Bill*'s focus on a female character that survives a shot to the head, a coma, a live burial, and a couple of unwanted injections could make the insight applicable to this artful generic hybrid as well. The one aspect that distinguishes the Bride from a man, besides her interrupted plans to marry another man at a chapel in El Paso, is her pregnancy. Yet both her conception and her delivery occur entirely off-screen. Moreover, when she wakes from the coma, neither she nor the viewer is initially aware of her own motherhood. Aside from the pregnancy test that prompts her brief life in hiding as Arlene, Uma Thurman's character engages in masculine pursuits, guns, martial arts, and swordplay. In art, if not life, Quentin Tarantino has found the perfect woman, a character described in the credits as "created by Q & U," the creative offspring of a platonic union between the director and his leading lady.

Its explicit narrative offering terms of legibility opposite those of critic Emanuel Levy's DVD commentary for *Reservoir Dogs*, *Kill Bill* can be said to pass off a filial figure as a lover, albeit now nominally

Figure 12. Uma Thurman as the Bride in *Kill Bill* (2003–2004). *Photo courtesy of A Band Apart/Miramax/Kobal Collection.*

female in continued deference to heterosexist strictures. Nevertheless, the revelation in the film's second volume that the Twin Pines Wedding Chapel Massacre—the attack by the Deadly Viper Assassination Squad that makes the Bride comatose and later vengeful toward her old colleagues—actually occurred during a wedding *rehearsal* helps foreground the ritualistic status of the pending ceremony. Film critic Dave Kehr's *New York Times* essay notes that the image of the Bride outside the chapel, with the backdrop of "a vast, blindingly bright Western landscape as framed through the doorway of a dark interior," recalls the work of director John Ford, most famously the closing shot in *The Searchers* (1956) that underscores Ethan Edwards's status as a perennial outsider. At the same time, Bill himself can be compared to Ethan, a searcher planning to kill the loved one adopted by another community but, this time making more of an effort to go through with his earlier decision. While Beatrix Kiddo is united with her daughter by the end of the story, no adult heterosexual couple is ever restored.

Regretting his attempt to kill her, but certain that he saved her from an unhappy future, Bill, a comic-book aficionado like Clarence in *True Romance*, provides the Bride with a reading of popular culture that is a more oblique and allegorical version of Sid's in *Sleep with Me*:

> As you know, I'm quite keen on comic books, especially the ones about superheroes. I find the whole mythology surrounding superheroes fascinating. Take my favorite superhero, Superman. Not a great comic book, not particularly well drawn, but the mythology is not only great, it's unique. . . . Now a staple of the superhero mythology is there's the superhero and there's the alter ego. Batman is actually Bruce Wayne; Spider-Man is actually Peter Parker. When that character wakes up in the morning, he's Peter Parker; he has to put on a costume to become Spider-Man. And it is in that characteristic that Superman stands alone. Superman didn't become Superman: Superman was born Superman. When Superman wakes up in the morning, he's Superman. His alter ego is Clark Kent. His outfit with the big red S, that's the blanket he was wrapped in as a baby when the Kents found him; those are *his* clothes. What Kent wears—the glasses, the business suit—*that's* the costume. That's the costume Superman wears to blend in with us. Clark Kent is how Superman views us. And what are the characteristics of Clark Kent? He's weak; he's unsure of himself; he's a coward. Clark Kent is Superman's critique on the whole human race—sort of like Beatrix Kiddo and Mrs. Tommy Plympton. . . . You would have worn the costume of Arlene Plympton, but you

> were born Beatrix Kiddo. And every morning when you woke up, you'd still be Beatrix Kiddo.

The Bride concedes that her future in El Paso would have been unfulfilling, but maintains, "I would have had a baby." Heterosexual marriage is just a means to an end, an assumed identity for "Arlene," just like for Mr. Orange in *Reservoir Dogs*.

Bill's lecture on alter egos, delivered shortly before his own demise near the conclusion of the film's second volume, retrospectively adds perspective to the lives that all the veterans of the Deadly Viper Assassination Squad—the Bride, Elle Driver, Bill, Budd, O-Ren Ishii, and Vernita Green—have chosen for themselves, marked mostly by a refusal to assimilate fully into heterosexuality. The making-of documentary in the DVD edition of *Kill Bill, Vol. 2* characterizes the Bride and Elle Driver as, respectively, the past "girl" and present "girl" of the unmarried Bill, the exact relationship otherwise left undefined. Bill's brother, Budd, lives alone in a trailer and is seen interacting with women solely, and always platonically, as co-workers, be they dancers at the topless bar where he works as a bouncer or, in the cases of the Bride and Elle Driver, fellow assassins from the old days. Although he denies that he still has one, the Bride discovers that Budd kept his own Hattori Hanzo sword, with that loving inscription from Bill, hidden in a golf bag in his bedroom closet, a place metaphorically alluding to a love that dares not speak its name. The eventual revelation of Bill's code name in the Deadly Viper Assassination Squad suggests a rather ambiguous, if clearly dominant, relationship with all his fellow assassins: While everyone else has an assassin code name that refers to a snake (Black Mamba for the Bride, California Mountain Snake for Elle Driver, Sidewinder for Budd, Cottonmouth for O-Ren Ishii, and Copperhead for Vernita Green), Bill's is listed in the closing credits of the film's second volume as Snake Charmer. Meanwhile, the Bride's voiceover in the feature film, when she is fast on Bill's trail, reveals that he himself has gone through several "father figures," the first being the aging pimp Esteban Vihaio, who deals with women exclusively as current and prospective prostitutes for his clients. Another past father figure of Bill's, Hattori Hanzo, who forges a new sword to help the Bride seek vengeance on his former disciple, is seen living with a male companion when she approaches him.

Since the squad's attack on the chapel, O-Ren Ishii remains both an active assassin and an outsider to heterosexual relationships, her closest companion being another woman, Sofie Fatale, from whom the Bride takes limbs but not her life so that she can report to Bill that Kiddo is coming for him. In contrast to her old co-conspirators at the El Paso shootout, Vernita Green, herself assuming a new alter ego, has taken a part in heterosexual marriage, parenthood, and middle-class domesticity before being killed in her new family's kitchen as payback for earlier denying the Bride a similar life in hiding. The prospect of Vernita's daughter, a witness to her mother's death, becoming a warrior herself pursuing the death of the Bride is acknowledged explicitly by the assailant, and the unresolved possibility keeps the door open for more volumes of *Kill Bill*, one Oedipal conflict after another. The 2004 *Entertainment Weekly* interview has Tarantino imagining the reconstitution of a nontraditional family from the surviving characters for the next installment:

> Uma won't be the star, though she'll be in it. The star will be Vernita Green's (Vivica A. Fox's) daughter, Nikki (Ambrosia Kelly). I've already got the whole mythology: Sofie Fatale (Julie Dreyfus) will get all of Bill's money. She'll raise Nikki, who'll take on the Bride. Nikki deserves her revenge every bit as much as the Bride deserved hers. I might even shoot a couple of scenes for it now so I can get the actresses while they're this age. It's exciting to know there's a little girl who'll grow up to be my leading lady. (Schilling, 26)

Parenthood does not require a partner.

Heterosexuality at a Distance

The terms of closure in Tarantino's narratives do not depend on the union of a man and a woman. The intertitle bridging the conclusion of *Kill Bill, Vol. 2*, and its closing credits reads, "The lioness has rejoined her cub, and all is right in the jungle." For all their talk about romantic possibilities with men, at least three of the female characters in *Death Proof* ultimately depend more on each other, and lingering concerns about Lee underscore the notion of heterosexuality as a nuisance at best. *Jackie Brown*'s title character leaves for Spain alone with freedom and financial independence. Rearranged chronologically, Butch's return to his girlfriend Fabienne is the last story event in *Pulp Fiction*, but as laid out for the viewer, the film actually ends with Jules's epiphany that he needs to leave his life of crime and "become he who, in the name of charity and good will, shepherds the weak through the valley of darkness," drifting from town to town, "just like Caine in *Kung Fu*," David Carradine's most famous character, always traveling alone. Even in the Tony Scott–directed *True Romance*, Alabama has to compete for Clarence's attention with Elvis Presley, after whom he names their son at the end of the movie. *Reservoir Dogs* concludes with the final tender moments between Mr. White and Mr. Orange before the latter's confession prompts the death of them both.

In the 2006 Oscar night edition of *Jimmy Kimmel Live*, the host jokes with Tarantino that the scene of male anal intercourse in *Pulp Fiction* was an important influence on director Ang Lee when he directed *Brokeback Mountain*, a suggestion that sets off an exchange of tasteless comments, which network censors alternately bleeped and muted. The point of those remarks is that Tarantino's work is very different from that evening's nominated contender for Best Picture, but perhaps the infamous scene from his second film really serves as an alibi that discourages a closer look at his work's heterosexual aspirations consistently undermined by an interest in manly pursuits, guns and swords more to the filmmaker's liking than a fishing trip, with marriage even less of an obligation.

Notes

1. DVD releases of his directorial efforts include *Reservoir Dogs (10th Anniversary Special Edition)* (Artisan Home Entertainment, 2002 [1992]), *Pulp Fiction (Special Edition)* (Miramax, 2002 [1994]), *Jackie Brown (Special Edition)* (Buena Vista Home Entertainment, 2002 [1997]), *Kill Bill, Vol. 1* (Buena Vista Home Entertainment, 2003), *Kill Bill, Vol. 2* (Buena Vista Home Entertainment, 2004), and *Grindhouse Presents "Death Proof"* (Dimension Home Entertainment, 2007). Warner Home Video released in 2002 Tony Scott's 1993 film of Quentin Tarantino's screenplay *True Romance*, almost simultaneously with that year's DVD releases of Tarantino's first three films, in a DVD edition subtitled *Unrated Director's Cut*, featuring, among the choice of commentary tracks, one by the screenwriter.

2. Robert E. Kapsis, who (with Kathie Coblentz) co-edited the Woody Allen volume, is himself keenly aware of how such studies alternately reinforce and redefine canons, as evidenced by his earlier (1992) scholarship.

3. *Top Gun* (Paramount Home Video, 2002 [1986]) and *Sleep with Me* (MGM DVD, 2004 [1994]).

4. In Tarantino 2003, 148–149, Tarantino and Brian De Palma actually talk about their shared fondness for the writing of Pauline Kael, the former calling her piece on the older director's film *Blow Out* (1981) "one of the best reviews she's written, and that's saying a hell of a lot!"

12

Harry M. Benshoff

A Straight Cowboy Movie

Heterosexuality According to *Brokeback Mountain*

My title is meant to be a play on the broadly held misperception that *Brokeback Mountain* (2005) is a "gay cowboy movie." On the contrary, neither Ennis Del Mar (Heath Ledger) nor Jack Twist (Jake Gyllenhaal) claims a gay, queer, or otherwise homosexual identity. ("You know I ain't queer," says Ennis. "Me neither," replies Jack.) Annie Proulx, who wrote the story on which the film was based, calls both characters "clearly homophobic" (130).[1] In fact, aside from their occasional sex together, both Ennis and Jack are quite publicly and obviously heterosexual, and the film focuses primarily on the daily routines of traditionally heterosexual institutions such as dating, marriage, child rearing, work, and extended family get-togethers. Ennis marries Alma (Michelle Williams), has two daughters, and after his divorce dates Cassie (Linda Cardellini), a sexy waitress. Jack rides the rodeo circuit where he meets and marries Lureen Newsome (Anne Hathaway), and together they raise a son. So which label—heterosexual or homosexual—actually comes closer to describing Ennis and Jack? Why does the public insist on characterizing their story as a "gay cowboy movie" when they are so visibly heterosexual in almost all aspects of their lives?

Perhaps it is because their intimate sexual relationship—whatever they may have called it, were they even able to speak of it in lucid terms—is thought to be the defining marker of their individual identities (and by extension, the film's identity). Similar to the "one drop of blood" rule invoked by racist discourses of previous eras—a maxim that labeled anyone of even a slight degree of mixed racial heritage as automatically a Negro—one instance of gay sex is all it takes to label someone as homosexual, or even an entire movie as "gay." By way of contrast, a self-identified gay man who sleeps with a woman is not immediately branded a heterosexual, his homosexual desires no longer thought to be of consequence. This simple reversal test reveals the power imbalance built into the hetero-homo binary. In a heterosexist and patriarchal world (that is, one obsessed with the supremacy of heterosexuality over homosexuality, and masculinity over femininity) "one drop" of same sex love or desire is all it takes to brand a person a homosexual, forever excluding him or her from the socially privileged space of heterosexuality and its sustaining institutions.

Yet, as has been noted repeatedly, this "one drop" rule varies a great deal in terms of the gender of the same sex coupling. Within Western heteronormative pornographic discourses, women are routinely paired with one another for the delectation of the male gaze. The need to label them as definitively gay or straight is not always necessary because they are still ultimately understood as sexual objects designed for the pleasure of straight men. Their absolute, essential heterosexuality is not as valuable as is a man's because within heteronormative patriarchal discourses women are already constructed as second-class citizens. Thus, when women act like men (by wearing pants, playing sports, kissing another woman), they disrupt the gender hierarchy by trying to move "up" it. Although this may cause consternation—fears that women are usurping men's privileged roles—it does not greatly destabilize the gender hierarchy itself. In fact, it further underscores masculinity's highly desirable and normative stature. However, when men pursue "feminine" activities (by wearing a skirt, playing with dolls, kissing another man), this is understood to be a betrayal of their allegedly superior masculine status. Within heteronormative patriarchal discourses, moving "up" the gender hierarchy is far less transgressive than is moving "down" it. Tomboys who play sports are generally less threatening to the social structures of heterosexuality than are sissy faggots who play with dolls.

This is precisely why *Brokeback Mountain* caused such a pop culture panic: it is a film about two heterosexual-seeming (that is, traditionally masculine) men who also have an intimate sexual relationship with one another. A similar film about two cowgirls in love (such as the Western-themed *Desert Hearts* [1985]) would not have caused such consternation, nor would a film about two "queer eye" interior decorators in New York City (Mendelsohn). *Brokeback Mountain*, however, posits that one of the most iconic images of heterosexual masculinity—the American Cowboy—may have had and might still have homosexual desires. As such, the film threatens the borders between straight and gay, between homosocial and homosexual. It causes one to wonder just what those stoic Marlboro Men might have been doing out there on the range for all those years, and it places much (if not all) homosocial bonding under suspicion—what really goes on during those buddy-buddy fishing trips? *Brokeback Mountain* is frightening to heteronormative patriarchy not so much because it is a gay cowboy movie, but because it looks so much like a straight cowboy movie. It must be labeled "THE gay cowboy movie" to particularize it, to let everyone know that it is indeed very different from all the other Westerns it so closely resembles both in terms of its mise-en-scène as well as its thematic concerns: civilization versus the wilderness, conformity versus freedom, and ultimately the preference for male-male bonding over heterosexual romance (Schatz, 45–80).

Figure 13. Ennis (Heath Ledger) and Jack (Jake Gyllenhall) in *Brokeback Mountain* (2005). *Author's personal collection.*

Brokeback Mountain—like its male couple—is thus not gay in the narrow, "identity-politics" sense, but it is queer in the broader theoretical sense. The film quite literally queers or makes strange the social institutions that define and delimit human sexualities so that they might be examined and critiqued. Like queer theoretical work in general, *Brokeback Mountain* focuses on a particular place and time to dissect the multiple discourses—including those of gender, class, and region—that produce complex and distinct human sexualities, sexualities that are so often simplistically labeled as either straight or gay. In doing so, the film has far more to say about heterosexuality than it does homosexuality, which (again like Ennis and Jack themselves) the film barely theorizes. Compared to the idyllic or even utopic simplicity of same-sex life on the open range, *Brokeback Mountain* depicts heterosexuality as a complex institution that structures the very bases of society and culture as well as the social and political identities, practices, and experiences of its characters (Richardson). Moreover, *Brokeback Mountain* judges that institution to be unhappy, unpleasant, and highly limited, fraught with rigid hierarchies, enforced silences, and the ever-present threat of violence. The film is indeed a love story about two queer males, but even more so a tragedy about the restrictions dominant heteronormative discourses placed on them. In examining those discourses, *Brokeback Mountain* sounds a strident critique of compulsory heterosexuality.

Rigid Roles and Capitalism

The idea that institutionalized heterosexuality traps men and women into narrowly-defined social roles derived from their biological sex has been a central tenet of feminist and queer theories for decades. As one theorist puts it, "Performing straightness entails rigid self-discipline. It is a state of monotony, repetition, and predictability" (Dixon, 8). Those adjectives clearly describe the characters in *Brokeback Mountain*, rural, uneducated people living on the extreme margins of second wave feminism. All of them lead lives circumscribed by heteronormative patriarchal capitalism. The women especially derive their identities solely from their location within heterosexual relations—as wife, girlfriend, daughter, or mother. (Commentators who complained that the film ignores the plight of Alma and Lureen seemed to miss this point: the film is not treating its female characters in a sexist manner; it is dramatizing how Midwestern American culture of the 1960s and 1970s was itself a limiting and sexist structure.[2]) Similarly, Jack and Ennis unthinkingly follow careers outlined for them by the tenets of traditional heteronormative patriarchal capitalism. They seem to marry not so much out of desire or love for their spouses, but because it is what is expected of them. Ennis is especially resigned to his place in this social structure, even though on some level he realizes it is destroying him. As he ruefully tells Jack at one point, "If you can't fix it . . . you gotta stand it." His stoicism—a conditioned part of his traditional masculinity—is in this case an attribute that works to confine him further within his limited and nearly loveless existence.

Brokeback Mountain also dramatizes how the gendered and heterosexed roles that its characters are expected to play are deeply imbricated with the discourses of class and capitalism in the United States. For example, at the start of the film, Jack and Ennis are literally handmaidens to heterosexist capitalism. Their job is to tend to sheep in the expectation that the animals will procreate and thus increase the herd's worth. Similarly, throughout the film Ennis is repeatedly called away from Jack and his family to attend to the birth and care of livestock. Ennis's ranching jobs—capitalist endeavors literally based on exploiting the heterosexual reproduction of other species—take precedence over all other areas of his life. Partly this is because as lower-class young men of the rural West, Ennis and Jack have next-to-no career options and little free time for exploring anything outside their limited frames of reference. (Ennis to Jack, "Makin' a livin' is about all I got time for now.") Their only luxuries seem to be beer, cigarettes, and the occasional camping trip, and the only skills they possess are those they acquired growing up on family ranches. With little or no formal education (Ennis attended high school for only one year before he was forced to go to work), their physical bodies are the only commodities they have to offer, and thus they compete on the job market by placing their bodies in the line of danger.

Although sheep herding is perhaps a relatively safe job (aside from the weather and the occasional bear), Jack's later need to make a living riding bulls on the rodeo circuit is far more hazardous. The film explicitly states that Jack is forced to ride bulls because he cannot afford a horse for the safer, more lucrative field of calf-roping. The film also implicitly ties this commodified use of young masculine bodies to the war in Vietnam. When Jack tells Ennis that his rodeo injuries kept him out of the war, making a connection between the two jobs (cowboy and soldier) is easy. Both are dependent on the exploitation of young male bodies, and both jobs are promoted within heteronormative patriarchal discourses as the epitome of masculinity. (As the Marines' slogan would have it, a young man should "be all that he can be," suggesting that "butching up" is an expansive process of human growth and not in fact a radical form of dehumanization.) In these senses, heteronormative patriarchal capitalism is not just rigid and limiting, it can be deadly, especially for those who are forced to pursue its more physically dangerous professions.

Although traditional heteronormative patriarchy dictates that men should be the sole breadwinners for their families—with women staying home to raise the children—*Brokeback Mountain* suggests that the realities of capitalism often make such an ideal impossible. For example, Alma explicitly states that she does not want to have any more children because Ennis cannot afford to take care of the ones he already has. She is forced to work in a grocery store to supplement the meager income Ennis earns as a ranch hand. Conditioned by patriarchy and not the exigencies of capitalism, Ennis becomes increasingly disquieted by Alma's job, frustrated that his marriage is not living up to his own idealized version of traditional heterosexual monogamy. He becomes angry when she leaves for an extra shift (even though she has already made dinner and left it on the stove), ranting, "No one's eatin' it unless you're servin' it!" Ennis also unquestioningly assumes his job is more important than Alma's, and he sees nothing wrong with dumping their kids at her place of work when his job comes calling. (The film also suggests that heterosexual desire is what allowed Alma to get and then keep her job at the grocery store: even after her children create a messy confusion in the aisles, her boss is happy to overlook it because he is sweet on her.) Still, Ennis remains the boss of the marriage in most other ways. He tells Alma what they as a couple are going to do without even discussing it with her, and he rarely considers let alone acts on her desires. Like many men regardless of their sexuality, Ennis is dismissive of women in general, and finds relating to them difficult. A telling moment toward the end of the film reveals that he is even unsure of what his girlfriend Cassie wants to do with her life, assuming it to be "nursin' school or somethin'."

Jack's wife Lureen seemingly has more options than does Alma because she comes from a higher socioeconomic class. Thus, Lureen is able to be more independent and forthright in her actions and desires. She actively pursues Jack when they first meet, and she is more sexually aggressive than he is. And as the film goes on, she cultivates a career as a successful businesswoman. Yet, all of these opportunities are the result of her father's status as a wealthy businessman, and he defines the limits of Lureen's relative freedom. Although she marries Jack against her father's wishes, her father still dominates both her career (he owns the business where she works) and her family life. Lureen's story ends with Jack's death and the phone call from Ennis. Trapped within a close-up frame that mirrors the closed up opportunities of her life, Lureen's barely audible sighs and squeaks hint at bitter knowledge that cannot be spoken: knowledge of just what Ennis and Jack meant to one another, as well as the knowledge that her own life—as defined by heteronormative patriarchal capitalism—has been an empty one.

Silence and Power

Traditional heteronormative patriarchy constructs a culture of silence for both men and women because speech is potentially challenging to the rigid roles of compulsory heterosexuality. Furthermore, as Monique Wittig has asserted, the "discourses of heterosexuality oppress us in the sense that they prevent us from speaking unless we speak in their terms" (25). Yet, these imperatives for silence are also gendered differently. Women may be permitted an occasional emotional outburst (because emotion is allegedly part of their sex's "weaker" nature), but men must be taciturn at all times. Silence is also a necessary component of most masculine, hierarchical professions, wherein men must unquestioningly take orders and obey their male superiors. Thus, when Ennis and Jack first meet outside ranch boss Mr. Aguirre's office they do not speak to one another, even though they are proximate. They continue to maintain their silence as Aguirre hires them—not asking questions about the job nor even inquiring about their wages. Aguirre himself communicates in terse sentences and nonverbal gestures, and he dismisses the young men with a curt look. His patriarchal authority is further underscored by his age, status, and vocal content—he refers snidely to Jack and Ennis as a "pair of deuces" with "scrawny asses"—as well as his blocking: Aguirre remains seated behind his desk while Jack and Ennis stand meekly before him, hats in hands. Only outside of Aguirre's hearing—on Brokeback Mountain itself—does Jack finally feel free to voice his complaints about Aguirre's authority, sounding a resentful critique of the inequities of patriarchal capitalism.

Ennis, on the other hand, rarely complains about anything because he rarely opens his mouth to speak at all. After the first few days on Brokeback Mountain, Jack comments that Ennis has finally started to open up and talk to him, and Ennis replies that his few statements have been the "most I spoke in a year." Most significantly, Ennis cannot state the nature of his desire or love for Jack. When their first summer together ends, Ennis retreats into a sullen silence rather than vocalize his disappointment. When he and Jack part, we see no kind words or gentle touches, merely the terse assertion, "I guess I'll see ya' around." And as he grows older, Ennis suffers from an almost complete emotional breakdown, unable to relate to anyone. By the end of the film and his abortive affair with Cassie, Ennis sits immobile in a diner slowly and joylessly eating a piece of pie. In an Oscar-nominated performance, Heath Ledger conveys much of Ennis's emotional blockage. Ennis's furrowed brow, firmly set mouth, and almost inaudible tones convey a man who has repressed not only his sexuality but also any capacity to connect with other human beings. In an apt and telling turn of phrase, he tells Jack's parents, "I can't begin to tell you how bad I feel." Similarly, his final words in the film, "Jack, I swear . . ." encapsulate his dilemma. Swearing indicates a deep emotional attachment, but exactly what Ennis is swearing on or about remains unspoken. Nearly 100 years after Oscar Wilde, Ennis's passion for Jack is still "the love that dare not speak its name."

Heteronormative patriarchy also demands silence from women, especially when they are in the company of men. Alma is consistently quiet and mousy; she does not confront Ennis even after seeing him passionately kiss Jack on the steps to their apartment. As young adults, Ennis's daughters Alma Jr. and Jenny are likewise silent, knowing that when they voice their desires they will inevitably be turned down, as when Alma Jr. asks if she might live with Ennis. Single women seem to have a bit more voice in the film and in culture-at-large. Both the young Lureen and Cassie are able to speak their minds—to a degree—even if they still ultimately cannot penetrate their men's silences. In a slightly different register, female silence is also the subject of the dance at the Childress social club, a scene that introduces Lashawn Malone (Anna Faris), a former sorority girl who cannot stop making idle chitchat. The film invites the audience to laugh at her vacuous logorrhea, but it also dramatizes how her talkativeness is a negative attribute within heteronormative patriarchy. Jack and her husband, Ray, leave the building to escape her endless prattle.

Jack and Lureen's Thanksgiving dinner scene also dramatizes Western culture's expectation of female silence, especially when confronted with the spectacle of "alpha" men competing for dominance. The scene centers on Jack and his father-in-law L. D. jockeying for masculine superiority while their wives sit by silently. As Jack begins to carve the turkey (traditionally the duty of the "man of the house"), L. D. grabs the utensils from Jack with the snide admonition that the "Stud Duck'll do the carvin' round here." To keep the peace, Jack defers to him, while Lureen suggests that she will have to turn off the televised football game if her son does not eat his dinner. Agreeing with Lureen, and out of respect to her efforts in preparing the meal, Jack turns off the television. L. D.—one of the film's most obvious symbols of traditional patriarchal attitudes—stops carving the turkey, crosses the room, and turns the television back on, admonishing, "You want your boy to grow up to be a man, don't ya? Boys should watch football." Now more agitated, Jack again rises and turns off the television. As L. D. once again makes his way toward the television to turn it back on, Jack finally bellows at him, "You sit down you old son of a bitch. This is *my* house, *my* child, and you are *my* guest. Now you sit down before I knock your ignorant ass into next week." Cut-away shots reveal that Lureen and her mother have remained silent throughout this exchange, although Lureen's slight smile indicates her approval of Jack asserting his dominance through traditional patriarchal means. In this one scene, *Brokeback Mountain* suggests that even so-called normal-looking heterosexual families are far from ideal, but are instead filled with rarely spoken tensions, rivalries, and the barely contained threat of physical violence.

Brutality and Violence

As one theorist of heterosexuality has expressed, "dominant culture's most repetitive message to men is that it is infinitely preferable for them to compete with each other viciously, to batter each other violently, even to murder each other brutally, than it is for them to fuck each other passionately" (Thomas, 98). Thus, even though Ennis and Jack are queer by reason of their shared homosexual relationship, most of their behaviors and attitudes are still derived from heteronormative patriarchal assumptions about competition and violence. Ennis, who is much more invested in a traditional model of masculinity than Jack, is especially prone to violent outbursts that serve to express what he will not or cannot say with words. For example, after brusquely dismissing Jack after their first summer together, Ennis suffers a violent emotional breakdown, punching a wall and vomiting. He uses masculine anger and its implied threat of physical violence—"What the fuck you lookin' at?"—to drive away an unsuspecting passerby. (Director Lee's use of chiaroscuro lighting in this doorway scene recalls similar effects in John Ford's *The Searchers* [1956], a more traditional Hollywood Western, albeit one with its own psychosexual traumas.) Similarly, when Alma finally confronts Ennis about the nature of his relationship with "Jack Nasty," Ennis brutally twists her arm and threatens to punch her. Realizing he cannot hit a woman, he heads into the streets where his anger and frustration are quickly displaced onto an attack on a random motorist. When, toward the end of their romance, Jack threatens to reveal his other homosexual experiences to Ennis, Ennis again responds with the threat of violence: "All them things that I don't know, might get you killed if I come to know them."

Even during Jack and Ennis's first summer together, their interactions are filtered through heterosexist discourses, including those of violence. Their first sexual coupling verges on rape, not same-sex desire, yet another moment in the film that belies the moniker "gay cowboy film." Indeed, at least one gay critic found their intimacies to be "the kind of sex that a person who's neither gay nor a cowboy imagines gay cowboys must have" (Carpenter, 13). (Another way to decode the scene is that it depicts homosexual sex between two heterosexual men.) In fact, not knowing anything about gay culture and its sexual mores—or in the case of Jack not admitting to such knowledge—Ennis and Jack mostly express their desires through discourses of heteronormative homosociality. We see them physically roughhousing, wrestling, punching, and teasing one another, but they never speak of desire or love, let alone tenderness and intimacy. And although they may appear on the surface to treat one another as equals, they repeatedly fall back into heterosexist assumptions about the nature of relationships—that is, that real relationships are composed of one top (the man) and one bottom (the woman). Sexually, Ennis seems to be the active, dominant top in the relationship (at least that is the only form of intercourse the film depicts). In broader terms, Ennis's silence, aloofness, and ability to dictate the terms of their relationship also help construct him as the dominant half of the relationship. Conversely, Jack's character is marked by attributes thought to be more feminine: he is more likely to voice his feelings and desires, and he is willing to accept—however grudgingly—most of the limits Ennis places on their relationship.

The fact that sexual intercourse between Ennis and Jack is depicted in the film only once and is envisioned almost as rape may have as much to do with characterizing Jack and Ennis as heteronormative as it does pandering to a straight audience for whom such scenes have traditionally been disquieting. As at least one queer theorist has argued, "anal pleasure is the single most interdicted of those pleasures open to male bodies in our culture—and, I argue, is also the 'thing' still that defines homosexuality. If the Phallus is the fetish, and masculinity the reified identity it signifies, the single most unthinkable event for the masculine is anal penetration *as pleasure*" (Yingling, 192–93). Thus, if and when heteronormative patriarchy imagines anal penetration at all, it is almost always figured as a violent rape that demeans and degrades one's masculine status. From virtually every prison movie to childhood abuse melodrama—from *Deliverance* (1972) to *Pulp Fiction* (1994)—popular culture figures anal intercourse as horrific; images of pleasurable anal intercourse between men are almost nonexistent in mainstream media. Thus, although one can infer that Jack and Ennis's off-screen sexuality includes willful and pleasurable anal intercourse, the film itself does not depict it. Within heteronormative discourses, such an event is literally unrepresentable. Instead, the film and its characters displace the erotic into the violent. The men's first summer ends with a fistfight as if to signal their return to the larger world of heterosexual, more forthrightly homosocial relations.

The violence of heteronormative patriarchy not only colors the film's homosexual relations, but it also polices the borders of permissible heterosexual relations. (As mentioned earlier, Ennis uses the threat of violence to control Alma, while Jack uses a similar threat to maintain order in his home.) The Fourth of July picnic scene explicitly dramatizes how violence is used to assert one form of heterosexuality over another. As Ennis and his family are about to enjoy the fireworks display, two male bikers sit down near them and begin to voice their heterosexual desires, drunkenly and loudly wondering about the best locales for finding "pussy on the hoof." The bikers' version of heterosexuality—and its overtly abusive approach to women—offends Ennis now that he has a wife and two young daughters. (One doubts that silent, passive Ennis would have made a stand against the bikers if he were not married with children.) Although Ennis first attempts to defuse the situation with a few words—rising above the violence inherent in the biker's belligerent attitude—he quickly descends to their level. The verbal altercation escalates into physical violence with Ennis punching and kicking the bikers until they back away.

This scene is especially telling for several reasons, not the least of which is that it queerly dramatizes the fact that a "diversity of meaning and social arrangements [exist] within the category 'heterosexuality,' rather than a unitary heterosexual subject and a unified, distinct heterosexual community" (Richardson, 2). Indeed, the scene makes one aware of the fact that seemingly polite and benign versions of heterosexuality (such as those espoused by Ennis's family values stand) exist, as well as more brutal versions the bikers embody. Yet the film also suggests that these two versions of heterosexuality are inextricably linked because both are dependent on women's status as second-class citizens. The brutal misogyny that passes as generic banter in male homosocial spaces such as locker rooms or biker clubs is simply a more obvious version of the violence done to women within more "kinder and gentler" modes of heterosexuality. (In this respect, Ennis is perhaps defending and thus distancing his version of heterosexuality from that of the bikers', rather than defending his family per se.) Furthermore, director Ang Lee uses this brief Fourth of July scene to tie these ideas about violent masculinity to American national identity. In one striking low-angle shot after Ennis has driven away the bikers, Lee frames Ennis standing tall and proud on the left side of the screen while Alma and the children huddle together on the right with fireworks—emblematic of America's founding national scene as well as the then-current war in Vietnam—bursting behind them.

Ennis's defenses aside, in *Brokeback Mountain* the brutal violence of heteronormative patriarchy extends to everyday family life. Heterosexuality is not the cornerstone of family values—in fact, every heterosexual family unit in *Brokeback Mountain* is disordered in significant ways:

neurotic, distant, and ultimately hostile to its own members. Ennis and Alma work hard at their version of heterosexuality—they produce two children but their marriage is empty and unbalanced because of his other desires. Their heterosexual life together is a vision of domestic hell, complete with sick and crying babies, and cramped and dingy apartments (compared to the open ranges where Ennis and Jack's relationship transpires). Repeated scenes show both Ennis and Alma fleeing from their apartment—he to the woods with Jack and she to her job at the grocery store. Jack's marriage to Lureen perhaps looks better on the surface, but he tells Ennis that it could be conducted over the phone equally as effectively. Importantly, Lureen's father never hides his contempt for Jack, and Jack believes that L. D. would actually pay him to leave Lureen.

In fact, in *Brokeback Mountain*, heterosexuality is even responsible for tearing families apart, as revealed by Ennis's childhood saga of domestic trauma. After his mother and father were killed in a car accident, Ennis was raised (briefly) by his sister and brother, both of whom abandoned him when they acted on their own heterosexual desires and married others. In this case the very cornerstone of family values—heterosexual courtship and marriage—is shown to be a destructive force: teenage Ennis was left alone with no economic or familial resources. Jack's own brutal and dysfunctional parents are revealed during the film's climactic moments. Earlier, Jack told Ennis that his father never taught him anything or supported any of his efforts, and in effect drove Jack away from home. When this bad father is finally revealed onscreen, he is surly and silent and as cold and remote as the stark off-white farm house in which he lives. On one level, he seems to know all about Jack and Ennis, but his inscrutable demeanor is haughty and hostile. Although Jack wanted his ashes to be spread on Brokeback Mountain (and Ennis has come there to do so), Jack's father cruelly insists on interring the ashes in the family plot, where presumably he can at last keep Jack under his ultimate control.

Homophobia, the Closet, and the Straight Mind

In *Brokeback Mountain*, the constitutive traits of heteronormativity—rigid and hierarchical gender roles, silence, and the threat of violence—construct and maintain compulsory heterosexuality. Those traits have also been shown to define and delimit clinical accounts of homophobia (Fone; Herek; Plummer). Indeed, the fear, loathing, and negation of same-sex desire arguably create and define heterosexuality in the first place. As one queer theorist puts it:

> The terror of being mistaken for a queer dominates the straight mind because this terror *constitutes* the straight mind; it is precisely that culturally produced and reinforced horror of/fascination with abjected homosexuality that produces and maintains "the straight mind" as such, governing not so much specific sexual practices between men and women (after all, these things happen) as the *institution* (arguably antisexual) of heteronormativity itself. (Thomas, 98–99)

Nowhere is this more apparent than in the character of Ennis, a man who maintains his own "straight mind" out of abject terror. As his backstory reveals, when Ennis was nine years old his father took him to view to the mutilated body of a murdered gay man, in what was meant to be an object lesson as to how violent masculinity justifiably punishes queers. The lesson was so successful that even as an adult Ennis fears that he and Jack will be murdered if their relationship is ever discovered. As he tells Jack, "If this thing gets out, we're dead." As he ages, he grows increasingly paranoid, imagining that people in town are staring at him, singling him out because they somehow know of his sexual relationship with Jack. Ennis is literally "scared straight"—perhaps like many people, Ennis defines himself as heterosexual less because of his sexual desires and more because he has been terrorized into accepting it as the normative identity.

Jack and Ennis both suffer ill effects from heteronormative homophobia and the need to keep their desires closeted. While the film's climactic scenes explicitly foreground actual closets in their mise-en-scène, Brokeback Mountain itself is also closet, albeit a huge and open-aired one; it is the place where Jack and Ennis express their sexuality, but it is also where they hide it from view. Indeed, arguably one of the film's most potent effects is its ability to create an almost palpable sense of the closet circa 1970s middle America (much as director Ang Lee created a palpable sense of 1970s sexual malaise in his film *The Ice Storm* [1997]). Jack and Ennis are so closeted that even after years of intimate sexual contact between them, they still lie to one another about the nature of their desires. Although Jack has been having sex with other men, he cannot admit that fact to Ennis for fear of losing his alleged heterosexual stature. Thus he tells Ennis that he has a thing going on with a "ranch foreman's wife," although the film clearly implies that Jack's "thing" is actually going on with the ranch foreman himself. Ennis's own internalized homophobia is made clear in that same scene when he practically accuses Jack of being a fag—sneering that he knows what "boys like you" are all about. He also blames Jack for making him "like this"—another euphemistic reference to his problematic homosexual desire. Even after Alma divorces him, Ennis is still unable to imagine a family that might include both his children and his male lover. In the end, his internalized homophobia destroys not only his chance for happiness with Jack, but it also ultimately works to incapacitate him entirely.

The closet that regulates the lives of Ennis and Jack also deforms those of their families. As one perceptive review of the film puts it, all the characters' lives are blasted not because Jack and Ennis are gay, "but because they pretend not to be; it's the lie that poisons everyone they touch" (Mendelsohn, 12). Lureen's climactic phone call from Ennis, shot in a static close-up and tersely enacted by Anne Hathaway, is riddled with pregnant ambiguity that hints at a lifetime of self-deception. One senses that Lureen might possibly know all about Jack and Ennis, but that her confronting that situation would be unthinkable. The possibility of same-sex love and desire remains repressed so that the heterosexual façade can be maintained. Similarly, Jack's parents seem to know all about Jack and Ennis, even though they too cannot speak directly about it. Jack's mother—mostly silent and fearful as befits her role—treats Ennis kindly and allows him to leave with the two shirts that symbolized Jack's love for Ennis. Jack's bitter and surly father, however, taunts Ennis by hinting that Jack had another male lover, that perhaps Ennis had been replaced in Jack's affections. Ultimately, the film leaves the "truth" of Jack's death as yet one more epistemological uncertainty the closet created. Did he really die in a freak roadside accident (as Lureen asserts), or is that a heterosexual cover story closeting a gay bashing (as Ennis imagines). Given the year of his death—1983—Jack may have also died from AIDS, a cause of death routinely denied or rewritten during that era because of widespread homophobia. Ultimately, by keeping the cause of Jack's death indeterminate, the film suggests that many things are fatal to rural closeted queers; Jack could just have easily been killed by any one of them.

"Heteronormativity, then, has something—itself—to prove, but it has no other proof of itself than its own repeated efforts at self-demonstration" (Thomas, 100). Thus heterosexuality is created and maintained via performative acts: marriage and dating, holiday meals, raising children, and the reiterated negation of homosexuality itself: "Just Say No" and "Don't Ask, Don't Tell." (Negation even inhabits the film's seemingly unimportant spaces: when we first meet Mr. Aguirre he is bellowing into his phone "No, no, not on yer fuckin' life!") In dramatizing these various rituals and negations, *Brokeback Mountain* exposes them as constitutive of the straight mind. But the film does more than just describe and delineate the functioning of heteronormative institutions, it also seeks to destabilize them, queerly teasing out connections between the interrelated discourses of homosexuality, heterosexuality, and male homosociality. In this respect, the scene between Jack and the ranch foreman outside the Childress social club is highly significant, and it encapsulates much of the film's subversive effect. In it, the ranch foreman invites Jack to a "cabin down on a lake" to "drink a little whiskey, fish some, get away, ya know?" The epistemological uncertainty of this brief exchange is highly disruptive of patriarchal heteronormative discourses and knowledge. Is the invitation strictly homosocial, or is it a not-so-thinly-veiled homosexual proposition? In queering what might be traditional heterosexual homosociality, this scene blurs the lines between homosexuality, heterosexuality, and homosociality, just as the film as a whole does.

Conclusion

To end where we started—it is precisely because *Brokeback Mountain* makes homosexuality look exactly like traditional heterosexual homosociality that the film must forcefully and repeatedly be labeled as overtly gay by the heteronormative discourses in which it circulates. Such labeling is a performative attempt to redraw the line between homosexuality and heterosexuality that the film so carefully blurs. (The fear and consternation among many filmgoers that the film created suggests that many indeed understood it as queerly subversive [Benshoff].) By depicting "normal" masculine heterosexual-seeming men who also are sexual intimates, the film raises suspicions about all homosocial practices and their meaning(s) within patriarchal heteronormativity. For many (if not most?) men, homosocial bonds are more important to the functioning of everyday life—not to mention everyday pleasure—than are heterosexual bonds between men and women. What "normal" straight guy does not long to get away from his wife and kids and spend a few days camping in the woods with his best buddy? *Brokeback Mountain* suggests that within the heterosexual matrix we currently inhabit, male homosocial and homosexual desires are closer in nature and function than perhaps either straight or gay men would like to admit. Both rest on patriarchal privilege that structurally excludes the female and the feminine.

Whereas most viewers (average audiences, critics for the popular media, and academic scholars alike) have tended to look at the story of Jack and Ennis as a homosexual love story, ultimately the film has as much (if not more) to say about the institution(s) of heterosexuality. *Brokeback Mountain* represents straight identity as a socially constructed role and speaks of the pressures placed on individuals to reenact such roles constantly. *Brokeback Mountain* is not a gay movie, nor is it a straight movie. It is a queer movie that attempts to unravel the various interlocking traits that comprise contemporary heteronormative identities and institutions. As such, the film dramatizes how the enforcement of heteronormativity has detrimental effects on everyone—gay, straight, or otherwise. One does not have to have same-sex desires to experience the stress, self-loathing, and possible violence that arise from the enforcement of heterosexual norms. Although Ennis stoically declares, "you gotta stand," those self-same norms, contemporary cultural criticism may at last be suggesting ways to "fix them."

Notes

1. On the same page Proulx also notes that "the urban critics dubbed it a tale of two gay cowboys. No. It is a story of destructive rural homophobia" (130).

2. For example, *Dallas Morning News* columnist Jacquielynn Floyd thought the overall film was "petty good," but in her opinion Alma and Lureen "came across not much more sympathetically than the horses and sheep. . . . The poor wives are written as stock characters: one is a tearful, frumpy, perpetually nagging drudge; the other is a brittle big-haired harpy" (B1–2).

Works Cited

Aaron, Michele. "Cinema's Queer Jews: Jewishness and Masculinity in Yiddish Cinema." In *The Trouble with Men: Masculinities in European and Hollywood Cinema*, edited by Phil Powrie, Ann Davies, and Bruce Babington, 90–99. London: Wallflower, 2004a.

———. "New Queer Cinema: An Introduction." In *New Queer Cinema: A Critical Reader*. 3–14. Edinburgh, Scotland: Edinburgh University Press, 2004b.

Ali, Lorraine, and Julie Scelfo. "Choosing Virginity." *Newsweek*, Dec. 9, 2002, 61–62.

Altman, Rick. *The American Film Musical*. Bloomington: Indiana University Press, 1987.

Amazonas, Lee. Pacific Film Archive program (Feb. 11, 2001), *A Free Soul* file. Film Archive, Academy of Motion Picture Arts and Sciences, Los Angeles, CA.

Astaire, Fred. *Steps in Time*. New York: Harper, 1959.

Avineri, Shlomo. *The Making of Modern Zionism*. New York: Basic, 1981.

Bach, Dr. George R., and Peter Wyden. *The Intimate Enemy: How to Fight Fair in Love and Marriage*. New York: Morrow, 1969.

Bailey, Kay. *From Front Porch to Back Seat: Courtship in Twentieth-Century America*. Baltimore, MD: Johns Hopkins University Press, 1988.

Barker, Olivia. "Mommie Hottest." *USA Today*, Jan. 25, 2005, D1.

———. "The Young and the Wed List." *USA Today*, Apr. 6, 2004, 9B.

Bazin, André. "The Evolution of the Western." In *Movies and Methods, Vol. 1*, edited by Bill Nichols, 150–57. Berkeley: University of California Press.

Becker, Ron. *Gay TV and Straight America*. New Brunswick, NJ: Rutgers University Press, 2006.

Bellafante, Ginia. "When Midlife Seems Just an Empty Plate." *New York Times*, Mar. 9, 2003, sect. 9, 1, 4.

Benshoff, Harry. "Brokering *Brokeback Mountain*: A Local Reception Study." *Jump Cut* 50 (Spring 2008), www.ejumpcut.org;currentissue/BrokbkMtn/index.html (accessed June 6, 2008).

Benshoff, Harry M., and Sean Griffin. *America on Film: Representing Race, Class, Gender and Sexuality at the Movies*. Oxford: Blackwell, 2003.

———. *Queer Images: A History of Gay and Lesbian Film in America*. Lanham, MD: Rowan and Littlefield, 2005.

Bernard, Jami. *Tarantino: The Man and His Movies*. New York: HarperPerennial, 1995.

Bernardi, Daniel, ed. *The Birth of Whiteness: Race and the Emergence of U.S. Cinema*. New Brunswick, NJ: Rutgers University Press, 1996.

Bhatia, Gautam. *Punjabi Baroque and Other Memories of Architecture*. Delhi, India: Penguin, 1994.

Biale, David. *Eros and the Jews: From Biblical Israel to Contemporary America*. New York: Basic, 1992.

Biskind, Peter. *Down and Dirty Pictures: Miramax, Sundance, and the Rise of Independent Film*. New York: Simon and Schuster, 2004.

Blumenfeld, Warren J. "History/Hysteria: Parallel Representations of Jews and Gay, Lesbians, and Bisexuals." In *Queer Studies: A Lesbian, Gay, Bisexual and Transgender Anthology*, edited by Brett Beemyn and Mickey Eliason, 146–62. New York: New York University Press, 1996.

Boo, Katherine. "The Marriage Cure." *New Yorker*, Aug. 18 & 25, 2003, 104–20.

Boone, Joseph A., and Michael Cadden. *Engendering Men: The Question of Male Feminist Criticism*. New York: Routledge, 1990.

Boyarin, Daniel. *Unheroic Conduct: The Rise of Heterosexuality and the Invention of the Jewish Man*. Berkeley: University of California Press, 1997.

———, Daniel Itzkovitz, and Ann Pellegrini. "Strange Bedfellows: An Introduction." In *Queer Theory and the Jewish Question*, 1–18. New York: Columbia University Press, 2003.

Breines, Paul. *Tough Jews: Political Fantasies and the Moral Dilemma of American Jewry*. New York: Basic, 1990.

Burnett, Frances Hodgson. *Little Lord Fauntleroy*. New York: Scribner, 1888.

Burt, Ramsay. *The Male Dancer: Bodies, Spectacle, Sexualities*. London: Routledge, 1995.

Butler, Judith. *Gender Trouble: Feminism and the Subversion of Identity*. New York: Routledge, 1990.

Califia, Pat. "Feminism and Sadomasochism." In *Feminism and Sexuality: A Reader*, edited by Stevi Jackson and Sue Scott, 230–37. New York: Columbia University Press, 1996.

Cannon, Regina. "Dancing Lady: Eleanor Powell's a Regular Gal." *Modern Screen*, Nov. 1935, 42–43, 66–67.

Carpenter, Dale. "The Other Side of the *Mountain*." *Txt Newsmagazine*, Dec. 23, 2005, 13.

Chauncey, George. *Gay New York: Gender, Urban Culture, and the Making of the Gay Male World 1890–1940*. New York: Basic, 1994.

Cheever, Susan. "Baby Battle." In *Mommy Wars: Stay-at-Home and Career Moms Face Off on Their Choices, Their Lives, Their Families*, edited by Leslie Morgan Steiner, 37–43. New York: Random, 2006.

Chura, Hillary. "Here Comes the Baby, and an Itch to Overbuy." *New York Times*, Jan. 8, 2006, 6.

Clover, Carol J. "Her Body, Himself: Gender in the Slasher Film." *Representations* 20 (Fall 1987): 187–228.

Cohan, Steven. "'Feminizing' the Song-and-Dance Man: Fred Astaire and the Spectacle of Masculinity in the Hollywood Musical." In *Screening the Male: Exploring Masculinities in Hollywood Cinema*, edited by Steven Cohan and Ina Rae Hark, 46–69. New York: Routledge, 1993.

———. *Incongruous Entertainment: Camp, Cultural Value, and the MGM Musical.* Durham, NC: Duke University Press, 2005.

Connelly, Tim. "'He Is Her Boss, You Know, as Well as Her Husband': Norma Shearer and the Place of Working-Wives in the Early 1930s." Paper presented at Society for Cinema Studies Conference, Washington, D.C., May 24–27, 2001.

Cook, David A. *A History of Narrative Film*, 3rd ed. New York: Norton, 1996.

Cousins, Norman. "Will Women Lose Their Jobs?" *Current History & Forum* 41 (Sept. 1939): 14.

Crafton, Donald. *The Talkies: American Cinema's Transition to Sound, 1926–1931.* New York: Scribner, 1997.

Croce, Arlene. "Dance in Film." *Afterimages*. New York: Random, 1977. 427–45.

Cronin, Anne. *Advertising and Consumer Citizenship: Gender, Images and Rights.* New York: Routledge, 2000.

De Cordova, Richard. "A Case of Mistaken Legitimacy: Class and Generation Difference in Three Family Melodramas." In *Home Is Where the Heart Is: Studies in Melodrama and the Woman's Film*, edited by Christine Gledhill, 255–67. London: British Film Institute, 1992.

Delamater, Jerome. *Dance in the Hollywood Musical.* Ann Arbor, MI: UMI Research Press, 1981.

Deleuze, Gilles. *Cinema One: The Movement Image*. Minneapolis: University of Minnesota Press, 1986.

D'Emilio, John, and Estelle B. Freedman. *Intimate Matters: A History of Sexuality in America*. New York: Harper and Row, 1988.

Didion, Joan. "A Problem of Making Connections." *Life*, Dec. 5, 1969, 34.

Dinnerstein, Leonard. *Anti-Semitism in America*. Oxford, England: Oxford University Press, 1994.

Dixon, Wheeler Winston. *Straight: Constructions of Heterosexuality in the Cinema.* Albany: State University of New York Press, 2003.

Doane, Mary Ann. "The Close-Up: Scale and Detail in the Cinema." *differences* 14.5 (2003): 89–111.

———. "Film and the Masquerade: Theorising the Female Spectator." In *Film Theory and Criticism*, 4th ed., edited by Gerald Mast, Marshall Cohen, and Leo Braudy, 758–72. Oxford, England: Oxford University Press, 1992.

Dooley, Roger Burke. *From Scarface to Scarlett: American Films in the 1930s.* New York: Harcourt Brace Jovanovich, 1981.

Doty, Alexander. *Making Things Perfectly Queer: Interpreting Popular Culture.* Minneapolis: University of Minnesota Press, 1993.

Douglas, Susan J., and Meredith W. Michaels. *The Mommy Myth: The Idealization of Motherhood and How It Has Undermined Women.* New York: Free, 2004.

Duberman, Martin, Martha Vicinus, and George Chauncey Jr., eds. *Hidden from History: Reclaiming the Gay and Lesbian Past.* New York: Meridian, 1990.

Duggan, Lisa. "Making It Perfectly Queer." In *Sex Wars: Sexual Dissent and Political Culture*, 155–72. New York: Routledge, 1996.

———. "The Social Enforcement of Heterosexuality and Lesbian Resistance in the 1920s." In *Class, Race, and Sex: The Dynamics of Control*, edited by Amy Swerdlow and Hannah Lesinger, 76–92. Boston: Hall, 1983.

Dyer, Richard. "'I Seem to Find the Happiness I Seek': Heterosexuality and Dance in the Musical." In *Dance, Gender and Culture*, edited by Helen Thomas, 49–65. New York: St. Martin's, 1993.

———. *White*. New York: Routledge, 1997.

Edelman, Lee. *Homographesis*. New York: Routledge, 1994.

Eisenberg, Noah. "Perennial Detour: The Cinema of Edgar G. Ulmer and the Experience of Exile." *Cinema Journal* 43.4 (2004).

Elsaesser, Thomas. "Tales of Sound and Fury: Observations on the Family Melodrama." In *Film Genre Reader II*, edited by Barry Keith Grant, 350–80. Austin: University of Texas Press, 1995.

———. "Vincente Minnelli." In *Home Is Where the Heart Is: Studies in Melodrama and the Woman's Film*, edited by Christine Gledhill, 217–22. London: British Film Institute, 1992.

Epstein, Joseph. "The Struggle for Sexual Identity." *Harper's*, Sept. 1970, 37–44, 49–51.

Evans, Harry. Review of *The Duke Steps Out. Life*, May 10, 1929, 25, 34.

Faderman, Lillian. *Odd Girls and Twilight Lovers: A History of Lesbian Life in Twentieth-Century America.* New York: Penguin, 1991.

Farmer, Brett. *Spectacular Passions: Cinema, Fantasy, Gay Male Spectatorship.* Durham, NC: Duke University Press, 2000.

Feingold, Henry L. *A Time for Searching: Entering the Mainstream, 1920–1945* (*The Jewish People in America*, vol. 4). Baltimore, MD: Johns Hopkins University Press, 1992. (Reprinted 2006.)

"Fight Together, Stay Together." *Time*, Feb. 21, 1969, 64, 66.

Fisher, Joe. "Clarke Gable's Balls: Real Men Never Lose Their Teeth." In *You Tarzan: Masculinity, Movies and Men*, edited by Pat Kirkham and Janet Thumim, 35–51. New York: St. Martin's, 1993.

Flanagan, Caitlin. "Bringing Up Baby." *New Yorker*, Nov. 15, 2004, 46–48, 50, 52.

———. *To Hell with All That: Loving and Loathing Our Inner Housewife.* New York: Little, Brown, 2006.

Floyd, Jacquielynn. "*Brokeback* Ignores Plight of Spouses." *Dallas Morning News*, Jan. 20, 2006, 1–2B.

Foertsch, Jacqueline. "In Theory if Not in Practice: Straight Feminism's Lesbian Experience." In *Straight with a Twist: Queer Theory and the Subject of Homosexuality*, edited by Calvin Thomas, 45–59. Urbana: University of Illinois Press, 2000.

Fone, Byrne. *Homophobia: A History*. New York: Metropolitan, 2000.

Forslund, Bengt. *Från Gösta Ekman till Gösta Ekman: en bok om Hasse, far och son.* Stockholm, Sweden: Askild och Kärnekull, 1982.

Foucault, Michel. *The History of Sexuality, Vol. I: An Introduction.* Trans. Robert Hurley. New York: Pantheon, 1978.

———. *The History of Sexuality, Vol. 2: The Uses of Pleasure*. Trans. Robert Hurley. New York: Pantheon, 1985.

———. *The History of Sexuality, Vol. 3: The Care of the Self.* Trans. Robert Hurley. New York: Pantheon, 1986.

Freeman, Elizabeth. *The Wedding Complex: Forms of Belonging in Modern American Culture*. Durham, NC : Duke University Press, 2002.

French, T. L. "The Comedies: Spectres at the Feast: European Viewpoints on Minnelli's Comedies." In *The Films of Vincente Minnelli: Program Notes to A Retrospective at Carnegie Hall and Bleecker Street Cinema* (Jan. 17–Mar. 9, 1978), edited by Penny Yates, 10, 38–39. New York: Thousand Eyes, 1978.

Freydkin, Donna. "These Serial Dads Have Full Houses." *USA Today*, Sept. 28, 2005, D3.

Furhammar, Leif. *Filmen i Sverige*, Stockholm, Sweden: Förlags AB Wiken, 1991.

———. *Folklighetsfabriken: porträtt av ett svenskt filmbolag*, Stockholm, Sweden: Norstedts, 1979, 1–10.

Fuss. Diana. "Introduction." In *Inside/Out: Lesbian Theories, Gay Theories*, 1–10. New York: Routledge, 1991.

Gaines, Jane. "*Lady Be Good*: Do Dogs Dance?" *Jump Cut* 31 (March 1986): 19–23.

Garrett, Roberta. *Postmodern Chick Flicks: The Return of the Woman's Film.* Basingstoke, England: Palgrave MacMillan, 2007.

Geller, Jaclyn. *Here Comes the Bride: Women, Weddings and the Marriage Mystique.* New York : Publishers Group West, 2001.

Gerstner, David A. "Queer Modernism: The Cinematic Aesthetic of Vincente Minnelli." *Modernity* 2 (2000), *http://www.eiu.edu/~modernity/modernity.html* (accessed Sept. 10, 2008.)

Gilman, Sandor. *Difference and Pathology: Stereotypes of Sexuality, Race and Madness.* Ithaca, NY: Cornell University Press, 1985.

Gilman, Sandor. *The Jew's Body*. New York: Routledge, 1991.

Goldman, Eric. *Visions, Images and Dreams: Yiddish Film Past and Present.* Ann Arbor, MI: UMI Research Press, 1983.

Gottlieb, Sidney, ed. *Alfred Hitchcock: Interviews.* Jackson: University of Mississippi Press, 2003.

Grant, Julia. "A 'Real Boy' and Not a Sissy: Gender, Childhood, and Masculinity, 1890–1940." *Journal of Social History* 37.4 (2004): 829–51.

Grant, Mark N. *The Rise and Fall of the Broadway Musical.* Boston: Northeastern University Press, 2004.

Greer, Germaine. *The Female Eunuch.* New York: Farrar, Straus and Giroux, 2001. (Originally published in 1970.)

Gregg, Ronald. "Gay Culture, Studio Publicity, and the Management of Star Discourse: The Homosexualization of William Haines in Pre-Code Hollywood." *Quarterly Review of Film and Video* 20 (2003): 81–97.

Guérif, François. *Vincente Minnelli.* France: Edilig, 1984.

Habel, Ylva. "Modern Media, Modern Audiences: Mass Media and Social Engineering in the 1930s Swedish Welfare State." PhD diss., Stockholm University, 2002.

Halberstam, Judith. *Female Masculinities.* Durham, NC: Duke University Press, 1998.

———. "Modern Love." *Flow: A Critical Forum on Television and Media Culture* 6:2 (June 2007), http://flowtv.org/?p=458 (accessed September 10, 2008).

Hall, Mordaunt. "Fractious Humor" (review of *The Girl Said No*). *New York Times*, Apr. 5, 1930, 3.

———. Review of *A Free Soul. New York Times*, June 3, 1931, 29.

Hall, Radclyffe. *The Well of Loneliness.* London: Jonathan Cape, 1929.

Hansen, Miriam. "Pleasure, Ambivalence, Identification: Valentino and Female Spectatorship." *Cinema Journal* 25.4 (Summer 1986): 6–32.

Haralovich, Mary Beth. "Advertising Heterosexuality." *Screen* 23.2 (July/August 1982): 50–60.

———. "Marlene Dietrich in *Blonde Venus*: Advertising Dietrich in Seven Markets." In *Dietrich Icon*, edited by Gerd Germudson and Mary Desjardins, 162–85. Durham, NC: Duke University Press, 2007.

Harvey, Stephen. *Directed by Vincente Minnelli.* New York: Harper Collins and the Museum of Modern Art, 1990.

Haskell, Molly. *From Reverence to Rape: The Treatment of Women in the Movies.* Chicago: University of Chicago Press, 1987.

Herek, Gregory M. "Beyond 'Homophobia': A Social Psychological Perspective on Attitudes Towards Lesbians and Gay Men." In *Bashers, Baiters, and Bigots: Homophobia in American Society*, edited by John P. DeCecco, 1–22. New York: Harrington Park, 1985.

Herrick, Christine Terhune. "Man, the Victim." *Munsey's Magazine* 27 (1902): 889.

Hill, Mike, ed. *Whiteness: A Critical Reader.* New York: New York University Press, 1997.

Hirdman, Yvonne. *Att lägga livet till rätta: studier i svensk folkhemspolitik.* Stockholm, Sweden: Carlsson, 1989.

———. *Genus: om det stabiles föränderliga former.* Malmö, Sweden: Liber, 2003.

———. *Genusanalys av välfärdsstaten: en utmaning av dikotomierna.* Stockholm, Sweden: Arbetslivsinstitutet, 1994.

Hoberman, J. *Bridge of Light: Yiddish Film between Two Worlds.* Philadelphia: Temple University Press, 1991.

Holahan, Catherine. "Actresses Inspire All Women to Sail Past 40 with Confidence." *Providence Journal*, June 28, 2006, H9.

Hopper, Hedda. "Astaire Way of Life Aims at Happiness." *Los Angeles Times* c. 1952–1953:1, 3. Clipping file, Margaret Herrick Library, Academy of Motion Picture Arts and Sciences, Los Angeles.

———. "The Neighborly Fords." Source unknown, Jan. 6, 1951. Clipping file, Margaret Herrick Library, Academy of Motion Picture Arts and Sciences, Los Angeles.

Humphrey, William. *Home from the Hill*. Baton Rouge: Louisiana State University Press, 1996. (Originally published by Knopf, 1957.)

Hunter, R. L. *The New Comedy of Greece and Rome*. Cambridge, England: Cambridge University Press, 1985.

Inden, Ronald. "Transnational Class, Erotic Arcadia and Commercial Utopia in Hindi Films." In *Image Journeys: Audio-Visual Media and Cultural Change in India*, edited by Christiane Brosius and Melissa Butcher, 41–66. New Delhi, India: Sage, 1999.

Ingraham, Chrys. *White Weddings: Romancing Heterosexuality in Popular Culture*. New York: Routledge, 1999.

Ignatiev, Noel. *How the Irish became White*. New York: Routledge, 1995.

Jacobs, Lea. *The Wages of Sin: Censorship and the Fallen Woman Film, 1928–1942*. Madison: University of Wisconsin Press, 1991.

Jayson, Sharon. "Autism Shouts in this Family." *USA Today*, Mar. 29, 2005, 8B, 9.

Jerselius, Kjell. *Hotade reservat: spelfilmerna med Edvard Persson*. Uppsala, Sweden: Filmförlaget, 1987.

Kapsis, Robert E. *Hitchcock: The Making of a Reputation*. Chicago: University of Chicago Press, 1992.

———, and Kathie Coblentz, eds. *Woody Allen: Interviews*. Jackson: University of Mississippi Press, 2006.

Katz, Jonathan Ned. *The Invention of Heterosexuality*, 2nd ed. Chicago: University of Chicago Press, 2007. (First publication, New York: Plume, 1999.)

Katz, Stephen, and Barbara Marshall. "New Sex for Old: Lifestyle, Consumerism, and the Ethics of Aging Well." *Journal of Aging Studies* 17 (2003): 3–16.

Kehr, Dave. "Charting the Tarantino Universe: The References of 'Kill Bill,' from East to West." *New York Times*, Apr. 11, 2004, 2, 11.

Kiley, David. "Chrysler Bets Big on Dion's Auto Endorsement Deal." *USA Today*, June 8, 2003, B4.

Kimball, Samuel A. "'Bad-Ass Dudes' in *Pulp Fiction*: Homophobia and the Counterphobic Idealization of Women." *Quarterly Review of Film and Video* 16.2 (1997): 171–92.

Klinger, Barbara. "'Cinema/Ideology/Criticism' Revisited: The Progressive Genre." In *Film Genre Reader 2*, edited by Barry Keith Grant, 74–90. Austin: University of Texas Press, 1995.

Knight, Arthur. *Saturday Review*, Mar. 1960, n. p. (Museum of Modern Art film clippings.)

Kobal, John. "Eleanor Powell." *People Will Talk*. New York: Knopf, 1985. 217–36.

———. *Gotta Sing Gotta Dance: A Pictorial History of Film Musicals*. London: Hamlyn, 1972.

Konigsberg, Ira. "'The Only 'I' in the World': Religion, Psychoanalysis and *The Dybbuk*." *Cinema Journal* 36.4 (Summer 1997): 22–42.

Kuhn, Annette. *Dreaming of Fred and Ginger: Cinema and Cultural Memory*. New York: New York University Press, 2002.

Kulkarni, Mangesh. "Is There Such a Thing as the Metrosexual Male?" *http://www.infochangeindia.org/agenda4_08.jsp* (accessed Apr. 4, 2007).

La Ferla, Ruth. "Sexy Singles, Make Way for Glamour Moms." *New York Times*, Nov. 10, 2002, sect. 9, 13.

Lang, Robert. *American Film Melodrama: Griffith, Vidor, Minnelli*. Princeton, NJ: Princeton University Press. 1989.

LaSalle, Mark. *Dangerous Men: Pre-Code Hollywood and the Birth of the Modern Man*. New York: St. Martin's, 2002.

Lehman, Peter, ed. *Masculinity: Bodies, Movies, Culture*. New York: Routledge, 2001.

Leonard, Suzanne. "Prematurely Gray: The 'Post-Sexual' Married Thirtysomething of Recent Cinema." Paper presented at Society for Cinema and Media Studies Conference, Vancouver, Canada, Mar. 2–5, 2006.

Levy, Ariel. "Dirty Old Women." *New York*, May 29, 2006a, 28–33.

———. *Female Chauvinist Pigs: Women and the Rise of Raunch Culture*. New York: Free, 2006b.

Loe, Meika. *The Rise of Viagra: How the Little Blue Pill Changed Sex in America*. New York: New York University Press, 2004.

Lugowski, David. "Queering the New Deal: Lesbian and Gay Representation and the Depression-Era Politics of Hollywood's Production Code." *Cinema Journal* 38.2 (1999): 3–35.

———. "Queering *Citizen Kane*." In *Film and Sexual Politics*, edited by Kylo-Patrick R. Hart, 38–48. Newcastle, England: Cambridge Scholars Press, 2006.

Lystra, Karen. *Searching the Heart: Women, Men, and Romantic Love in Nineteenth-Century America*. New York: Oxford University Press, 1989.

Macleod, David I. *Building Character in the American Boy: The Boy Scouts, YMCA, and Their Forerunners, 1870–1920*. Madison: University of Wisconsin Press, 1983.

Mankekar, Purnima. "Brides Who Travel: Gender, Transnationalism and Nationalism in Hindi Film." *positions* 7.3 (1999): 731–61.

Mann, William J. *Wisecracker: The Life and Times of William Haines, Hollywood's First Openly Gay Star*. New York: Penguin, 1999.

McLean, Adrienne L. *Being Rita Hayworth: Labor, Identity, and Hollywood Stardom*. New Brunswick, NJ: Rutgers University Press, 2004.

———. "Feeling and the Filmed Body: Judy Garland and the Kinesics of Suffering." *Film Quarterly* 55.3 (2002): 2–15.

McNamara, Sallie. "Georgette Heyer: The Historical Romance and the Consumption of the Erotic, 1918–1939." In *All the World and Her Husband: Women in Twentieth-Century Consumer Culture*, edited by Maggie Andrews and Mary M. Talbot, 82–96. London: Cassell, 2000.

Mechling, Jay. *On My Honor: Boy Scouts and the Making of American Youth*. Chicago: University of Chicago Press, 2001.

Mehta, Monika. "Globalizing Bombay Cinema: Reproducing the Indian State and Family." *Cultural Dynamics* 17.2 (2005): 135–54.

Mendelsohn, Daniel. "An Affair to Remember." *New York Review*, Feb. 23, 2006, 12–13.

Miller, D. A. "Anal *Rope*." In *Inside/Out: Lesbian Theories, Gay Theories*, edited by Diane Fuss, 119–141. New York: Routledge, 1991.

Millett, Kate. *Sexual Politics*. New York: Doubleday, 1970.

Minnelli, Vincente. *I Remember It Well*. Hollywood, CA: Samuel French Trade, 1990. (originally published 1974.)

Mosse, George L. *The Image of Man: The Creation of Modern Masculinity*. New York: Oxford University Press, 1996.

Mulvey, Laura. *Visual and Other Pleasures*. Bloomington: Indiana University Press, 1989.

Myrdal, Alva, and Myrdal, Gunnar. *Kris i befolkningsfrågan*. Stockholm, Sweden: Bonnier, 1934.

Naremore, James. *The Films of Vincente Minnelli*. New York: Cambridge University Press, 1993.

Negra, Diane. *Off-White Hollywood: American Culture and Ethnic Female Stardom*. New York: Routledge, 2001.

"The New Feminists: Revolt against 'Sexism.'" *Time*, Nov. 21, 1969, 53–54, 56.

Newsome, Melba. "Not Just for Kids." *Time*, Sept. 5, 2005, W11, W12.

"No Girls. Please, We're Indian." *Hindu* (Aug. 29, 2004), http://www.hinduonnet.com/mag/2004/08/29/stories/2004082900130100.htm (accessed Sept. 14, 2008).

"Obscenity? It's in Your Jeans," *Times of India*, Nov. 11, 1999.

O'Neill, Nena, and George O'Neill. *Open Marriage: A New Life Style for Couples*. New York: Evans, 1972.

Otnes, Cele C., and Elizabeth H. Pleck. *Cinderella Dreams: The Allure of the Lavish Wedding*. Berkeley: University of California Press, 2003.

Otto, Herbert A. "Has Monogamy Failed?" *Saturday Review*, Apr. 25, 1970, 23–25, 62.

Ozment, Katherine. "A Winter of Discontent, Then Along Comes Baby." *New York Times*, May 14, 2006, 9.

Paskin, Sylvia, ed. *When Joseph Met Molly: A Reader on Yiddish Film*. Nottingham, England: Five Leaves, 1999.

Paul, William. *Laughing/Screaming: Modern Hollywood Horror and Comedy*. New York: Columbia University Press, 1994.

Peary, Gerald, ed. *Quentin Tarantino: Interviews*. Jackson: University of Mississippi Press, 1998.

Penley, Constance, and Sharon Willis, eds. "Male Trouble" (Special Issue). *Camera Obscura* 17 (May 1988).

Philips, Adam. *On Flirtation*. Cambridge, MA: Harvard University Press, 1994.

Plummer, David. *One of the Boys: Masculinity, Homophobia, and Modern Manhood*. New York: Harrington Park, 1999.

Polan, Dana. *Power and Paranoia: History, Narrative, and the American Cinema, 1940–1950*. New York: Columbia University Press, 1986.

———. *Pulp Fiction (BFI Modern Classics)*. London: British Film Institute, 2000.

Proulx, Annie. "Getting Movied." In *Brokeback Mountain: Story to Screenplay*, 129–38. New York: Scribner, 2006.

"Quentin Tarantino—Wikipedia, the Free Encyclopedia." *http://en.wikipedia.org/wiki/Quentin_Tarantino#Personal_life* (accessed Sept. 5, 2008).

"QT's Dream Team." *Entertainment Weekly*, Apr. 16, 2004, 28.

Qvist, P. O. *Folkhemmets bilder: Modernisering, motstånd och mentalitet i den svenska 30–talsfilmen*. Lund, Sweden: Arkiv, 1995.

Rao, Harshita. "In Quest of the Real Metrosexual" (Oct., 8, 2005) *http://www.dnaindia.com/report.asp?NewsID=4932&CatID=*7 (accessed Apr. 15, 2007).

"Repairing the Conjugal Bed." *Time*, May 25, 1970, 49–52.

"Report XI, Is Fred Astaire Washed-Up?" (May 15, 1940). *Gallup Looks at the Movies: Audience Research Reports 1940–1950*. Wilmington, DE: American Institute of Public Opinion and Scholarly Resources Inc., 1979. n.p., on microfilm.

Rich, Adrienne. "Compulsory Heterosexuality and Lesbian Existence." In *The Lesbian and Gay Studies Reader*, edited by Henry Abelove, Micehele Aina Barale, and David M. Halperin, 227–54. New York: Routledge, 1993.

Rich, B. Ruby. "Homo Pomo: The New Queer Cinema." In *Women and Film: A Sight and Sound Reader*, edited by Pam Cook and Philip Dodd, 165–75. Philadelphia: Temple University Press, 1993.

Richardson, Dianne, ed. *Theorising Heterosexuality: Telling It Straight*. Philadelphia: Open University Press, 1996.

Rimmer, Robert. *The Harrad Experiment*. Amherst, NY: Prometheus, 1990. (Originally published by Sherbourne Press in 1966.)

Rogin, Michael. *Blackface, White Noise: Jewish Immigrants in the Hollywood Melting Pot*. Los Angeles: University of California Press, 1996.

Rothman, Ellen K. *Hands and Hearts: A History of Courtship in America*. New York: Basic, 1984.

Rubin, Martin. *Showstoppers: Busby Berkeley and the Tradition of Spectacle*. New York: Columbia University Press, 1993.

Russo, Vito. *The Celluloid Closet: Homosexuality in the Movies*. New York: Harper and Row, 1981.

Sachar, Howard. *A History of the Jews in America*. New York: Vintage/Random House, 1992.

Sales, Nancy Jo. "Sex and the Single Mom." *Vanity Fair*, June 2005, 80–88, 145–48.

Saul, Stephanie. "Record Sales of Sleep Pills Cause Worry." *New York Times*, Feb. 7, 2006, A1, C4.

Schaefer, Eric. *Bold! Daring! Shocking! True! A History of Exploitation Films, 1919–1959*. Durham, NC: Duke University Press, 1999.

Schatz, Thomas. *Hollywood Genres: Formulas, Filmmaking, and the Studio System*. New York: MacGraw–Hill, 1981.

Schilling, Mary Kaye. "The Second Coming." *Entertainment Weekly*, Apr. 16, 2004, 26.

Schultz, Margie. *Eleanor Powell: A Bio-Bibliography*. Westport, CT: Greenwood, 1994.

Sedgwick, Eve Kosofsky. *Between Men: English Literature and Male Homosocial Desire*. New York: Columbia University Press, 1985.

———. *The Epistemology of the Closet*. Berkeley: University of California Press, 1990.

———. *Tendencies*. Durham, NC: Duke University Press, 1993.

Seidman, Steven. *Romantic Longings: Love in America, 1830–1980*. New York: Routledge, 1991.

Sherwood, R. E. "The Silent Drama" (review of *Slide, Kelly, Slide*). *Life*, Apr. 14, 1927, 24.

Sicular, Eve. "Gender Rebellion in Yiddish Film." In *When Joseph Met Molly: A Reader on Yiddish Film*, edited by Sylvia Paskin, 245–54, Nottingham, England: Five Leaves, 1999.

———. "Outing the Archives: From the Celluloid Closet to the Isle of Klezbos." In *Queer Jews*, edited by David Schneer and Caryn Aviv, 199–214. New York: Routledge, 2002.

———. "A yingl mit a yingl hot epes a tam: Lesbian and Gay Subtext in Yiddish Film." Presentation at the New Festival, the New York Lesbian and Gay Film and Video Festival (June 10, 1995).

Siroto, Janet. "When Two Is Not Enough." *Redbook*, Oct. 1998, 168–73.

Slide, Anthony. "The Silent Closet." *Film Quarterly* 52.4 (1999): 24–32.

Sklar, Robert. *City Boys: Cagney, Bogart, Garfield*. Princeton, NJ: Princeton University Press, 1992.

Soila, Tytti. "Kvinnors ansikte: stereotyper och kvinnlig identitet i trettiotalets svenska film." PhD diss. Stockholm University, 1991.

———. "Valborgsmässoafton: Melodrama and Gender Politics in Swedish Cinema." *Popular European Cinema*, edited by Richard Dyer and G. Vincendeau, 232–44. London: Routledge, 1992.

Sterritt, David, ed. *Jean-Luc Godard: Interviews*. Jackson: University of Mississippi Press, 1998.

Stork, Joe, and Sharon Rose. "Zionism and American Jewry." *Journal of Palestine Studies* 3.3 (Spring 1974): 39–57.

Straayer, Chris. *Deviant Eyes, Deviant Bodies: Sexual Re-Orientation in Film and Video*. New York: Columbia University Press, 1996.

Studlar, Gaylen. *This Mad Masquerade: Stardom and Masculinity in the Jazz Age*. New York: Columbia University Press, 1996.

Sullivan, Nikki. *A Critical Introduction to Queer Theory*. New York: New York University Press, 2003.

Tarantino, Quentin. "Emotion Pictures: Quentin Tarantino Talks with Brian De Palma." In *Brian De Palma: Interviews*, edited by Laurence F. Knapp, 135–49. Jackson: University of Mississippi Press, 2003.

———. *Jackie Brown: A Quentin Tarantino Screenplay*. New York: Hyperion, 1997.

———. *Natural Born Killers: The Original Screenplay*. New York: Grove, 2000a.

———. *Pulp Fiction: A Quentin Tarantino Screenplay*. New York: Hyperion, 1994.

———. *Quentin Tarantino's 'Death Proof': A Screenplay*. New York: Weinstein, 2007.

———. *Reservoir Dogs: The Screenplay*. New York: Grove Press, 2000b.

———. *True Romance: The Screenplay*. New York: Grove Press, 2000c.

Tasker, Yvonne, and Diane Negra. "Feminist Politics and Postfeminist Culture." In *Interrogating Postfeminism: Gender and the Politics of Popular Culture*, edited by Yvonne Tasker and Diane Negra, 1–26. Durham, NC: Duke University Press, 2007.

Thomas, Calvin. "Introduction: Identification, Appropriation, Proliferation." *Straight with a Twist: Queer Theory and the Subject of Heterosexuality*, edited by Calvin Thomas, 11–44. Urbana: University of Illinois Press, 2000.

Tinkcom, Matthew. *Working Like a Homosexual: Camp, Capital, Cinema*. Durham, NC: Duke University Press, 2002.

Uberoi, Patricia. *Freedom and Destiny: Gender, Family and Popular Culture in India*. Delhi, India: Oxford University Press, 2006.

Udovitch, Mim. "Tarantino and Juliette." In *Quentin Tarantino: Interviews*, edited by Gerald Peary, 166–75. Jackson: University of Mississippi Press, 1998.

Valentin, Guido. *Gösta Ekman: ett kasseri*. Stockholm, Sweden: Hökerberg, 1919.

Vasan, Akhila. "Sex Books and the Mediation of Masculinities." *http://www.infochangeindia.org/agenda4_11.jsp* (accessed Apr. 4, 2007).

Wallace, Carol. *All Dressed in White: The Irresistible Rise of the American Wedding*. New York: Penguin, 2004.

Warner, Michael. "Introduction: Fear of a Queer Planet." *Social Text* 4, 29 (Spring 1992): 3–8.

———. *The Trouble with Normal: Sex, Politics and the Ethics of Queer Life*. New York: Free Press, 1999.

Waugh, Thomas. "Queer Bollywood, or 'I'm the player, you're the naïve one.'" In *Keyframes: Popular Cinema and Cultural Studies*, edited by Matthew Tinkcom and Amy Villarejo, 280–97. London: Routledge, 2001.

Wearing, Sadie. "Subjects of Rejuvenation: Aging in Postfeminist Culture and Feminist Critique." In *Interrogating Postfeminism: Gender and the Politics of Popular Culture*, edited by Yvonne Tasker and Diane Negra, 277–310. Durham, NC: Duke University Press, 2007.

Wexman, Virginia Wright. *Creating the Couple: Love, Marriage, and Hollywood Performance*. Princeton, NJ: Princeton University Press, 1993.

"Who Stays Married Longer." *U S. News and World Report*, Oct. 30, 1972, 39.

Wild, David. "Quentin Tarantino, Violence and Twisted Wit." *Quentin Tarantino: Interviews*, edited by Gerald Peary, 124–35. Jackson: University of Mississippi Press, 1998.

Wiles, Mary M. "Not that There's Anything Wrong with That: Reading the Queer in *Seinfeld*." In *Straight with a Twist: Queer Theory and the Subject of Heterosexuality*, edited by Calvin Thomas, 165–90. Urbana: University of Illinois Press, 2000.

Williamson, Catherine. "Swimming Pools, Movie Stars: The Celebrity Body in the Post-War Marketplace." *Camera Obscura* 38 (May 1996): 4–29.

Willis, Sharon. "The Fathers Watch the Boys' Room." *Camera Obscura* 32 (May 1995): 40–73.

Wilson, Anna. "Little Lord Fauntleroy: The Darling of Mothers and the Abomination of a Generation." *American Literary History* 8.2 (1996): 232–58.

Wittig, Monique. *The Straight Mind and Other Essays*. Boston: Beacon Press, 1992.

Wylie, Philip. *Generation of Vipers*. Normal, IL: Dalkey Archive Press, 1996. (Originally published 1942.)

Yagoda, Ben. "My Heart Belongs to 'Mother.'" *New York Times*, May 14, 2006, 14.

Yingling, Thomas E. "Homosexuality and the Uncanny: What's Fishy in Lacan." In *The Gay '90s: Disciplinary and Interdisciplinary Formations in Queer Studies*, edited by Thomas Foster, Carol Siegel, and Ellen E. Berry, 191–98. New York: New York University Press, 1997.

Yosef, Raz. *Beyond Flesh: Queer Masculinities and Nationalism in Israeli Cinema*. New Brunswick, NJ: Rutgers University Press, 2004.

Contributors

Harry M. Benshoff is an Associate Professor of Radio, Television and Film at the University of North Texas. He has published essays on *Dark Shadows* fan cultures, blaxploitation horror films, Hollywood LSD films, and *The Talented Mr. Ripley* (1999). He is the author of *Monsters in the Closet: Homosexuality and the Horror Film* (Manchester University Press, 1997). With Sean Griffin, he co-edited *Queer Cinema, The Film Reader* (Routledge, 2005), and he co-authored *America on Film: Representing Race, Class, Gender and Sexuality at the Movies* (Blackwell Publishers, 2004) and *Queer Images: A History of Gay and Lesbian Film in America* (Rowman & Littlefield, 2006).

Allan Campbell, a doctoral candidate at the University of Texas at Austin, writes on the social and historical aspects of popular culture in the United States, particularly its cinema, with recurring interest in stars, film censorship, sexual issues, and popular music.

Michael DeAngelis is an Associate Professor at DePaul University's School for New Learning, where he teaches in the areas of media and cultural studies. He is the author of *Gay Fandom and Crossover Stardom: James Dean, Mel Gibson, and Keanu Reeves* (Duke University Press, 2001), as well as essays on stardom, authorship, and historiography.

David A. Gerstner received his PhD in the Department of Film and Television at UCLA. He is Associate Professor of Cinema Studies at the City University of New York's College of Staten Island and Graduate Center where he is a member of the Doctoral Faculty in the Department of Theatre. He is author of *Manly Arts: Masculinity and Nation in Early*

American Cinema (Duke University Press, 2006); editor of *The Routledge International Encyclopedia of Queer Culture* (Routledge, 2006) which was awarded "Best of Reference 2007" by the New York Public Library; and co-editor with Janet Staiger of *Authorship and Film* (Routledge, 2003). His work has appeared in *Film Quarterly*, *The Stanford Humanities Review*, *Cine-Action*, *The Velvet Light Trap*, *Cultural Critique*, *Wide Angle*. His recent publications include essays on Marcel Duchamp, Andy Warhol, and Spike Lee. His research-project now underway studies twentieth-century black-queer aesthetics and cultural identity in the works of Richard Bruce Nugent, James Baldwin, and Marlon Riggs. Dr. Gerstner was principle organizer and co-curator of 'Another Wave: Global Queer Cinema' at the Museum of Modern Art during July and September 2006.

Sean Griffin is an Associate Professor of Cinema-Television at Southern Methodist University. He has published essays on soap operas, *Mystery Science Theater 3000*, and the musical genre. He is the author of *Tinker Belles and Evil Queens: The Walt Disney Company from the Inside Out* (NYU Press, 1999). With Harry M. Benshoff, he co-edited *Queer Cinema, The Film Reader* (Routledge, 2005), and he co-authored *America on Film: Representing Race, Class, Gender and Sexuality at the Movies* (Blackwell Publishers, 2004) and *Queer Images: A History of Gay and Lesbian Film in America* (Rowman & Littlefield, 2006).

Mary Beth Haralovich teaches television and film history and is Director of Internships in Media Arts at the University of Arizona in Tucson. Among her publications on television drama are studies of the popular appeal of *Magnum P.I.* and the geo-politics of civil rights in *I Spy*. Her essay on the 1950s suburban housewife in the domestic family situation comedy has been reprinted several times. In film studies, she is the author of several articles on film posters and on genre (the 1930s proletarian women's film; Sherlock Holmes films; color in 1950s melodrama). Co-editor of *Television, History, and American Culture: Feminist Critical Essays* (Duke Unversity Press, 1999), she is a founder of the International Conference on Television, Video, New Media, Audio and Feminism: Console-ing Passions.

Kevin Heffernan teaches in the Division of Cinema-Television in the Meadows School of the Arts at Southern Methodist University. He is the author of *Ghouls, Gimmicks and Gold* from Duke University Press as well as co-author of *My Son Divine* from Alyson Publications with Frances Milstead and Steve Yeager. He was associate producer and co-screenwriter on two documentary features, *In Bad Taste* (1999) and *Divine Trash*, the latter of which won the Filmmakers' Trophy at the 1998 Sundance Film Festival. He is currently writing a book on east Asian popular cinema after 1997 tentatively titled *A Wind from the East* and another book on Dumb White Guy culture and politics in the new millenium tentatively titled *Nuts and Gum.*

David Lugowski is an Associate Professor of English and Director of the interdisciplinary Communication Studies program at Manhattanville College. He has written on American, European and Asian film for *Cineaste*, *Cinema Journal*, *Senses of Cinema*, *Baseline*, *Arizona Quarterly*, *The Encyclopedia of Documentary Film* and *The International Encyclopedia of Queer Culture*, among other publications. He also has essays in such anthologies as *Film and Sexual Politics*, *American Cinema of the 1930s: Themes and Variations*, and *Looking Past the Screen: Case Studies in American Film History and Method.*

Adrienne L. McLean is an associate professor of film studies at the University of Texas at Dallas. She is the author of *Being Rita Hayworth: Labor, Identity, and Hollywood Stardom* (Rutgers University Press, 2004), and the co-editor of *Headline Hollywood: A Century of Film Scandal* (Rutgers University Press, 2001).

Diane Negra is Professor of Film and Television Studies at the University of East Anglia. She is the author of *Off-White Hollywood: American Culture and Ethnic Female Stardom* (Routledge, 2001), editor of *The Irish in Us: Irishness, Performativity and Popular Culture* (Duke, 2006) and co-editor of *A Feminist Reader in Early Cinema* (Duke, 2002) and *Interrogating Postfeminism: Gender and the Politics of Popular Culture* (Duke, 2007). Her book *What a Girl Wants?: Fantasizing the Reclamation of Self in Postfeminism* will be published by Routledge in 2008.

Bashkar Sarkar, Associate Professor of Film Studies at UC Santa Barbara, is the author of *Mourning the Nation: Indian Cinema in the Wake of Partition* (Duke University Press, forthcoming). He has published articles in several anthologies, and in journals like *Quarterly Review of Film and Video*, *Visual Anthropology Review*, *Rethinking History*, and *Journal of Postcolonial Studies.*

Victoria Sturtevant is an Assistant Professor of Film and Video Studies at the University of Oklahoma. Her publications focus on race, class, gender, and performance in Classical Hollywood Cinema. Her first book, *Punctured Romance: Marie Dressler's body of work*, is forthcoming from the University of Illinois Press.

Louise Wallenberg is Assistant Professor of Cinema and Fashion at Stockholm University, Sweden. She holds a doctorate in Cinema Studies (2002) and is currently the director at the Centre for Fashion Studies at Stockholm University. She has published on queer and mainstream cinema and feminist and queer philosophies.

Index